The Northern Ireland Peace Process

Ending the Troubles?

The Northern Ireland Peace Process

Ending the Troubles?

THOMAS HENNESSEY

Gill & Macmillan

Gill & Macmillan Ltd
Hume Avenue, Park West, Dublin 12
with associated companies throughout the world
www.gillmacmillan.ie
© Thomas Hennessey 2000
0 7171 2946 2
Index compiled by Cover To Cover
Design and print origination by Sally O'Leary
Printed by ColourBooks Ltd, Dublin

This book is typeset in Ehrhardt 11pt on 12pt.

A CIP catalogue record for this book is available from the
British Library.

5 4 3 2 1

For Mum

Contents

Acknowledgements

Many people have assisted me in writing this book, often through exchanges of opinion and debates on the Peace Process. Many of those I wish to thank would not agree with the arguments and conclusions in this book. If the text has one obvious flaw it is that it focuses on the divisions and agreement between Irish Nationalism and Ulster Unionism. This is not to belittle the contribution of other parties such as the Alliance Party or the Women's Coalition to negotiations, but to emphasise where the real conflict of identity and ideology lay and where I feel the centre of gravity in the Multi-Party Talks rested. In particular, I would like to take this opportunity to thank the following: David Adams; Professor Antony Alcock; Jack Allen; Dr Arthur Aughey; Professor Paul Bew; David Brewster; David Campell; Jeffrey Donaldson MP; Sir Reg Empey MLA; Dr Richard English; Steven Farrey; Kate Fearon; Arlene Foster; Jim Gibney; Dr Graham Gudgen; Tom Hartley; Toby Hardenson; Dr Alvin Jackson; Dr Denis Kennedy; David Kerr; Peter King; Stephen King; Alan Leonard; Gordon Lucy; Mitchel McLaughlin MLA; Gary McMichael; Dr Austin Morgan; Dermot Nesbitt MLA; Ian Paisley Jnr MLA; Professor Henry Patterson; Patrick Roche MLA; Lord Rogan; Rt Hon. John Taylor MLA MP; Peter Taylor; Rt Hon. David Trimble MLA MP; and Peter Weir MLA. Thanks also go to those British and Irish civil servants who, for obvious reasons, cannot be named. A special mention is reserved for Robin Wilson at Democratic Dialogue for access to his unrivalled collection of newspaper cuttings and to Yvonne and Ciaran of the Northern Ireland Political Collection at the Linen Hall Library, Belfast, where the papers from the Multi-Party Talks are now deposited.

Abbreviations

CAC	Continuity Army Council
CIRA	Continuity Irish Republican Army
CLMC	Combined Loyalist Military Command
DAAD	Direct Action Against Drugs
DUP	Democratic Unionist Party
EC	European Community
ECHR	European Convention on Human Rights
EEC	European Economic Community
EPA	Emergency Powers Act
EU	European Union
GOC	General Officer Commanding
INLA	Irish National Liberation Army
LVF	Loyalist Volunteer Force
NIO	Northern Ireland Office
PIRA	Provisional Irish Republican Army
PTA	Prevention of Terrorism Act
PUP	Progressive Unionist Party
RUC	Royal Ulster Constabulary
SDLP	Social Democratic and Labour Party
SF	Sinn Féin
UDA	Ulster Defence Association
UDP	Ulster Democratic Party
UDR	Ulster Defence Regiment
UFF	Ulster Freedom Fighters
UUC	Ulster Unionist Council
UUP	Ulster Unionist Party
UUUC	United Ulster Unionist Council
UVF	Ulster Volunteer Force
UWC	Ulster Workers' Council

Note on Terminology

In the text the terms Unionist, Nationalist, Loyalist and Republican are capitalised to denote parties or organisations and their members; without capitals they refer to supporters within the wider community. In direct quotation, the casing is as set out in the original printed source. Terms such as Ulster and Londonderry, used predominantly by members of the unionist community, and the Six Counties, the North and Derry, used mainly by members of the nationalist community, in referring to Northern Ireland and its second city, reflect the different political and cultural perceptions the two communities hold on the same political and geographical entities. Although not all Protestants are unionists and not all Roman Catholics are nationalists in Northern Ireland, it is a commonly held perception that religious belief or upbringing corresponds to political allegiance. These terms are used in the text as they are employed by a particular individual or organisation whose perception, more often than not, merges political allegiance with communal membership. For reasons of convenience, the terms 'Republic of Ireland' and the 'Irish Government' – rather than 'Ireland' and the 'Government of Ireland' – are used in the text to avoid confusion for readers unfamiliar with the correct constitutional usage.

Introduction

This book attempts to answer two questions: why it was possible for the parties to the Northern Ireland conflict to reach agreement in 1998, and why previous attempts failed. At the outset it is important to realise that what complicated the Northern Ireland conflict was the range of options which the central protagonists – Unionists and Nationalists – viewed as their preferred solution. Historically, the Ulster Question has been a dispute concerning sovereignty and identity. Or to put it another way, it has been a conflict between states and nations. But neither Unionists nor Nationalists could agree which states were legitimate or the legitimacy of the opposing group's national identity.

One of the enduring features of the Northern Ireland conflict has been the clash between the claim to British sovereignty in Ireland and the claim to Irish national self-determination. In the period 1800-1922, this concerned the Irish Nationalist denial of any part of the Irish nation, which was deemed to be co-terminus with the island of Ireland, to be part of the British state of the United Kingdom of Great Britain and Ireland. Some Nationalists, however, were prepared to compromise and accept membership of the British state if the Irish nation were granted limited self-government: an Irish devolved parliament within the United Kingdom. But, following the secession of the Irish Free State from the British state in 1922, the issue increasingly became whether or not 'Northern Ireland' – the six Irish counties which remained within the United Kingdom of Great Britain and Northern Ireland – and the Protestant majority therein, had a right to opt out of the Irish nation. As the independent Irish state evolved it challenged British sovereignty in any part of Ireland as a denial of the right to Irish national self-determination.

What was to become Northern Ireland became part of the United Kingdom in 1801. Article 1 of the Union with Ireland Act 1800 enacted that the Kingdoms of Great Britain and Ireland would, from 1 January 1801, and 'for ever after, be united into one kingdom, by the name of the United Kingdom of Great Britain and Ireland'.[1] The Act of Union was and remained the legal basis of British sovereignty over Ireland, and later, over Northern Ireland. Ever since, the right of the United Kingdom Parliament to sovereignty in Ireland has been contested by Nationalists. They demanded the right of Irish national self-determination.

The problem, however, was defining the Irish nation. And, to complicate matters in the Irish case, the United Kingdom of Great Britain and Ireland was a multi-national state. Whereas Nationalists saw themselves as Irish only, Unionists possessed a dual identity. In pre-partition Ireland, Irish Unionists, who tended to be Protestants, were violently opposed to Home Rule. This was particularly true of Protestants in the northern, nine-county province of Ulster. In 1911, Ulster Protestants organised themselves into an armed paramilitary force, to resist the extension of a Home Rule Bill to the whole of Ireland. Unionists feared that a Home Rule Parliament would preside over a confessional Roman Catholic state. Irish Unionists also saw Home Rule as a threat to their Britishness and feared that the establishment of Irish self-government would lead ultimately to an Irish Republic.

Many Unionists at that time thought of themselves as both Irish and British, and, like the Scots or Welsh, saw no contradiction in this. They saw Home Rule as a dilution of their Britishness and their part in a British nation which stretched throughout the globe, via the British Empire. For Unionists it was the natural geographical unit of the British Isles, not Ireland, which constituted their political nation. They also, at this point, denied that Irish Catholics formed a separate national group within the United Kingdom. Irish nationalists, on the other hand, did not possess a British identity. They saw Irish unionists not as a separate British nation within the island of Ireland, but as a religious minority within the Irish nation.

A settlement of the Irish Question was postponed by the outbreak of the First World War. The War radically altered the dimensions of the Irish Question. At its commencement Irish Nationalism was represented by a political movement committed to securing Irish self-government within the United Kingdom; by the end of the War, the Home Rule Party was electorally swept away by Sinn Féin, which apparently sought an Irish republic outside the British Empire. In 1918, as the Great War drew to a close, the British Government once more attempted to settle the Irish Question by framing a fourth Home Rule scheme for Ireland. Ulster Unionists would only accept a Home Rule scheme for Ireland if the island were partitioned, with at least six of the nine Ulster counties remaining outside the jurisdiction of an Irish Parliament. Ulster Unionists held the view that the new 'province' should consist of the six counties of Armagh, Antrim, Londonderry, Down – with Protestant majorities – alongside Fermanagh and Tyrone which had Catholic majorities but substantial Protestant minorities. These six counties were the maximum territory which Unionists could hold; but the new boundary contained almost a third of the population, which were Roman Catholic and non-unionist.

The Government of Ireland Act 1920 partitioned Ireland, creating two new jurisdictions with their own devolved Parliaments within the island of Ireland, but also within the United Kingdom. 'Northern Ireland' was to consist of the aforementioned six counties; 'Southern Ireland' was to consist of the remaining twenty-six Irish counties. The Act provided for the establishment of a Northern Ireland Parliament. Section 75 of the Act stated that:

> ... the supreme authority of the Parliament of the United Kingdom shall remain unaffected and undiminished over all persons, matters and things in Ireland and every part thereof.

This was later mistaken by Nationalists for a territorial claim by Britain to Ireland. But Section 75 was a 'saving provision', that is a section inserted for political purposes; it was not a declaration of British sovereignty in Ireland. British sovereignty was inherent in the Act: the Westminster Parliament was sovereign over all persons and things in His Majesty's dominions. The new regional unit of Northern Ireland was part of the United Kingdom because of the Act of Union, not the Government of Ireland Act. And it remained part of the United Kingdom because of the Act of Union.

The Government of Ireland Act looked forward to the ultimate reunion of Ireland by consent. Irish unity would occur with the separate consent of both devolved Irish Parliaments, and made provision for a Council of Ireland to help facilitate this. The British Government was not, therefore, opposed to a united Ireland. The Council of Ireland was to be composed of members of the Northern Ireland and Southern Ireland Parliaments, making decisions on an all-Ireland basis. Ironically, the originator of this North-South body was the leader of Irish Unionism, Sir Edward Carson. In 1917, Carson proposed a National Consultation Assembly of Ireland, composed of a committee of Ulster MPs, elected to the Westminster Parliament, and Irish MPs, elected to any Southern Irish Parliament. This would hold annual sessions to consider legislative proposals for the whole of Ireland.[2] But this was a united Ireland *within* the United Kingdom and *under* the British Crown.

However, the new political realities in Nationalist Ireland, demonstrated by the 1918 General Election results, led to a violent confrontation between the armed wing of the Sinn Féin movement, the Irish Republican Army (IRA), and British forces in Ireland. A united Ireland within the United Kingdom and under the British Crown was unacceptable to diehard Irish Republicans. Divisions within Sinn Féin were exposed after a military stalemate between the IRA and British forces, in 1921, led to negotiations between the British Government and Sinn Féin. The result was a Treaty which saw the Irish delegates accept 'Dominion Status' for twenty-six Irish counties. On paper this independence seemed limited: the British King was head of state, represented by a Governor-General, and all elected representatives had to take an Oath of Allegiance to the King.

The terms of the Treaty produced a split within Sinn Féin causing a bloody civil war during 1922-1923 and the formation of two new political parties: the pro-Treaty Cumann na nGaedheal, later Fine Gael; and the anti-Treaty Fianna Fáil party of Éamon de Valera. The political unity of the British Isles was therefore ended by the establishment of the Irish Free State or Saorstát Éireann (encompassing the twenty-six counties of 'Southern Ireland', defined in the Government of Ireland Act) as an Irish Dominion, within the British Empire, or British Commonwealth of Nations, but outside what was now the United Kingdom of Great Britain and Northern Ireland.

This agreement was expressed in the Articles of Agreement for a Treaty, commonly called the 'Treaty' and was given force of law in the United Kingdom by the Irish Free State (Agreement) Act 1922. It gave 'Ireland' the name of the Irish Free State. However, and crucially, the reference in Article 1 to 'Ireland' *did not* include Northern Ireland. This had profound consequences for issues of sovereignty in Ireland.

In 1925, the Irish Government formally recognised the borders between the Irish Free State and the United Kingdom of Great Britain and Northern Ireland, in an Agreement negotiated by it and the British and Northern Irish Governments. The Agreement declared that 'the British Government and the Government of the Irish Free State, being united in amity in this undertaking with the Government of Northern Ireland, and being resolved mutually to aid one another in a spirit of neighbourly comradeship' agreed that the territory of Northern Ireland was to be that set out in the Government of Ireland Act 1920. It was also agreed that the powers of the Council of Ireland were to be transferred to the Parliament and Government of Northern Ireland. The Agreement was confirmed in domestic law by the Free State and British Parliaments.

The succession of de Valera's Fianna Fáil party to power in the Free State, in 1932, witnessed a reversal of the policy of mutual co-existence between the Irish and Northern Irish Governments. De Valera progressively dismantled the Treaty and promoted his vision of a united sovereign Irish republic. He removed the Oath of Allegiance in 1932; deleted all constitutional references to the King in 1936; abolished the office of the Governor-General; and introduced, in 1937, a new written Constitution, Bunreacht na hÉireann. The official name of the Free State was now 'Éire', or in the English language, 'Ireland'. The effect of these changes was to establish a republic in all but name. It was really at this point that Southern Ireland can be said to have formally severed its connection with the British Commonwealth; however, neither the British nor the Irish Governments were willing to push this point. Ulster Unionists were particularly angered by the South's territorial claim, in Bunreacht na hÉireann, to the territory of the whole of the island. Article 2 of the Constitution, defining the Irish Nation, declared that:

> The national territory consists of the whole island of Ireland, its islands and the territorial seas.

Article 3 stated that:

> Pending the re-integration of the national territory, and without prejudice to the right of the parliament and Government established by this Constitution to exercise jurisdiction over the whole of that territory, the

laws enacted by the parliament shall have the like area and extent of application as the laws of Saorstát Éireann and the like extra-territorial effect.[3]

This was a territorial claim. According to the Irish Constitution, Northern Ireland was a part of both the Irish nation and the independent Irish state. It was not part of the United Kingdom. Thus the Irish state formally challenged the right of British sovereignty in Northern Ireland. When the Government of Ireland – to use the official title of the state – announced in 1948 that it was to formally become a republic, the British Government, after consultations with the Northern Ireland Government, passed the Ireland Act, in 1949. This recognised that Ireland/Éire, now commonly called the Republic of Ireland, had ceased to be part of His Majesty's Dominions. With reference to Northern Ireland the key clause of the Act was Clause 1 (1) B. For the first time the province's secession from the United Kingdom was made conditional on the consent of the Northern Ireland Parliament. The clause stated that:

> Parliament hereby declares that Northern Ireland remains part of His Majesty's Dominions and of the United Kingdom and affirms that in no event will Northern Ireland or any part thereof cease to be part of His Majesty's Dominions and of the United Kingdom without the consent of the Parliament of Northern Ireland.[4]

Within Northern Ireland, the combination of a guaranteed Protestant majority in government, a sense of being under siege from the South, and the presence of an occasionally violent, trapped and profoundly reluctant minority within its borders, led to the creation of a state apparatus designed to ensure survival. This included emergency legislation such as the power of internment without trial to combat periodic threats from IRA splinter groups. These laws were enforced by the overwhelmingly Protestant police force, the Royal Ulster Constabulary (RUC) and its exclusively Protestant special constable reserve, the B-Specials. One-party rule, that of the Ulster Unionist Party, was guaranteed by the 'first past the post' electoral system, ensuring the political dominance of one community over the other. Catholics were rarely recruited to the institutions of the regional government because of their alleged 'disloyalty'.

The phrase, used by Lord Craigavon, Northern Ireland's Prime Minister from 1921 until 1940, that he presided over a 'Protestant Parliament for a Protestant people', has to be understood in the context of the perceptions Ulster unionists had of the independent Irish state. The Free State's provisional government, under the direction of Michael Collins, had, during the early 1920s, supported IRA attacks upon the Northern state, hoping to force it into union with the South. Unionists regarded Northern Ireland as the Protestant part of Ireland and the South the Catholic part. The problem was that a third of the North's population was not Protestant or Unionist.

The consequence was, almost inevitably, a society which treated the minority with, at best, suspicion and, at worst, discrimination and bias. Yet the primary grievance of Northern Nationalists was not discrimination but that the partition of Ireland was unnatural. There was, consequently, a general refusal to accept its legitimacy and, particularly in the early years, to participate in its institutions. Northern Nationalists, like their counterparts in the South, were overwhelmingly drawn from the Catholic community. On both sides of the border there was a Catholic-Nationalist consensus – Northern Ireland was an abomination; it was artificially created by the British Government; it had no right to exist; and the best way to end its existence was to persuade the British Government to terminate its existence against the wishes of the Protestant majority there.

Added to these perceptions was the attitude of the Northern Ireland Government. Northern Nationalists complained that the Northern Ireland Parliament refused to give justice to the minority and their representatives. Every attempt to have the grievances of the minority discussed at Westminster was defeated by the existence of a 'convention' which prevented discussion of matters within the competence of the Northern Ireland Parliament. Northern Nationalists protested at discrimination against Catholics in the civil service, the creation of a Protestant-dominated paramilitary police force, and the gerrymandering of electoral wards to produce artificial Unionist majorities. In turn Ulster Unionists regarded Northern Nationalists as enemies determined to destroy the devolved administration.

The new Irish state was equally unable to understand that the Northern unionists were not just posturing in their determination to remain British, and that their Protestantism was an important and unbargainable part of their position. The power of the Roman Catholic Church in the South was obvious and public and a religiously homogeneous southern Irish state was assumed and legislated for. The Gaelicisation of Saorstát Éireann also alienated Unionists from their sense of Irishness. Ulster Unionists saw 'Pro-Gaelic' as 'Anti-British'. Neither Unionists nor Nationalists could comprehend the other.

Solutions

Following the explosion of communal violence in Northern Ireland, in 1969, attempts were periodically undertaken to resolve the crisis. This did not take place within a vacuum. Outside Northern Ireland international law had evolved, and was to continue to evolve, during the following thirty years of conflict. There were other significant changes: both the British and Irish Governments became partners within the European Economic Community in 1973; both sought to contain the violence in Northern Ireland; both sought a political accommodation within Northern Ireland, between Northern Ireland and the Republic of Ireland and between the United Kingdom and the Republic.

Attempts at resolving the ethno-national conflict in Northern Ireland involved two aspects: an internal accommodation between the unionist and nationalist communities; and an external accommodation between Northern Ireland and the Republic of Ireland. The internal accommodation was to be based on the concept of powersharing or consociationalism. The most straightforward form that this might take was that of a grand coalition cabinet in a parliamentary system. But Ulster unionists, although a minority in the United Kingdom, constituted a majority in Northern Ireland. As such they wished to retain regional autonomy, by majority rule, because they did not regard their national government as sufficiently able, or willing, to withstand the demands of Irish Nationalists for the termination of Northern Ireland's membership of the United Kingdom. Majoritarian devolved self-government was seen as a bulwark against absorption by the Irish state. Unionists feared that the problem with consociational democracy in Northern Ireland was that a substantial section, if not the majority, of the Catholic/Nationalist minority was determined to break the surrounding constitutional settlement by which Northern Ireland remained part of the United Kingdom.

This perception had a profound impact on the second aspect of conflict resolution in Northern Ireland – a possible external accommodation between Unionists in Northern Ireland and Nationalists in the Republic of Ireland. This was based on two fundamentally different views concerning the relationship between the two parts of Ireland. The major causes of dissension occurred between Unionists and Nationalists over the form that North-South institutions might take. Northern Nationalists were less keen on internal power-sharing schemes than on institutionalising their national identity on a North-South basis. The problem was that whereas most Unionist schemes for the internal governance of Northern Ireland were to involve the retention of majority rule, most Nationalist schemes for an institutional North-South dimension involved the possibility of Northern Ireland either being absorbed by the Republic of Ireland – through the creation of a unitary or federal Irish state – or being governed by joint authority. Broadly, after the imposition of Direct Rule by London in 1972, the options preferred by Unionists and Nationalists were as follows:

Full Electoral and Administrative Integration within the UK (Unionist solution)
Unionists argued that the British state was a modern pluralist state which accommodated multi-national and multi-ethnic identities. Therefore, full integration into the British state, with its respect for diversity, was the best method for dealing with Northern Ireland's inter-communal tensions. This could take a number of forms: electoral integration whereby mainland British parties would organise in Northern Ireland; or administrative integration whereby Northern Ireland would not be treated as a place apart but would be administered like Scotland and Wales prior to devolution in those countries. The continuation of Direct Rule seemed to offer the best long-term hope for this model.

Devolved Northern Ireland Assembly with Majority Rule (Unionist solution)
A return to the situation where there was a devolved parliament/assembly
within the UK to control Northern Ireland's domestic affairs would ensure
that political power would be wielded by whichever party or parties could
secure an overall electoral majority. In the traditional model it was assumed that
the elected representatives of the unionist community would form a cabinet. In
a reformed majority rule system there could be an element of low-level power-
sharing. Unionist, Nationalist and other non-Unionist/Nationalist parties
might have places on backbench committees according to the number of votes
secured in elections. This was known as proportionality. The committees
would have a role scrutinising the functions of the assembly/parliament. There
would be no automatic places for opposition parties in any cabinet.
Assembly/parliament decisions, subject to certain voting thresholds as a
safeguard for minorities, would be determined by majority voting.

Confederal North–South Consultative Body (Unionist)
The creation of a consultative North–South body with no executive power
would provide an institutional but confederal relationship, i.e. a loose link
recognising the separate nature of the Republic of Ireland on the one hand and
Northern Ireland as part of the United Kingdom on the other – with both
agreeing to co-operate on certain matters. It would be composed of
representatives from a devolved Northern Ireland administration and the Irish
Government. Ministers from both jurisdictions would meet and consult on
cross-border initiatives. Agreed all-Ireland or cross-border projects would be
authorised by a devolved Northern Ireland assembly/parliament and the Irish
Parliament in their separate jurisdictions.

Confederal British–Irish Consultative Body (Unionist)
The creation of a British–Irish consultative council encompassing the geographical
entity of the British Isles would ensure an institutional confederal link between the
sovereign states of the United Kingdom and the Republic of Ireland as well as any
devolved structures therein. It could be composed of representatives from the
sovereign UK and Irish Governments; from devolved Northern Ireland, Scottish
and Welsh administrations established within the UK; as well as those from
outside the UK but within the British Isles such as the Channel Islands.

North–South Body with Executive Power establishing Joint Authority (Nationalist)
A powerful North–South body with executive power to make decisions on an all-
Ireland basis would be composed of representatives from a devolved Northern
Ireland administration and the Irish Government. It could eventually
accumulate enough executive functions to act as an all-Ireland government.
Authority would flow from the North–South body and not the Northern Ireland
Assembly or the Irish Parliament. This could constitute Belfast-Dublin joint
authority.

British–Irish Joint Authority (Nationalist)

The British and Irish Governments would share executive authority over Northern Ireland. The British Government would retain sovereignty but would choose to exercise that sovereignty by agreeing to jointly administer Northern Ireland with another sovereign state, the Republic of Ireland.

Devolved Northern Ireland Assembly with Power-Sharing (Nationalist/Unionist)

This option was also known as consociationalism and co-determination. A devolved Northern Ireland assembly would be established in which Unionist and Nationalist political parties would share executive power on an entrenched basis. It would probably take the form of a power-sharing cabinet. This option was favoured by many Nationalists and a minority of Unionists.

Federal Irish State (Nationalist)

Northern Ireland would leave the United Kingdom to be absorbed within an all-Ireland state but would retain a high degree of autonomy. In a composite Irish state, executive and legislative powers would be shared and divided between the central all-Ireland government and the regional Northern Irish government. This option was favoured by many constitutional Nationalists and some Republicans.

A Unitary Irish State (Nationalist)

A sovereign independent united Ireland with no devolved or federal autonomy for Northern Ireland would involve the expulsion of Northern Ireland from the United Kingdom and its absorption by the Republic of Ireland. This option was favoured by most Republicans and many constitutional Nationalists.

Given the different perceptions and aspirations of Unionists and Nationalists it appeared unlikely that there could ever be any agreement between the opposing groups. Unionists looked to internal Northern Ireland institutions which guaranteed Nationalists a minimalist access to power. Unionists hoped to maintain their internal dominance and a low-level external relationship with the Republic of Ireland. Nationalists refused allegiance to a system of government which did not recognise their communal identity either internally or externally. In particular the favoured Nationalist institutions for North-South relations included mechanisms which appeared to have the potential for a fast-track approach to the political integration of Northern Ireland and the Republic.

The picture was compounded by two other factors. Firstly, neither Unionists nor Nationalists really accepted the legitimacy of the other. Many Unionists regarded nationalists as British whether they liked it or not. Furthermore, they believed that the symbols of the region and its institutions should be British in all their manifestations. Many Nationalists could not accept that unionists were British with the implications this had for the concept of the Irish nation. Instead they considered unionists to be members of the Irish nation who should have no veto over the short-term or long-term unification of the country. Secondly, there was the factor of violence. Substantial sections of Northern Ireland society were prepared to aggressively demonstrate the righteousness and moral superiority of their world-view by supporting, or at least acquiescing in, the use of violence. Violence acted as a pressure point for both communities. It could be seen as not only advancing a particular point of view, but also as acting as a check on undesirable outcomes.

Dummy Run: Sunningdale and its Failure

The outbreak of the modern phase of the Troubles destroyed the old political order in Northern Ireland and this led to the first Anglo-Irish governmental attempt to resolve the conflict. The failure of this attempt led to the multitude of preferred solutions outlined above. From the early 1970s, the Ulster Unionist Party tore itself apart after more than fifty years in power. Its dominance of Unionist politics was challenged by the Reverend Ian Paisley's Democratic Unionist Party. Within the Catholic community the Nationalist Party was swept aside by the young Turks of the Social Democratic and Labour Party. The Republican Movement split over the question of recognising the 'partitionist' parliaments in Ireland. Provisional Sinn Féin, the political wing of the emerging Provisional IRA, held true to the traditional policy of abstentionism. Almost by default the SDLP became the representatives of the nationalist community as the Republican constituency in Northern Ireland opted out of politics.

The latent cold war between the two communities snowballed into terror and counter-terror as the PIRA attacked the institutions and personnel of the state, while Loyalist paramilitaries, such as the Ulster Defence Association/Ulster Freedom Fighters and the Ulster Volunteer Force, took their bloody revenge on the Catholic population. Faced with escalating violence the British Government suspended the Northern Ireland Parliament and in 1972, London imposed Direct Rule. Stormont's powers were vested in a newly-created Secretary of State of Northern Ireland. A new Northern Ireland Office took over the running of the Northern Ireland Government's ministries which were turned into six departments to be administered by civil servants. For the first time since 1920, the local unionist community had lost control of its political destiny. From now on all Northern Ireland legislation would be passed at Westminster by Order in Council, with minimal parliamentary time and debate.[5] Northern Ireland's Unionist politicians were powerless.

Violence peaked in 1972, by far the worst year of the entire Troubles. To find a way out of the downward spiral of civil disorder, the British and Irish Governments began the search for a new political accommodation. This involved two aspects. First, they sought a greater role for the Catholic community in the government of Northern Ireland. Second, they developed an 'Irish Dimension'. Since both of these strategies appeared to be aimed at appeasing nationalist alienation from the state, the British Government also sought to reassure the unionist community. Westminster passed the Northern Ireland Constitution Act 1973 which transferred the principle of consent from the suspended Northern Ireland Parliament to the Northern Ireland electorate. This reassured the unionists that there could be no change in the constitutional status of Northern Ireland without the consent of a majority of the people there. For Unionists this was the 'constitutional guarantee', but for Nationalists it was the 'Unionist Veto' – a mechanism to block political progress. The Act defined Northern Ireland as the unit of self-determination which would decide if Northern Ireland was to remain within the United Kingdom. The relevant section stated:

> It is hereby declared that Northern Ireland remains part of Her Majesty's dominions and of the United Kingdom, and it is hereby affirmed that in no event will Northern Ireland or any part of it cease to be part of Her Majesty's dominions and of the United Kingdom without the consent of the majority of the people of Northern Ireland voting in a poll held for the purposes of this section ...

The Act also provided for power-sharing between Catholics and Protestants. There would have to be a 'broadly based' Executive, or cabinet. Otherwise there would be no Northern Ireland Assembly.[6] So, to regain any political influence in Northern Ireland, Unionists had to share political power with Nationalists. This was too much of a shock for many in the unionist community who had been used to 50 years of political dominance.

The British Government set out its vision of the 'Irish dimension' in October 1972. They returned to an old idea: the Council of Ireland. This would operate at an intergovernmental and interparliamentary level between Northern Ireland and the Republic. Any Northern Ireland executive might '(a) consult on any matter with any authority of the Republic of Ireland' and (b) 'enter into any arrangements with any authority of the Republic' in respect of any matters transferred to it by Westminster.[7] Unionists would regain control of their domestic affairs and be reassured by the principle of consent. Nationalists would share political power in Northern Ireland and have their political identity recognised in a North–South institution.

The UUP, led by Brian Faulkner, would only agree to a North–South body on certain conditions. Firstly, the Republic of Ireland had to recognise the right of the people of Northern Ireland to self-determination. This meant altering Articles 2 and 3 of the Irish Constitution. Secondly, a North–South Inter-Governmental Council could be established. Members would be drawn equally from the Northern Irish and Republic's governments to discuss mutual co-operation in economic and social matters. But the UUP was adamant in its rejection of any attempt by the Republic to interfere in Northern Ireland's internal affairs. It would not allow any Council of Ireland to 'become a stage on the road to Irish unity'.[8] The key point here was that the UUP's

Intergovernmental Council was *consultative*: it would be a forum where Ministers from Northern Ireland and the Republic would meet to discuss matters of mutual interest and concern. The Intergovernmental Council would not of itself have any executive power – it would not have the power to implement decisions arrived at in consultations between Northern and Southern Ministers. It was to be Faulkner's retreat from this position which would split his party.

Faulkner encountered widespread opposition from within the UUP to his decision to accept power-sharing. He thought power-sharing would integrate Catholics into Northern Ireland. But those who opposed power-sharing took a different view. They feared that the SDLP would seek to destroy Northern Ireland's position within the UK from inside a power-sharing executive. However, the opponents of power-sharing were unable to command a majority within the key institutions of the UUP. This allowed the power-sharing Executive to take its first faltering steps to assuming power in the province. In November 1973, the make-up of the Executive was announced. Faulkner was made Chief Executive and Gerry Fitt, leader of the SDLP, Deputy Chief Executive. Six other Unionist members, five SDLP members, and two Alliance members completed the Executive. For the first time since 1920, Nationalists were at the heart of Northern Ireland's government. Many within the unionist community were prepared to tolerate power-sharing, but few were prepared to accept the form which the Irish dimension was about to take.

In September 1973 the British Government succumbed to Nationalist pressure and accepted a Council of Ireland with *executive* functions. This was fundamentally different from the *consultative* Intergovernmental Council the UUP had envisaged. A Council of Ireland with executive powers could be an embryonic all-Ireland government. From the Irish Government's point of view the Council appeared to be a fair settlement for both unionists and nationalists in Northern Ireland. It was after all a retreat from the standard demand for rapid unity. Garret FitzGerald, Minister for Foreign Affairs in the Republic's Fine Gael-Labour Coalition Government, described the Council as designed to respond in a balanced way to the different aspirations of Nationalists and Unionists. On the one hand it would be open ended, with the capacity in principle to evolve towards an all-Ireland political institution. This responded to Nationalist aspirations. On the other hand, both its initial functions and any extension of its role were to be subject to Unionist agreement. Unionists were to be reassured by (a) the Irish Government accepting equal representation for North and South on the Council's Ministerial body, despite the fact that the South had twice the population of the North; (b) providing that all decisions within the Council were to be taken by unanimity, thereby granting Unionists a veto; and (c) giving to the representatives of the Northern majority a determining voice in the timing and method by which the Council would evolve.

In December 1973, at the Sunningdale Conference in England, the British and Irish Governments as well as the SDLP and the cross-communal Alliance Party agreed the structure of the Council of Ireland. Crucially, so did Faulkner and this was to have far-reaching consequences. It was agreed that in addition to harmonising laws between North and South, as proposed by Paddy Devlin of the SDLP, the Council would have, from the beginning, certain executive functions in sectors where there was currently North-South duplication, e.g. tourist promotion, electricity generation, and agricultural and industrial research. Ministerial Council decisions were to be unanimous; but the *extension* of the Council's functions were to be determined by a majority vote in a second-tier Council Assembly.[9] It was this ability for the Council to evolve, and extend, its executive power, which was to give the institution the appearance of an embryonic all-Ireland government. Nationalists could envisage the slow, but steady, growth of a joint Belfast-Dublin executive body, by-passing the Northern Ireland Assembly and supplanting the Irish Parliament. A *de facto* all-Ireland state could evolve without any formal transfer of sovereignty from Westminster to Dublin.

This clearly pleased the SDLP. Their preferred model was far closer to the Sunningdale model than that proposed by the UUP. The SDLP had originally proposed that the British and Irish Governments agree to impose joint London-Dublin sovereignty over Northern Ireland. Two British and Irish Commissioners would act as the 'Representatives of the Sovereign Powers' to jointly sign all legislation passed by a Northern Ireland Assembly. The SDLP also proposed a National Senate of Ireland which would have equal representation from the Dublin Parliament and a Northern Ireland Assembly. The basic function of the Senate would be to plan the 'integration of the whole island by preparing the harmonisation of the structures, laws and services of both parts of Ireland and to agree on an acceptable constitution for a New Ireland and its relationships with Britain'. The SDLP envisaged that this would lead to the 'emergence of a Parliament for the whole of Ireland'.[10] Clearly, then, the Council of Ireland could fit in with the SDLP's aim of creating a 'New Ireland'. While there would not now be British-Irish joint authority, there would effectively be Belfast-Dublin joint authority.

If the form that the North-South body finally took at Sunningdale represented a fundamental setback for Faulkner – despite his subsequent attempt to disguise this by his description of it as 'necessary nonsense' to appease Nationalists – he fared no better with the Republic's territorial claim to Northern Ireland. When he stressed the need to settle the issue of Northern Ireland's constitutional status as a precondition to establishing the Council of Ireland, one of the Irish delegation, Conor Cruise O'Brien, responded that a simple proposal to delete Articles 2 and 3 from the Irish Constitution would certainly be rejected by the people of the Republic in a referendum; the Irish Government should not be pushed on the issue, he said. A working group was set up to draft reciprocal declarations that would be made by the two Governments.[11] The fudging of this issue was to significantly undermine Faulkner's position within the unionist community.

Aside from the constitutional issues, the Irish Government had also wanted significant changes made to policing in Northern Ireland, and this reflected Northern nationalist alienation from Northern Ireland's security forces such as the RUC. Nationalists wanted to change the name of the RUC and break it into a number of local forces based on the British model.[12] While the British wanted the police forces, North and South, to stay under their respective governments, the Irish, on the other hand, favoured allowing the Council of Ireland to direct policing on an all-Ireland basis. This, the Irish believed, would help the Northern minority to identify with the RUC, particularly as it seemed the British would not change the name of the force, which the Irish felt reflected the ethos and symbolism of the unionist community alone.[13]

The Irish proposed a common law enforcement area comprising the whole of the island, with a court consisting of an equal number of judges from North and South to be appointed by the Council of Ireland. This would try persons accused of scheduled – terrorist – offences in the jurisdiction where they were arrested. The Irish Government proposed this as a means of circumventing the difficulties created by the Republic's High Court, which had rejected extradition to Northern Ireland for 'political' – or terrorist in Northern Ireland – offences on constitutional grounds.[14]

Faulkner, however, believed that unless the Northern Ireland Executive had real policing powers, he could not sell the overall agreement to unionist opinion. The SDLP saw no way of overcoming nationalist alienation from the police unless the RUC were seen to be in some way responsible to the Council of Ireland, in which the Republic would have a key role.[15] Eventually, the British Government, which was reluctant to return control of security to the Province, agreed to meet Faulkner's requirement by conceding that 'as soon as the security situation problems were resolved and the new institutions were seen to be working effectively, they would wish to discuss the devolution of responsibility for normal policing and how this might be achieved with the Northern Ireland Executive and the Police.' On the other hand, in order to meet the SDLP's requirements, it was agreed that the Irish and Northern Ireland Governments would co-operate on policing 'under the auspices of the Council of Ireland' through their respective police authorities.[16]

The final agreement was published in the form of a joint British and Irish Government Communiqué. It announced that the Council of Ireland was to have a Council of Ministers consisting of seven members from the Northern Ireland Executive, and seven members from the Irish Government. It was to have 'executive and harmonising functions and a consultative role', but with decisions only being made by a unanimous vote. There would be a

Consultative Assembly, with 30 members from the Northern Ireland Assembly, and the same number from the Dáil, having advisory and review functions. There would also be a permanent secretariat to service the institutions of the Council and to 'supervise the carrying out of the executive and harmonising functions and the consultative role of the Council'.

Co-operation on security matters saw Article 10 of the Communiqué promise an Anglo-Irish special commission to discuss amending laws on extradition, the creation of a common law enforcement area in which an all-Ireland court would have jurisdiction, and the extension of domestic courts to enable them to try extra-territorial offences. Article 15 provided for the Republic and the Executive to set up two Police Authorities to which appointments would be made after consultation with the Council of Ministers; the Authorities would then seek to improve 'community identification with and support for the police services'. Article 5 dodged the question of the Republic's territorial claim to Northern Ireland in the form of parallel declarations by the Irish and British Governments:

> The Irish Government fully and solemnly declared that there would be no change in the status of Northern Ireland until a majority of the people of Northern Ireland desired a change in that status.

> The British Government declared that it was, and would remain, their policy to support the wishes of the majority of the people of Northern Ireland. The present status of Northern Ireland is that it is part of the United Kingdom. If in future the majority of the people of Northern Ireland should indicate a wish to become part of a united Ireland, the British Government would support that wish.[17]

While both declarations stated that Northern Ireland's status could not be changed without the consent of a majority of its people, only the British declaration defined Northern Ireland as part of the United Kingdom. The Irish declaration could not. In Irish law Northern Ireland was part of the Republic of Ireland; it was not part of the United Kingdom. From a Unionist perspective the Irish declaration was worthless.

In his memoirs, Faulkner persuaded himself that the Unionist delegation at Sunningdale had come off best during the negotiations. This was clearly at odds with the recollection of the other delegations as well as his own. But Faulkner was satisfied that formal co-operation against terrorism had been agreed for the first time, and on the question of the recognition of the constitutional status of Northern Ireland, he claimed that not since de Valera laid claim to Northern Ireland had Unionists achieved a recognition by the Republic of Northern Ireland's right to self-determination within its existing boundaries. They had also received an *informal* commitment that the constitutional claim would be removed at the earliest opportunity.

Faulkner argued that the price Unionists had to pay for this progress lay in the Council of Ireland. The Council of Ministers would have a valuable practical role in formalising co-operation on security and social and economic matters. In a very real sense getting the Irish Government to treat Northern Ireland representatives as equals on an inter-governmental body would underline their acceptance of partition. The other 'appendages' of the Council – the Consultative Assembly, the Permanent Secretariat, the executive functions of the Council of Ministers – 'fell in my mind into the "necessary nonsense category"'. They were necessary to get the co-operation of the SDLP and the Dublin Government. But nothing agreed at Sunningdale infringed on the powers of a Northern Ireland Assembly by which everything would have to be approved and delegated. Given the overwhelmingly Unionist composition of that body and the unanimity rule in the Council of Ministers, Faulkner was 'satisfied that the constitutional integrity of Northern Ireland was secure'.[18]

But Faulkner's optimism was soon shown to be misplaced. Immediately after the Sunningdale Agreement, the Taoiseach, Liam Cosgrave, gave an interview in which he stated: 'There is no question of changing our Constitution with regard to our claim of sovereignty over all of Ireland.' Effectively, Cosgrave was confirming that the Irish declaration at Sunningdale did not admit that Northern Ireland was part of the United Kingdom. The Irish Government was worried by a legal action taken by a former Irish cabinet minister, Kevin Boland, who claimed its declaration was unconstitutional and recognised Northern Ireland as part of the United Kingdom. Therefore, as Garret FitzGerald pointed out, 'we must be able to deny and disprove *all* the claims made by Boland.' This involved being able to deny that the two declarations made by the Irish and British Governments were part of an international agreement, since Northern Ireland was a domestic issue according to the Irish Constitution; deny that the Irish declaration acknowledged that Northern Ireland was part of the United Kingdom; or that it purported to limit the national territory to a portion of the island of Ireland.

The Irish Government also had to deny that the declaration limited the right of the Irish Parliament and Government to exercise jurisdiction over the whole island of Ireland, or to preclude Irish courts exercising jurisdiction over the whole island of Ireland. And, explained FitzGerald, the Irish Government had to assert that its declaration at Sunningdale merely enunciated the *policy* of the Irish Government as to the manner in which a united Ireland could come about. As FitzGerald subsequently admitted, 'Legally we had an impeccable defence – and it succeeded. Politically, in its impact on unionist opinion, it was totally disastrous.'[19] The Irish Government's successful defence of its position meant that Faulkner could no longer claim that the South had recognised Northern Ireland's constitutional status as part of the United Kingdom.

The power-sharing arrangement and the Sunningdale Agreement

eventually collapsed in May 1974. The Ulster Workers Council and anti-Sunningdale Unionists called for a general stoppage which paralysed Northern Ireland. Effectively this was an insurrection by Northern Ireland's Protestant community. The anti-Sunningdale Unionists had converged into what was to be a short-lived coalition, the United Ulster Unionist Council. Faulkner and his supporters were swept aside. At the Northern Ireland Constitutional Convention, in 1976, the UUUC demanded the return of a Northern Ireland Parliament with majority rule and emphatically rejected power-sharing.[20] Instead, it proposed that a parliamentary system of backbench committees be established, covering each department of government. The committees would consist of members drawn equally from government and opposition. In addition, the committees would be empowered to scrutinise all the activities of their departments, and each committee would be involved in the process of legislation relating to its department. To protect the rights of the Catholic minority the UUUC proposed a Bill of Rights. There would be no institutionalised North-South relationship with the Irish Republic – not even a consultative forum. Issues of common concern between Northern Ireland and the Republic would be dealt with separately by the respective governments.[21]

The fall of Faulkner and his supporters in the UUP resulted in a political ascendancy within Unionism which demonstrated a distinct lack of tactical or strategic imagination. The call for simple majority rule and the rejection of consociational government offered no chance of attracting moderate Nationalism into acknowledging the legitimacy of Northern Ireland's position within the United Kingdom. But Nationalists appeared unaware of the contribution they might have made to the collapse of the Executive and the Sunningdale Agreement. Many Nationalists saw the fall of the Executive as a result of the inability of the incoming British Labour Government to send in troops to quell what was a communal insurrection. They did not advocate this when their supporters where rebelling against the state. For years they looked with disdain on the limited vision of the new Unionist political élite. But this was partly their fault – Faulkner and moderate Unionism had been as much destroyed by the excessive demands of Irish Nationalism as by the irreconcilables of Unionism.

A subtler analysis would be to appreciate the following: firstly, the shock for the unionist community of losing their majority-controlled Parliament was immense, as was the realisation that Unionists would have to share power with Nationalists. At one level many Protestants plainly did not want to share power with Roman Catholics on a theological basis; on another level, many unionists believed that Nationalists would seek to destroy Northern Ireland's constitutional position from within the heart of government. Added to this was the fact that Faulkner had been unable to secure constitutional recognition and stability for Northern Ireland. He had not received from the Irish Government a recognition of Northern Ireland as part of the United Kingdom; and by being pressurised into accepting a North-South body with executive rather than consultative powers, as well as a Consultative Assembly which would add to those powers by a majority vote, he had accepted what many Nationalists inside and outside Northern Ireland regarded as a fast-track route to an embryonic all-Ireland administration through joint Belfast-Dublin authority.

This was to be the fundamental error of 1973-1974: the acceptance of an internal consociational settlement by Unionists was only possible if constitutional stability was accepted by Nationalists in the longer term. In all probability such a settlement was not possible in 1973-1974. Neither Unionists nor Nationalists understood or accepted the legitimacy of each other's position. The next two decades were indeed, in the words attributed to Seamus Mallon, to be a case of 'Sunningdale for slow learners' – but for both Unionists and Nationalists.

PART I

From the Anglo-Irish Agreement to Inter-Party Talks

Defining an 'Agreed Ireland': Constitutional Nationalism 1976-1984

It was in the failure of the Sunningdale Agreement that the route to the Anglo-Irish Agreement was conceived. The UWC Strike convinced many within the SDLP, and its deputy leader John Hume in particular, that an alternative strategy was required to circumvent traditional Unionist intransigence and unwillingness to share power with Catholics. Over the next twenty years Hume would dominate Nationalist thinking on Northern Ireland. It was he who would revive the Anglo-Irish process and impose the parameters of Nationalist-Unionist dialogue. Yet his major failing was, and remained, an inability to grasp that Unionist resistance to reaching agreement with the SDLP might not be because Unionists refused to compromise but because every solution sought by the SDLP was blatantly geared towards moving to a Nationalist solution. This meant either rapid movement towards a united Ireland – by the Council of Ireland or Joint British/Irish sovereignty – or a united Ireland full stop, as with their proposal for a federal Ireland.

Hume consistently saw Unionism in simple terms. In 1978 he compared Northern Ireland to the situation in Rhodesia. He asked if the minority white community there would have bothered to talk to the majority blacks if they, like the Unionists, had been assured of continuing British support regardless of their actions. Hume was referring to the 'constitutional guarantee' contained in the 1973 Northern Ireland Constitution Act which he had come to regard as a Unionist veto on any political change. He believed that the major question in the North was how Unionist intransigence could be ended. The Unionist policy of exclusiveness, he argued, was bound to lead to violence; but the British Government had the power to alter the situation. Hume concluded that the problem in the North was essentially one of identity for the majority population.[1] Unionists did not know whether they were Irish or British or just Protestant.

By now, the SDLP had abandoned their proposals for joint British-Irish rule over Northern Ireland but instead came up with the solution of absorbing Northern Ireland into a federal united Ireland. Hume believed that the British Government had three options open to it. The first was to maintain the position that Northern Ireland would remain part of the United Kingdom for as long as a majority of people there wanted it to remain so. This meant that Unionists had no reason to look at any other alternative. The second option was to make, as the Provisional IRA wanted, a declaration of intent to withdraw from Northern Ireland. The SDLP and Hume rejected this option because 'we believe it would not leave behind a united and peaceful Ireland. In fact, we believe there is a serious risk that it might leave behind a much more divided Ireland. What happens when this declaration of intent is made? Does everybody think the Unionist population will be prepared, like lambs, to sit around the table? I don't believe the majority of them would rise up. ... But I believe there is a serious risk that a significant number of them would react violently.' That being the case, violent action and reaction would leave, at best, a repartitioned Ireland after a lot of bloodshed. An additional weakness in this approach was that a political party that committed itself to securing a declaration of intent, as a first step to progress, completely handcuffed itself if that declaration was not made. The third option open to the British Government was to declare that its objective in Ireland was the bringing together of both Irish traditions in reconciliation and agreement:

> Another way of putting that is bringing them together in unity. We believe that this is a reasonable objective, one which no one can object to, particularly when it's made clear that agreement is essential to it. We believe that this should be the basis of British policy now, instead of the maintenance of the Union. They should commit all their resources, all their powers of persuasion towards that end in the same way as they have committed all their resources in the past to maintaining the Union.

The British Government would therefore become persuaders for Irish unity. But, added Hume, Nationalists had to spell out to Ulster Protestants what they meant by unity. In the past, Irish Nationalist political parties had failed to spell out what they meant by unity, or their vision of it. This meant that Loyalists had easily been able to interpret unity as something the Protestant people of the North ought to be afraid of, something that could trample on their rights or coerce them into a hostile state. Hume believed that 'one concept which would instantly, I think, do a lot to remove Loyalist fears – or so called fears that are whipped up by politicians – would be to spell out that one form of agreed Ireland would be in fact a power-sharing Ireland. There is one specific form of a power-sharing Ireland that I'm actually talking about and that would be the North ruling itself inside a federal Ireland. That, I believe, would represent power-sharing. This would allow the Northern people to protect themselves in the areas where they felt they needed protection and it would allow full-scale co-operation and partnership between both Irish traditions. It would also give the Northern people much more influence ... on fundamental issues in relation to agriculture and Europe.'

Hume believed the Unionists had few options – to continue as they had been doing and seek a restoration of their ascendancy with a majority parliament in Northern Ireland; or pursue integration with Britain. Either of these options ignored the Catholic minority and its aspirations. Thus they were doomed to failure and would lead only to continuing violence. Another option for Unionists was the realisation that 'unity is inevitable – and many say so privately. If this is so, is the right approach not to begin now to negotiate ... the future of Ireland rather than to wait until some British Government arbitrarily forces them into something that they don't like? I believe this second object is much more attractive, particularly when the offer being made for reconciliation both by the South and the Northern minority is one which will reassure them that the end objective is not domination.'[2]

Hume argued that if a new, more inclusive form of Irishness could be embodied within an independent pluralist Irish state, then the unionist community, which would retain a significant degree of self-government in a federal Irish state, could be persuaded to accept unity. But this could only occur if the British Government encouraged them to believe that their long-term interests lay with that destiny. In 1980, Hume, by now leader of the SDLP, espoused many of the core elements that became the foundation of his political philosophy. He believed that 'Unionists will not be able to bring themselves to entertain seriously the notion of Irish unity unless Dublin unambiguously spells out what it understands by unity and gives clear evidence of its commitments.' The Southern state was seen by many Unionists as a lay expression of sectarian Catholic values, and as such was unacceptable to them. Unionists had a right to be convinced that the South was serious when it declared its intention to embody pluralist values in the law of the united Ireland to which it aspired. Even more seriously, those who avowed a united Ireland had to clarify how they would implement this.

Hume thus called for a positive and decisive initiative by London and Dublin acting together. Firstly, they would make it clear that there were no longer any unconditional guarantees for any section of the Northern community; there would only be a commitment to achieving a situation in which there were guarantees for all. Secondly, they would make it clear that there was no solution as such, only a process that would lead to the solution: 'They should declare themselves committed to such a process, a process designed to lead to an agreed Ireland with positive roles for all.' An invitation for all parties would be issued to participate in this process, and although some groups would undoubtedly react with an initial refusal, the 'process should continue without them, leaving the door always open for their participation at any stage'.[3]

In July 1980, the full impact of Hume's strategy on the Irish Government's Northern policy was illustrated when both it and the SDLP endorsed a common policy. The Taoiseach, Charles Haughey of Fianna Fáil, represented the unreconstructed Nationalist *par excellence* and was committed to a simple British declaration of intent to withdraw from Northern Ireland. But Hume persuaded Haughey to modify this simplistic approach. Both now agreed three areas: the need for the British Government to declare its interest in Irish unity; that any settlement should take the Irish dimension into account; and that the situation should be raised to a new inter-governmental level and considered in the context of closer co-operation between the British and Irish Governments. Both parties insisted that the 'way would be opened towards political progress if the British Government were to declare their interest in Irish unity, by consent, and in peace, and their willingness to participate in the process for achieving it'.[4]

Progress towards this goal appeared feasible when Anglo-Irish co-operation was initiated in the same year by Margaret Thatcher and Haughey. Both premiers were committed to 'develop new and closer political co-operation between their two governments,' and with this purpose in mind, to hold regular meetings. The first meeting, in December 1980, promised to give special consideration to the 'totality of relationships within these islands', and commissioned a series of joint studies. An Anglo-Irish Intergovernmental Council was created following talks between the British and Irish Prime Ministers during 1981 and 1982. It met at Head of Government, ministerial or official level. The framework of the Council would allow for discussion of matters of common interest and concern to the two Governments, including cross-border co-operation and other matters of common concern between the Republic of Ireland and Northern Ireland.[5]

None of this meant that Mrs Thatcher's Conservative Government was wedded to this Anglo-Irish process. As relations between Haughey and Thatcher were soured during the Falklands War, the British sought a purely internal Northern Ireland settlement. Mrs Thatcher's sympathies were instinctively Unionist and in 1982 the British Government established a new Northern Ireland Assembly. Its scope was strictly limited: it had no legislative powers and merely possessed 'scrutinising, deliberative and consultative functions' which sought to improve the processes of Direct Rule by establishing committees entrusted with the monitoring of the NIO Departments. Essentially it was a talking shop. But there was the possibility that the Assembly could evolve through a process of 'rolling devolution'. Unionists saw in this the hope of eventually regaining control of Northern Ireland's domestic affairs.[6]

But Hume's primary aim was to destroy the Assembly. As far as he was concerned it was an irrelevance which did not address the core elements of the conflict. The SDLP boycotted the Assembly and since it required 'cross-community' support in order to acquire more powers, the SDLP's refusal to participate meant it was dead in the water. Hume dismissed the British devolution proposals as unworkable because of Unionist intransigence and unacceptable because they represented a dilution of power-sharing and the Irish dimension. The SDLP believed that a solution should be sought 'once again in its proper framework. It is abundantly clear that a purely internal solution to the problem of Northern Ireland is not possible. A solution must deal with the problem which is one of relationships not only within Northern Ireland but within Ireland and between Britain and Ireland. The Anglo–Irish framework is therefore the proper framework for a solution.'[7]

Hume concluded that there should be a new Irish 'Constitution on the table at the time when the British Government may change its mind about Northern Ireland'.[8] Therefore the SDLP proposed to the Irish Government that a 'council for a new Ireland' be set up with membership from the Dáil and the Northern Ireland Assembly and tasked with producing a blueprint dealing with the problems in the way of an agreed Ireland. Hume argued that this would give political parties in the South an opportunity to state their positions on the economic, social and constitutional obstacles to Irish unity. The council would be open to 'elected democratic parties' who believed in 'a new Ireland'. This would automatically exclude even elected members of Sinn Féin, as it would be confined to Nationalists 'who believed in the ballot box not the Armalite'.[9]

Hume stressed that while any final solution had to be acceptable to Ulster Protestants, that 'right is not an absolute right. It's a right that's qualified by the right of the [Northern] minority to an acceptable solution and by the rights of the British and Irish governments who will be called upon to enforce or pay for any settlement.' Ideally, this would lead to Unionists asking for independence from Britain. But this would be unattainable because it would not have the consent of the Northern minority nor that of the British and Irish Governments. At this point Nationalists would say to Unionists, 'We're not agreeable to independence but we are agreeable to autonomy'. Northern Ireland would be offered federal autonomy within an independent Irish state. There would also be an external Anglo–Irish Council, an institutional link with Britain, to recognise the British identity of Unionists.[10]

The rise in electoral support for Sinn Féin, following the Hunger Strikes of 1981, now provided an important catalyst to the Anglo–Irish process. In an effort to consolidate the SDLP's position in Northern Ireland, constitutional Nationalism throughout Ireland sought to reinvent their ideology through a variation of Hume's council for an agreed Ireland – the New Ireland Forum. In the New Ireland Forum Report of 1984, the parties to the Forum, consisting of the major Southern political parties, and the SDLP, reaffirmed their shared aim of a united Ireland, pursued only by democratic political means. Perhaps the most significant ideological result of the Forum was the recognition that Irish Nationalists had 'hitherto in their public expression tended to underestimate the full dimension of the unionist identity and ethos'.[11]

The Forum identified three elements of what they perceived unionists wanted to preserve: 'Britishness'; Protestantism'; and the 'economic advantages of the British link'.[12] This amounted to the first time that the representatives of constitutional Irish Nationalism, North or South, had officially recognised the right of unionists to their British identity. But, crucially, the description of unionist Britishness as a 'tradition' still allowed Nationalists to define unionists as a minority within the Irish nation. Therefore, the Forum did not allow its recognition of the unionists' sense of Britishness – by defining them as a separate national community – to undermine its goal of an 'agreed Ireland'. To do this would be an admission that there were two nations in Ireland and would destroy the fundamental basis of Irish Nationalist ideology. For example, it was re-emphasised that the fault for partition lay not with unionist resistance to a united Ireland, but remained the 'imposed division of Ireland' by the British Government which 'created an artificial political majority in the North'.[13]

The Forum concluded that the solution to the Northern Ireland conflict required new structures which would accommodate two sets of legitimate rights: 'the right of nationalists to effective political, symbolic and administrative expression of their identity' and 'the right of unionists to effective political, symbolic and administrative expression of their identity, their ethos and their way of life'.[14] The Forum defined 'agreement' in Ireland as meaning that the 'political arrangements for a new and sovereign Ireland would have to be freely negotiated and agreed to by the people of the North and the people of the South' – in other words a united Ireland. The particular structure of political unity which the Forum wished to see established was a 'unitary state, achieved by agreement and consent, embracing the whole island of Ireland and providing irrevocable guarantees for the protection and preservation of both the unionist and nationalist identities'. A second model considered was that of a two-province non-denominational federal or confederal state based on the two existing entities of North and South. The third option suggested by the Forum was 'Joint Authority', described as the 'equal sharing of responsibility and authority for all aspects of the government of Northern Ireland by the governments of Great Britain and Ireland' including external relations and diplomatic representation.[15]

However, the Forum Report revealed deep divisions between the main Southern political parties. Charles Haughey and Fianna Fáil would only endorse the Report if the preferred choice was a unitary state. As his special advisor on Northern Ireland, Martin Mansergh, explained, a confederal Ireland was unacceptable because it would not be a united Ireland in any strict sense. Effectively it would involve an independent Northern Ireland co-operating with the Republic for certain purposes. Furthermore, it was Haughey's belief that Northern Ireland was a failed political entity. This automatically precluded a federal Ireland because it would involve the revival of a parliament at Stormont albeit in an all-Ireland context. Mansergh feared that every difference of opinion could escalate into a constitutional conflict between the two parts of Ireland. He was also sceptical as to whether the nationalist community in Northern Ireland would be happy to settle down again under a majority-rule Stormont – there would be little point of having a federal system if Unionists were 'not allowed a relatively free hand'.[16]

The Forum's final option had been joint authority which clearly owed much to the SDLP's proposals of 1972. In their unpublished section on joint authority, members of the Forum had decided to avoid the complicated question of sovereignty. Instead they set up a sub-committee of all the parties, including the SDLP, to consider the merits of joint authority. According to the report:

> Joint authority is the equal sharing of responsibility and authority for all aspects of the government of Northern Ireland by the governments of Great Britain and Ireland. Power over all matters relating to Northern Ireland would be vested in and exercised by an Executive Joint Authority of the two governments. The Executive Joint Authority would appoint a Joint Authority Commission to run Northern Ireland. Beneath this there could be whatever levels of local responsibility that the Executive Joint Authority might wish to establish and were agreed by local representatives. A binding agreement or treaty between the two governments would establish the Executive Joint Authority.

Choosing joint authority rather than joint sovereignty would avoid the conflict between the provisions of Articles 2 and 3 (which stated that Northern Ireland was part of the Republic) and Section 1 of the Northern Ireland Constitution Act (which stated that Northern Ireland was part of the United Kingdom) while preserving the 'essential element of joint sovereignty', i.e. responsibility for all aspects of government and international relations. The report proposed two different models of joint authority. One was a system of 'shared direct rule' in which the Joint Authority Commission exercised all executive powers; the other was a system in which certain powers would be reserved to the Commission while the main executive authority was elected by a local executive supported by a locally-elected Assembly.[17]

In 1984 joint authority was the preferred choice of the Republic's Fine Gael-Labour Government, led by Garret FitzGerald. The opportunity to push for this came with mounting concern in London at the electoral rise of Sinn Féin. Anglo-Irish negotiations were spurred on by the fear that Sinn Féin could overtake the SDLP as the dominant Nationalist party in Northern Ireland. Sensing the British concern, in May 1984, FitzGerald authorised an approach to the British based on the Forum Report. This involved taking up the unitary state model; if that was unacceptable to the British, the federal or confederal model; and if that in turn proved unacceptable, a set of ideas incorporating joint authority in a form that would be durable and provide for the possibility of Irish unity. The Irish Government indicated the possibility of movement on Articles 2 and 3, but only in return for British movement in the direction of joint authority.[18]

However, Margaret Thatcher's response to the Forum's proposed conclusions was that each option was 'out ... out ... out'. As she admitted: 'My own interests are profoundly Unionist. ... I felt the greatest sympathy with the Unionists while we [the Conservatives] were in Opposition. I knew that these people shared many of my own attitudes, derived from my staunchly Methodist background. Their warmth was as genuine as it was usually undemonstrative. Their patriotism was real and fervent, even if too narrow. They had often been taken for granted.' Thatcher's imperative, however, started from the need for more security. If this meant making limited concessions to the South, much as she disliked this kind of bargaining, then 'I had to contemplate it.' From Thatcher's perspective, despite the fact that she had a 'great deal of respect for the old Stormont system' and believed that Catholic claims of discrimination were 'exaggerated', she accepted that the political realities of Northern Ireland prevented a return to majority rule.

The Prime Minister also rejected the analysis of Enoch Powell, the former Conservative minister, who was now a UUP MP, and the influence he had within his adopted party and with its leader, James Molyneaux. Powell's aim was 'integration', which would have meant eliminating any difference between the government of Northern Ireland and the rest of the United Kingdom, ruling out a return to devolution and any special role for the Republic. Powell's view was that terrorists thrived on uncertainty about Ulster's constitutional position and that this uncertainty could be ended by full integration combined by a tough security policy. Thatcher disagreed with this for two reasons. Firstly, she did not believe that security could be disentangled from wider political issues. Secondly, she saw devolved government and an assembly for Northern Ireland, not as weakening the Union, but rather strengthening it. Like Stormont before it, it would provide a clear alternative focus to Dublin, without undermining the sovereignty of the Westminster Parliament.[19]

As far as Thatcher was concerned the PIRA were the 'core of the terrorist problem; their counterparts on the Protestant side would probably disappear if the IRA could be beaten.' Thatcher considered that the best chance of beating them would occur if three conditions were met. Firstly, the PIRA had to be rejected by the nationalist community on whom they depended for shelter and support. This required that the minority should be led to support or at least acquiesce in the constitutional framework of the state in which they lived. Secondly, the PIRA had to be deprived of international support, whether from well-meaning but naïve Irish Americans, or from Arab revolutionary regimes like that of Colonel Gaddafi. This, explained Thatcher, required constant attention to foreign policy with the aim of 'explaining facts' to the misinformed and cutting off the supply of weapons from the mischievous. Thirdly, and linked to the other two, relations between Britain and the Republic of Ireland had to be carefully managed. Although the PIRA had plenty of support in areas like west Belfast, 'very often it is to the South that they go to be trained, to receive arms and to escape capture after crimes committed within the United Kingdom'. The border was of crucial significance to the security problem. Thatcher concluded that much depended on the willingness and ability of the political leaders of the Republic to co-operate effectively with British intelligence, security forces and courts. So it was that throughout Thatcher's time in office, security and political initiatives were intertwined.[20]

Consequently, while Thatcher rejected the Irish Government's proposals for joint authority she was prepared to develop the idea of a *consultative* role for the Republic in Northern Ireland. While the idea of amending Articles 2 and 3 was attractive to Thatcher it was 'clear that the Irish would expect a good deal in return, and I ... doubted their capacity to deliver the referendum vote.' The British, instead, pressed the Irish for some kind of firm declaration committing them to the principle that unification could only come about with the consent of the majority in Northern Ireland. This, it was hoped, would reassure the Unionists.[21]

On 15 November 1985, the British and Irish Governments signed the Anglo-Irish Agreement. For the first time the Irish Government was given a consultative role in the affairs of Northern Ireland. An Inter-Governmental Conference was formed, dealing with political matters, security and related matters, legal matters and the promotion of cross-border co-operation. Under Article 2(b) the British Government committed itself 'in the interests of promoting peace and stability' to make determined efforts to resolve any differences which arose within the conference with the Irish Government. Article 5(a) stated that the Conference would look at measures to 'recognise and accommodate the rights and identities of the two traditions in Northern Ireland, to protect human rights and prevent discrimination'. Matters to be considered in these areas included measures to foster the culture and heritage of both traditions, changes in electoral arrangements, the use of flags and symbols and the avoidance of social and economic discrimination. Article 5(c) of the Agreement stated that 'if it should prove impossible to achieve and sustain devolution on a basis which secures widespread acceptance in Northern Ireland, the conference shall be a framework within which the Irish government may, where the interests of the minority community are significantly or especially affected, put forward views on proposals for major legislation and on major policy issues, which are on the purview of the Northern Ireland departments.'[22] For Unionists, in particular, nothing was going to be the same again.

Republicanism: Towards an Electoral Strategy

Throughout the 1970s and 1980s the main threat to political stability in Northern Ireland remained the paramilitary campaign of the Provisional IRA. According to Republican ideology, the PIRA were the direct descendants of the 1919 Dáil Éireann parliament, elected in 1918, the occasion of the last all-

Ireland parliamentary election. As such, the Army Council of the PIRA was the 'legal and lawful government of the Irish Republic which has the moral right to pass laws for, and to claim jurisdiction over, the whole geographical fragment of Ireland, its maritime territory, air space, mineral resources, means of production, distribution and exchange and all of its people regardless of creed or loyalty'. As the PIRA's leadership was the lawful government of the Irish Republic, all other parliaments and assemblies in Ireland were 'illegal assemblies, puppet governments of a foreign power, and willing tools of an occupying force'. PIRA Volunteers were urged to believe 'without doubt' that all PIRA orders were the legal orders and actions of the Government of the Irish Republic.[23]

While Republicans remained locked in an ideological time warp, not all Republican thinking was out of synch with constitutional Nationalist thinking. For the PIRA, and its political wing, Provisional Sinn Féin, the Irish conflict resulted from the British claim of sovereignty in Ireland and the consequent denial of self-determination to the Irish nation. Unionists in Northern Ireland were a religious minority within the Irish nation and to accommodate them, the Provisionals announced, in the 1970s, their Dáil Uladh policy which would see the establishment of a nine-county Ulster Parliament in a federal Ireland. The stumbling block to any solution, according to the Republican Movement, had always been the Unionist fear of being swamped in a Catholic-dominated Republic. Therefore, the Republican Movement recognised the civil and religious concerns of Protestants, but not their Britishness, as a core element of their desire to remain within the United Kingdom.[24] The fundamental difference between Republicans and constitutional Nationalists was not the goal of a united Ireland but how to achieve it; Republicans believed that armed struggle was crucial to the endgame.

In July 1972 the Provisionals had the opportunity to put their proposals to the British Government. A PIRA delegation including a young Gerry Adams and Martin McGuinness met William Whitelaw, the Secretary of State for Northern Ireland for talks in London. The Republican delegation demanded that the British Government publicly recognise the right of the people of Ireland, acting as a unit, to decide the future of Ireland and to declare its intention to withdraw all British forces from Irish soil, such a withdrawal to be completed on, or before, the first day of January 1975. A fundamental difference between the British and the Provisionals occurred on the question of all-Ireland elections and Irish self-determination. For the British the unit of self-determination was Northern Ireland, while for the Provisionals it was the island of Ireland.

Whitelaw brought up the objection that the British Government had several times given constitutional guarantees to the majority in Northern Ireland. This was rejected by the Provisionals, who protested that this guarantee came from the Ireland Act 1949, passed in the British House of Commons, and that 'no act of that parliament could not be set aside by another.' In the Republican view these guarantees 'were not insurmountable problems. All that was required to remove them was a simple majority in the House of Commons'. Therefore, in the Provisionals' view, the solution to the Irish Question rested, not on persuading the unionist community to accept a united Ireland, but on persuading the British to legislate for a united Ireland in the British House of Commons.[25] Whitelaw later described the meeting as a 'non-event', calling their ultimatums 'absurd' suggestions which no British Government could ever concede.

The Republican Movement remained undeterred by this apparent knock-back. Optimistic that victory was near, the PIRA declared a temporary unilateral ceasefire, leading to a truce which effectively lasted for most of 1975. Talks with British Government officials convinced the Provisionals that the British were prepared to disengage from Northern Ireland. According to the Provisional leader, Ruairí Ó Brádaigh, the PIRA were in receipt of a message from the British over the Christmas period that 'H[er] M[ajesty's] G[overnment] wished to devise structures of disengagement from Ireland.' But what did this mean? Merlyn Rees, the Secretary of State, claimed it really meant that if a permanent cessation of violence was achieved, security would be reduced to a 'peacetime level'.[26] The truce broke down when it became clear that the British administration was not leaving Ireland.

The 1975 ceasefire sowed a deep distrust of the British Government among Republicans. It did not, however, dent the Republican Movement's capacity for optimism. In March 1977, convinced of the inevitability of their victory, the Ulster Executive of Sinn Féin had observed, 'The signs of British withdrawal from the Six Counties are becoming more and more obvious with each passing day.' Republicans, throughout the North, could clearly see the evidence of dwindling troop numbers, fewer road blocks, and fewer patrols. This was based on a 'deteriorating security situation, the British Army's inability to defeat the risen people, and the collapse of economic life here'.[27] By 1978, *An Phoblacht* concluded that since no Irish war, in over 800 years, had lasted so long, the 'war cannot be lost and, indeed, the evils of our adversaries, military and political, will become more obvious, along with the obvious justice of our cause, in the months ahead. This should make possible the mass support needed to force the invader to withdraw, thus ending the war of liberation. This phase cannot be far off now.'[28]

The Republican Movement's political fortunes, and in particular those of its political wing, Sinn Féin, were boosted by the emotional trauma caused in the Catholic-Nationalist community by the events of the 1981 Hunger Strikes. It allowed the Republican Movement to develop a second front. Ten Republican prisoners died, evoking a similar reaction among many of the nationalist population of Northern Ireland as the 1916 executions had throughout nationalist Ireland over 60 years earlier. The election of hunger striker Bobby Sands as an MP opened up a new strategy for the Republican Movement. The following electoral success enjoyed by Sinn Féin encouraged the Republican Movement to adopt a two-fold strategy, symbolised by a senior Republican, Danny Morrison, at the party's Ard Fheis in October 1981. There, he asked the delegates, 'Who here really believes we can win the war through the ballot box? But will anyone here object if, with a ballot paper in one hand and the Armalite in the other, we take power in Ireland?' In elections to the new Northern Ireland Assembly in October 1982, Sinn Féin obtained 64,191 votes, or 10.1 per cent of the valid poll, while the SDLP polled 118,891 votes, or 18.8 per cent of the poll.[29]

Electoral success encouraged younger elements of the Republican Movement, centred around those from the North, such as Gerry Adams, Martin McGuinness and Danny Morrison, to advocate ending the boycotting of elected institutions in Ireland. Up to this point abstentionism had been a core element in Republican thinking. It was proposals to follow a similar path which in 1969 had led to a split in the IRA and the formation of the Provisionals. In the first stage the proposed change in policy was to be limited to Southern Irish parliamentary institutions. A change in Sinn Féin's stance occurred in 1983, when its Ard Chomhairle proposed that the party contest the forthcoming European Economic Community Parliamentary elections. This, and a decision to abandon the Dáil Uladh policy, led to the resignation of Ruairí Ó Brádaigh as President of Sinn Féin.[30] The new Ard Chomhairle saw Gerry Adams elected as President in his place. Adams reaffirmed his militant Nationalism in traditional terms:

> All casualties and fatalities in Ireland or Britain as a result of the war are sad symptoms of our British problem. ... Ireland geographically, historically and culturally is one nation. We as one people have the right to be free, and in that freedom the divided sections of our people will find the will to unite, regardless of religious affiliations, in establishing a society which meets the needs of all our people.[31]

Likewise, *An Phoblacht* criticised Dublin politicians for their 'rush' to recognise the 'existence' and 'rights' of unionism. As far as the Republican Movement was concerned:

> Historically, the ranks of unionism have included people of all religions who for political, social and/or economic reasons have defended the British connection. Their primary incentive was not patriotism but the realisation that their own personal or sectional interests were best guaranteed in the context of British imperial rule. This type of unionism – often described as Britishness – has never been peculiar to Ireland. In India, Uganda, and indeed all of its colonies, Britain maintained its control by creating, 'promoting' and defending similar sectional interests. As a reward for suppressing the majority, these élites were deemed British as a badge of superiority. As the sun began to fade rapidly on the empire and these colonial 'allies' arrived at Heathrow with their British passports, they were not made welcome. Like Northern loyalists, the Indian Sikhs and Ugandan Asians are resented as

foreign intruders on the streets of London, Manchester, etc. In the colonies the only criteria demanded of an aspiring British 'citizen' was and is support for the imperial institutions – crown and parliament.

The most zealous Northern unionists qualify on the basis of the above criteria. Their support for the crown is conditional on the crown remaining in Protestant hands, and they have regularly threatened to subvert the authority of the Westminster parliament if it suits their ends. British, Ulster/British and Ulster/Scots have all been used to describe the 'identity' of Northern unionists. But in all of this confusion, the only thing to emerge clearly is that unionists suffer from a crisis of identity. Modern unionism is a legacy of Britain's colonisation policy in Ireland. Every Irish county was colonised or 'planted' at one time or another but in most cases the descendants of these colonists, whether Norman, English, Scottish, Welsh, Palatine or Huguenot, were assimilated simply because, in time, they came to identify with the land and people of Ireland. In Ulster the story was different because there the plantation was so extensive that the colonists could form an exclusive social network, isolated from the native Irish, who were forced to flee to the mountains and bogs. Encouraged by Britain, the political, social and economic advantages of these colonists have been defended over the past 300 years through a system which is akin to apartheid.[32]

This was the immoral system which legitimised the PIRA's violence. In his first presidential address Gerry Adams elaborated on Sinn Féin's attitude to armed struggle: it was a 'necessary and morally correct form of resistance in the six counties against a government whose presence is rejected by the vast majority of Irish people'. But, in defending and supporting the right of the Irish people to engage in armed struggle, it was important for those engaged to be aware of the constant need and obligation they had to continuously examine their tactics and strategies. Revolutionary force 'must be controlled and disciplined so that it is clearly seen as a symbol of our people's resistance'. To those who said that the British Government would be unmoved by armed struggle, Adams observed that the history of Ireland and British colonial involvement throughout the world told Republicans that the British would not be moved by anything else.

On the broader front, Adams embraced the new stance on the EEC elections, perceiving it as an outlet to arrest the stagnation which had afflicted the Republican Movement since the mid to late 1970s. That, identified Adams, was the period in which anti-imperialist politics and the struggle for Irish independence had become isolated and restricted to its active base. There had been an 'unconscious slipping into "spectator politics"' whereby people who had been previously involved in the struggle were pushed into the sidelines. The situation had required a clear and conscious reappraisal which, in turn, led to the conscious reorientation of Sinn Féin towards an electoral strategy. This process was accelerated by the sacrifices of the Hunger Strikers. Their deaths emphasised that it was no longer sufficient to be passive supporters of the PIRA; more and more people began to realise that, insofar as the PIRA had established a military alternative to the British war machine, they as Republicans had a duty and a responsibility to establish alternatives to all the other facets of British involvement on the island.[33]

Retrospectively, Adams identified the early years of the 'liberation struggle' as a period in which there had been a popular base for Republicanism. At this stage Sinn Féin really was a 'second cousin' to the PIRA, and a 'very poor cousin at that'. It was a protest organisation capable, in moments of emotionalism, of mobilising for a short period of time a very large section of people. However, it did not have the organisation necessary for keeping those people or a sizeable section of them involved in the struggle. For example, Adams recalled that following Bloody Sunday, 'we had thousands of people heading towards us, but six months later we were back to ourselves again.' This was because Sinn Féin lacked a clearly perceived and wide-ranging strategy or policy to cope with the difficulties facing it. Sinn Féin could only stand and watch the increase in political collaboration between the Irish and British Governments, such as at Sunningdale – 'basically sell-outs'. The organisation was also faced with the problem in which, with spectator politics, 'a person [who] couldn't join the fight or was worn out after a period in prison, couldn't really do much.' Adams believed that Sinn Féin had become even more of a second cousin to the PIRA because of the emergence of plastic bullets, which forced people off the streets, and because the effect of 'marching up and down streets for six or seven years made people feel useless'.

The impact of the 1975 PIRA ceasefire was also crucial. The duration of the cessation was a mistake. Once the PIRA had been removed from the scene, and because there were no other manifestations of the struggle, it meant that the British were 'able to confuse republicans. We had people believing that the British government was about to leave.' Instead, it was clear that far from leaving, the British were increasing their counter-insurgency in a more sophisticated form, manifested in 'normalisation' and 'criminalisation'. Towards the end of this period, the Republican leadership had sat down and conducted a number of major reviews of the whole situation, not only to establish what had happened, but also to analyse what to do about it. This review took between three and four months, after which a number of basic decisions were taken: 'that we had to get back to and update our republicanism and that we had to establish a basic ideological unity so that the mistakes which were made in 1969 wouldn't happen again.'

It was agreed that the Republican base had to be broadened, that the community support which had previously existed had to be won back, that spectator politics had to cease and that Republicans had to build a party which would develop on the basis of a thirty-two county strategy. There was also a return of confidence within Republican circles that the armed struggle was not over. This occurred with Jimmy Drumm's speech at Bodenstown, which formally announced the 'Long War' strategy with the admission that the British were not leaving Ireland. At the same juncture spokespersons announced in numerous interviews that the PIRA had undertaken a review and re-organisation and were able to rebuild strength and confidence. While it had been suggested that electoral interventions might be introduced, Adams insisted that none of this was a part of a grand plan; in fact, 'Nobody had actually worked this strategy out, only that it was within the broad framework that an ideologically sound and united Republican Movement could use the electoral system to achieve its political objectives.'

Thus, in 1978-79, it was decided simply and in principle that a positive attitude towards an electoral strategy should be taken by Sinn Féin. The coincidence of the Hunger Strikes allowed an acceleration of this process. With the embracing of an electoral strategy, the Republican Movement 'wanted to build an electoral machine, do away with spectator politics, and bring about a situation where Sinn Féin would be every bit as relevant as the IRA. We want to build an opposition to the SDLP and show up the contradictions of the six-county state.'[34] Adams rejected any notion that the Northern Ireland statelet could be reformed to accommodate Northern Nationalists. He believed that the SDLP's position was flawed because:

> Hume will push his party towards whatever form of internal settlement satisfies the Dublin establishment, the British establishment, is acceptable to a section of the unionists, and at the same time accommodates some outward recognition of a nationalist identity. But there is a total difference between the person living in a British colony in the six counties, having the right to fly the Tricolour and speak Irish, and an Irish person living in an independent Ireland. What Hume will go for is some symbol of nationalist aspirations. But history proves that you cannot fulfil those aspirations without actually having national rights themselves.

Adams considered the SDLP a populist party. Both it, and Hume, could be 'all things to all men'. Seamus Mallon, the SDLP's deputy leader, could appeal to the Nationalist wing of his party by 'shouting' about RUC and British Army excesses, and Hume could woo the 'not so nationalist' wing by talking of joint sovereignty. The danger for nationalists, feared Adams, was that the personal and electoral popularity of Hume would mean that loyalists and their British allies, who perceived the SDLP as the softer Nationalist option, would believe that a significant section of the nationalist electorate were prepared to go for such a 'softer option'.[35]

By 1984, the electoral strategy was proving a welcome companion to armed struggle because, as the PIRA admitted, the ability to inflict casualties on the British military was becoming more difficult. British security personnel were better protected, through improved body armour and strengthened armoured vehicles. Nevertheless, the PIRA warned that 'these vehicles, British soldiers, local forces and out-of-uniform RUC and Ulster Defence Regiment men are still vulnerable to landmine and gun attacks and we will make full use of these methods'. Occasional bombing sorties in Great Britain, such as the no-warning Harrods bomb – which killed six people – were designed to inflict damage against enemy political and military targets and bring to the attention of the British public the fact that its government was engaged in a war in Ireland. Such a strategy relied on the premise that the British people did not support British Government 'sponsored murder' in Ireland. They would want their troops withdrawn, because of the cost of the war, the attrition rate, a sense of demoralisation and war-weariness. The Provisionals warned, 'This war is to the end. There will be no interval. ... When we put away our guns, Britain will be out of Ireland and an Irish democracy will be established.'[36]

The Brighton bomb, in 1984, which narrowly failed to kill Margaret Thatcher, was part of the strategy to 'wear down their [Government] political resolve'. Britain, after 15 years of conflict, 'cannot defeat us, so her occupation of Ireland is going to keep on costing her dearly until she quits'. Eventually, the British would have to say, 'We lost Airey Neave, Lord Mountbatten, Margaret Thatcher etc – is it worth it'? The PIRA speculated that had they been able to kill Thatcher, the British would have responded with widespread repression; but the Provisionals estimated that the bulk of the PIRA would have remained intact. From this political crisis – the inability of the British to cope with the situation and the inestimable, expensive cost to their political system – it would have dawned on them that the war could not be won and would have led to a major and radical rethink along the lines of withdrawal. The PIRA were adamant that 'nothing they say or do has ever, or can ever, convince us that we cannot break them [the British]. We can break them.'[37] Subsequently, Gerry Adams concluded that the 'attempted execution of the British cabinet ... has helped to apply Thatcher's mind to the question of Ireland, and at least give it a greater priority than it had before.'[38]

But while the military purists remained convinced that they could break British rule in Ireland, it remained unclear, in the absence of killing the British Cabinet, precisely what could actually achieve a critical mass in the struggle and force the British to leave Ireland. Gradually, the Sinn Féin leadership began an attempt to reach outside the Republican Movement and search for allies in their liberation struggle. In December 1983, Adams had already written to Dr Cathal Daly, the Roman Catholic Archbishop of Down and Connor, requesting a meeting. Adams, by now MP for West Belfast, claimed that this was in order to discuss issues that might be of some benefit to the people of his constituency. The Archbishop's reply indicated the problems Sinn Féin had in trying to adopt a more respectable image as a legitimate political party. Daly politely declined the request. In his reply he pointed out that the organisation which Adams led was one which openly and publicly supported a campaign of physical force and demanded from its members 'unambiguous support' for an armed struggle, which it declared to be 'morally correct'. Daly found this completely contrary to the moral teaching of the Roman Catholic Church, which condemned the physical force campaign as 'morally evil'. Daly noted that Adams's letter gave no indication that as President of Sinn Féin he was prepared to revise his stated positions which were at variance with this teaching. In the light of this, Daly could not at that time agree to a meeting.

Adams, unsurprisingly, was disappointed on the grounds that 'if a solution to our present colonial difficulties is to be found, then dialogue without preconditions is of paramount importance.' Adams argued, 'We all have a duty to seek ways to resolve the present conflict. This can only be done by means of dialogue and by an honest and frank exchange of views.'[39] Daly's response also drew sharp criticism from the PIRA leadership, which on the sixty-fourth anniversary of the Easter Rising not only proclaimed the right to armed struggle but also pointed to the lack of an alternative:

> Today we commemorate and honour the patriots of Easter Week 1916, who – with no blessing or mandate other than that inherent in the natural right of all nations to national sovereignty and self-determination – went out to do 'bloody and deadly violence' against our enemy whose susceptibility to reasonable persuasion is as absent today as it was then. .... The IRA's use of revolutionary force results from the inescapable fact that we are left with no peaceful or democratic alternative by which to achieve the national rights of our people. ... But we will not lie down. We cannot lie down. Our martyrs, our people, our children and the unborn generations demand that we pursue this struggle to a successful conclusion and end this evil forever.[40]

The lack of a 'peaceful or democratic alternative' mentioned by the PIRA was to become a key justification for the continuation of the armed struggle. The reality was that the Republican Movement remained unaware of the compromises it would have to make in order to come in from the political wilderness. For Sinn Féin, as the only true keepers of the Nationalist Holy Grail, it was the Southern Irish political parties and the SDLP which had betrayed the faith. At the annual Bodenstown commemoration, in 1984, Jim McAllister, from south Armagh, gave the Republican Movement's response to the New Ireland Forum. McAllister described the Forum as an attempt to save the SDLP from becoming a 'galloping irrelevance'. Likewise, to protect their collective political back, the Republic's parties had advocated the 'preferred' option of a unitary state. But, true to their political practice of supporting the *status quo*, their real partitionist position, concealed as alternatives 'worthy of consideration', was embodied in the federal and joint sovereignty proposals. The Forum Report was a 'dead duck'. Its immediacy lay, not in bringing about any short-term change in the political arrangement existent in Ireland, however superficial, but in fortifying the flagging nationalist *bona fides* of the conservatives who participated in its formation. The Forum's intent was psychological – to deceive Irish nationalists and thus bolster the position of Irish and British conservatives. While, in the long term, joint sovereignty/federation was a potentially important political weapon, it had been put into cold storage, to be dragged out at some future period of heightened crisis for the *status quo* of partition. Sinn Féin now clearly stood as the only all-Ireland Republican party.[41]

Adams, in turn, criticised the Forum Report for failing to contest the reality of British claims to sovereignty in Ireland and for failing to assert the right of the Irish nation to national self-determination.[42] The President of Sinn Féin concurred with Danny Morrison's view that among the many dangers of the Forum was the fact that it would raise nationalist expectations and that when the British 'knocked the Forum down ... those nationalists who had expectations would suffer humiliation. That is what has happened.'[43] The way forward for Irish Nationalists was to recognise that one had to take a 'dogmatic and principled stand' towards the British connection and partition. 'There can be no such thing', claimed Adams, 'as an Irish nationalist accepting the loyalist veto and partition.' Sinn Féin, far from being excluded from the Forum, should have had the same rights to put across its point of view, for it represented a sizeable section of nationalist opinion in the Six Counties. 'Had we had our say in the Forum', speculated Adams, 'and we had been listened to, I think there would have been a much different outcome today. We would not have agreed to go to the British government with a report which was a dolly-mixture of various options, and we certainly would not be trying to negotiate with a government which showed no willingness to talk to us.'

Adams felt that for decades the revisionists and the pro-British ethos of the Dublin establishment had diluted Irish national pride. Mrs Thatcher had showed how little respect the London administration had for Dublin, for the British had no reason to respect a partitionist government which had been consistently subservient to British interests and reluctant to press the Irish case for self-determination. What was required was the 'restoration of national pride'. This could not be done by meaningless nationalist rhetoric; it needed 'firm action, a united approach and a steadfast maintenance of our principles'. It would involve stopping the extradition of terrorist suspects between the North and South and ending any cross-border collaboration.[44]

For Adams, the subsequent London–Dublin talks, leading to the Anglo-Irish Agreement, were necessary from a British point of view because: 'The sustained resistance of recent years has made the unionist methods redundant ... and Britain is seeking new ways to repress or neutralise opposition to their rule.' On the role of the Dublin government, Adams argued that before the rise of Sinn Féin, the British–Unionist alliance had meant that the use of the Orange card was always successful. The Unionists, in British propaganda terms, were the guarantors of the Union. Now that the Unionist failure to accommodate or defeat Nationalist opposition was clear,

Britain no longer needed the Orange excuse as much as it did before. In recent times, and especially since the Hunger Strikes, London and Dublin interests, always complementary, had become clearer, with the urgent merging of their objectives. Therefore, whatever the outcome of the current talks, and with agreement likely, London's role would be to confront the Unionists while Dublin's role would be to lower Nationalist aspirations, so that both Governments could pursue their joint objective of defeating Republicanism.[45]

Martin McGuinness was equally dismissive of the proposed Anglo-Irish co-operation, recalling how twice the British, with the co-operation of the Irish Government, had sought to 'rationalise and sanitise' partition in Ireland. Settlements that 'ignore reality, that ignore history, that do not confront the real issue, are not solutions at all, but devices that enable Britain to refine its repression of republicans and its partition of Ireland. ... The only talks that will ever have any relevance and hope for Ireland will be talks that involve the Republican Movement, talks with two items on the agenda – namely the disengagement of Britain from our country and self-determination for the Irish people.'[46]

Sinn Féin remained equally dismissive when the Anglo-Irish Agreement was finally signed. As far as Adams and Sinn Féin were concerned, the Agreement consisted of two major elements. Firstly, it institutionalised the British presence in Ireland and pledged Dublin's formal recognition of the Six-County state, partition, the loyalist veto and the British connection. Secondly, it contained a promise of concessions to improve the quality of life for nationalists in the Six Counties. Here, Adams argued that the 'establishment' had made the major mistake of believing their own propaganda. They believed that Sinn Féin flourished on deprivation, unemployment, poverty and one-sided laws. They ignored, or failed to note, Sinn Féin's commitment, whilst smashing partition, to work alongside ordinary people in an endeavour to win as many gains as possible within the twenty-six counties and Six Counties. Dublin and London readily admitted that their agreement was partly aimed at isolating Sinn Féin by introducing concessions. According to Adams the equation was therefore a simple one: support for Sinn Féin equalled concessions from the British. Adams pointed out that concessions, even for the wrong reasons, were good. They showed that the establishment could be moved. If they were substantial they whetted the appetite for more; if they were unsubstantial they exposed the claims of Sinn Féin's opponents as hollow. Sinn Féin realised that the Agreement was a long-term process aimed at ensuring that its electoral support did not increase.

Adams concluded that both Dublin and Unionism feared Sinn Féin for different reasons. Dublin feared Sinn Féin because it exposed the shallowness of Dublin's Nationalist credentials and the anti-working class nature of their policies on the national question and on other social, economic and cultural issues. Dublin was also dismayed by the fact that the

SDLP could no longer claim to be the sole representatives of anti-Unionists in the Six Counties, and feared that a parallel development in the twenty-six counties could herald unprecedented changes in voting patterns there. The Unionists feared Sinn Féin because of what it and the PIRA represented: the only real opposition to their supremacist politics, for 'Most loyalist leaders would not notice the difference, apart from climate and colour, if they lived in South Africa'.[47] Adams did not accept that Dublin's new involvement in the Six Counties was a positive development. If Dublin were committed to the 'reconquest of Ireland, to the decolonisation of the six counties, to the principle of Irish national self-determination and if the agreement was aimed at these objectives and geared towards a timetable, then there might be some merit in Dublin's involvement'. However, the Agreement did the opposite: one of its aims was to re-establish Stormont, albeit in modified form. This flew in the face of Dublin and SDLP assertions that no internal arrangement would be viable or acceptable.[48]

The joint military/electoral strategy, in contrast, appeared to offer increasing dividends for the Republican Movement. By September 1986, senior members of the Republican Movement now believed that Sinn Féin could hold the balance of power after the next Dáil elections if it ended abstentionism. Journalists were briefed that Sinn Féin expected to win up to five seats in an Irish general election, and then vote on whom would be the Taoiseach. Martin McGuinness believed that Sinn Féin had been damaged electorally in the Republic because of its abstentionist policy. He added that if the policy continued the party was unlikely to win any seats in a general election; but if the policy were dropped 'we'd probably get several seats, possibly five, though no more than that.' The previous year the Ard Fheis had rejected proposals for the removal of abstentionism; however, the issue resulted in an intense debate and the motion was defeated by only 25 votes.[49] In November 1986 the Ard Fheis voted to drop the abstentionist policy, securing the necessary two-thirds majority from the 628 delegates, by 429 votes to 161 votes, a majority of ten. Following the vote, at the Mansion House in Dublin, Ruairí Ó Brádaigh led his abstentionist supporters out of the hall. The dissidents established a new Republican organisation, pledging its support to the 'right of the Irish people to use whatever degree of control and disciplined force is necessary in resisting English oppression'. The chairman of the new organisation, Dáithí Ó Conail, denied that it intended to set up a new IRA 'at this stage'.[50]

The SDLP-Sinn Féin Talks

But, however optimistic the Republican Movement were about their long-term aims, it was also clear to some within Sinn Féin that the armed struggle on its own might be insufficient to redirect British policy towards eventual withdrawal. The electoral strategy had its limitations. Sinn Féin consistently failed to break the SDLP's dominance of Nationalist politics in Northern Ireland. With only modest electoral success there appeared little way, apart from armed struggle, in which Republicans could sustain their influence. There appeared to be a growing frustration for Adams, and Republicans generally, which lurked behind many of their confident comments. The PIRA were finding it increasingly hard to kill British soldiers from mainland regiments. This reflected the policy of Ulsterisation employed by the British from the mid-1970s. The overwhelmingly Protestant RUC and UDR were placed in the front-line battle against terrorism. This allowed a reduction in the number of troops from mainland regiments. Protestant members of the security forces now bore the main brunt of PIRA attacks. This highlighted a fundamental contradiction at the heart of Republican ideology. The armed struggle was waged against the British state in Ireland. But this involved killing a large number of Protestant police officers and soldiers who were supposedly part of the Irish nation.

Violence clearly dashed the Republican hope of reconciliation between Protestant, Catholic and dissenter. Adams revealed his frustration at the effectiveness of Ulsterisation, in 1988, when he explained that, from Sinn Féin's point of view, the killing of soldiers from British mainland regiments was 'vastly preferable' to the killing of members of the RUC and UDR. One reason for this was that the deaths of mainland British soldiers had a far greater impact on political and public opinion in Britain. But besides this: 'Callous as it may sound, when British soldiers die it removes the worst of the agony from Ireland.' Adams complained, without any hint of the implications this had for the ideology of Irish Nationalism, that one of the most malign results of Ulsterisation was that the British had been able to 'reduce the violence to Irish people killing each other'.[51]

Increasingly, Sinn Féin tried to reach out beyond the Republican constituency. Adams's attempt at dialogue with Cardinal Daly was part of this. But Sinn Féin's support for violence meant that they remained politically beyond the pale. However, an opportunity for dialogue arose from an interview with Adams published in *Hot Press*. Adams was asked if he personally would have the courage to call a halt to the armed struggle. He answered:

> Certainly. Certainly if there could be a total demilitarisation of the situation and an end to offensive action by all military or armed organisations. I would have no problem. I've already gone further. ... I [have] said that I would be prepared to consider an alternative, unarmed struggle, to attain Irish independence. If someone would outline such a course I would not only be prepared to listen, but I would be prepared to work in that direction. The difficulty is that no one has outlined a scenario by which unarmed struggle would achieve Irish independence and peace. ... Most of my discussions, and most of my statements ... are aimed at ... opening up a dialogue to seek an end to the causes of violence. ... There's no military solution, none whatsoever. Military solutions by either of the two main protagonists only mean more tragedies. There can only be a political solution. And Dublin has failed

to show any vestige of any political solution. They don't give a damn at all as far as I can see.[52]

This interview did not go unnoticed. John Hume read it, and the origins of what became known as the 'Peace Process' – that is the attempt to draw Republican paramilitaries away from armed struggle and into non-violent politics – began in talks between the SDLP and Sinn Féin in 1988. Hume attracted considerable criticism for embarking upon this course of action, particularly as it had followed so soon after one of the PIRA's most infamous bombings, that of a Remembrance Day service, in Enniskillen, County Fermanagh, in November 1987. Eleven people, all Protestants, had been killed in the attack.

But Hume remained undeterred. Sources close to him indicated that the SDLP leader had become interested in developing some form of dialogue with Sinn Féin following the *Hot Press* interview, and considered Adams's admission that no military solution was possible in the North to be a departure from previous hardline Sinn Féin sentiment. In December 1987, Hume had expounded on radio that there could be room for political progress if both Sinn Féin and the Unionists could be encouraged towards separate negotiations.[53]

This represented a fundamental shift in Hume's position. He now advocated a situation in which everybody, including Sinn Féin, would sit around a conference table, with the 'guns and bombs silent'. He rejected the accusation that Sinn Féin had bombed its way to the conference table, although he accepted that in the 1970s this would have been a correct interpretation: 'What has changed is that Sinn Féin stands for elections and they would be at the conference table on the same basis as anybody else would be at the conference table – on the basis of an electoral mandate.' It was 'easy to dismiss ... the Sinn Féin/IRA thing that they are a lot of gangsters and criminals. That is a simple way. If that were true, if they were only those things, if they were gangsters and criminals, they would be very easily dealt with. But they are not. They are completely dedicated to what they are doing. I disagree with them profoundly. They are a handed-down tradition which is out of date in modern Ireland.'

Hume believed that sitting down with Sinn Féin, face to face, which nobody had ever done, and engaging in what he thought both sides recognised as genuine dialogue, was 'the business of politicians because politics was the alternative to war'. At the heart of the Republican philosophy was the view that the Irish people had the right to self-determination and the right to sovereignty: 'I would accept that. But I would point out that the right of self-determination is a right which belongs to the people. What the people of this island are divided about is how to exercise that self-determination. Only when the people of this island reach agreement to exercise that right and how to exercise it will you get permanent peace.'[54]

The two parties now agreed to meet. Mitchel McLaughlin, a member of

Sinn Féin's delegation, indicated his party's attitude towards the talks. The time had come for all shades of Nationalism to 'agree one simple proposition, namely, the Irish people's right to national self-determination'. McLaughlin believed that the talks could be extended to cover all strands of political opinion in Ireland:

> We are out to persuade Irish nationalists that nothing but self-determination will suffice. Irish self-determination is a principle to which every Irish nationalist can subscribe. The SDLP, Fianna Fáil and the other parties in the 26 counties are on record supporting the concept of independence in one way or another. This support must now become a practical campaign with a minimum objective of a negotiated British withdrawal. After that it will be up to Irish men and women to decide in an amicable fashion the structures within which the Irish people can live and prosper.

McLaughlin emphasised that there could be no British solution or partitionist settlement. For example, the Anglo-Irish Agreement did not confront the real issue, which was the continuance of British rule in Ireland.[55] Tom Hartley, general secretary of Sinn Féin, posed the question: 'Should we attempt a strategy to push the SDLP and Fianna Fáil to adopt republican issues?' He argued that confrontation with the SDLP was counter-productive to the achievement of Sinn Féin's basic objective. Sinn Féin, said Hartley, had now to 'start looking at the SDLP in a more structured and political way'.[56] It was as part of this strategy that Adams called on Fianna Fáil and other political parties in the Republic to join in a 'national consensus on Irish reunification' and to adopt a joint strategy to achieve it. Speaking to Sinn Féin's Ard-Comhairle, he pointed out that while unification was the declared policy of most of the political parties in Ireland, it was no more than a stated ideal unless backed by a strategy to achieve it: 'British governments do not move of their own volition; they have to be pushed.' Calling for a broad consensus to include 'Irish nationalists, Republicans, socialists and democrats' to press for national self-determination, it was imperative for all parties supporting the ideal of unification, 'and particularly the Dublin Government party of the day', to adopt it as a policy objective and then draw up and implement a strategy to bring it about. 'Sunningdale was not part of such a strategy. The Hillsborough treaty is not part of such a strategy. Their end objective was, and is, the maintenance of partition.'[57]

But the talks were to emphasise the differences rather than the similarities between Sinn Féin and the SDLP. Hume and Adams met for the first time in January 1988. Sinn Féin presented a document, *Towards A Strategy for Peace*, to the SDLP. The document began by restating the traditional Republican view of the history of partition: 'For as long as Britain remains in Ireland its presence distorts the political landscape. Britain's interference has been and continues to be malign because its presence has been and continues to be based on its own self interests.' Given the lengths to which the British went to remain in Ireland, to consolidate their position, Sinn Féin concluded that Britain believed it to be in its interests to maintain the Union, to finance the Union, to let its soldiers die for the Union and, at times, to be internationally scandalised for the Union. The only solution to the current political conflict in Ireland was the ending of partition, a British disengagement from Ireland and the restoration to the Irish people of their right to sovereignty, independence and national self-determination. Sinn Féin's view was that the British Government needed to be met with a firm, united and unambiguous demand from all Irish Nationalist parties for an end to the Unionist Veto and for a declaration of a date for withdrawal. This would effectively solve the conflict because:

> Within the new situation created by these measures, it is then a matter of business-like negotiations between all representatives of all the Irish parties, and this includes those who represent today's Loyalist voters, to set the constitutional, economic, social and political arrangements for a new Irish state. We assert that the Loyalist people must be given, in common with all other Irish citizens, firm guarantees of their religious and civil liberties, and we believe that, faced with a British withdrawal and the removal of partition, a considerable body of Loyalist opinion would accept the wisdom of negotiating for the type of society which would reflect their needs as well as the needs of all other people in Ireland. The establishment of a society free from British interference, with the Union at an end, will see sectarianism shrivel and with the emergence of class politics a realignment of political forces along left and right lines.

The Irish democracy thus created would usher in the conditions for a permanent peace, a demilitarisation of the situation, and the creation of a just society. Within their general strategy, the political aim of Sinn Féin was to 'popularise opposition to British rule, and to extend that opposition into some form of anti-imperialist campaign. Our main political task is to turn political opposition to British rule in Ireland into a political demand for national self-determination.' That demand would be eventually realised when the will of the British Government to remain in Ireland was eventually eroded. The intended political effects of Sinn Féin's political strategy was to bring the British Government to the point where they wanted to leave by:

- frustrating British efforts to physically control the Six Counties
- highlighting the coercive and colonial nature of the Six-County state
- creating a broad based anti-imperialist movement
- developing the process of winning the confidence of the Unionist population
- winning widespread public opinion around to the correctness of this analysis.

Sinn Féin sought to create conditions which would lead to a permanent cessation of hostilities, an end to the long war and the development of a peaceful, united, independent and democratic society. Such objectives would only be achieved when a British Government adopted a strategy for decolonisation. This had to begin by repealing the Government of Ireland Act and publicly declaring that the Northern Ireland statelet was no longer a part of the United Kingdom. Furthermore, the British Government had to declare that its military forces and its system of political administration would remain only for as long as it took to arrange their permanent withdrawal. This needed to be accomplished within the shortest practical period. A definite date within the lifetime of a British government would need to be set for the completion of this withdrawal. Such an irreversible declaration of intent would minimise any Loyalist backlash and would go a 'long way towards bringing around to reality' most Loyalists and their representatives genuinely interested in peace and negotiation. It would be the business of such negotiations to set the constitutional, economic, social and political arrangements for a new Irish state through a Constitutional Conference.

On the issue of armed struggle, Sinn Féin argued that it should be 'seen as a political option' with its use considered in terms of achieving national political aims and the efficacy of other forms of struggle. This need to wage an armed struggle arose from the political experience of the Northern nationalist community which had been taught that the inherent undemocratic nature of the Union was maintained through the superior use of force by the British state; that the British state still acted against the democratic wish of a majority of the Irish people by its commitment to maintain the Union; and that Britain had no intention of withdrawing its political, military and economic interests from the Six Counties. Added to this was 60 years of ineffectual leadership by constitutional Nationalist politicians whose unwillingness to confront the British helped lock the Northern Catholic population into a state of second-class citizenship. Sinn Féin argued:

> It should be noted that armed struggle is forced upon the IRA. Neither the IRA nor Sinn Féin wants this war but the ineffectualness of all other forms of struggle, the conditions of repression that we have experienced, and British attitudes, have made armed struggle inevitable. The deaths and injuries caused by the war are all tragedies which have been forced upon the people by the British presence. Your party's [the SDLP's] bargaining leverage, plus the continuous need for Britain to apply time and energy through the mechanism of its various political initiatives, are proof enough that the armed struggle has been beneficial to the political aspirations of the nationalist community.

Sinn Féin rejected any reform of the Six Counties because the degree of political, civil and economic rights afforded to nationalists depended on the degree to which Loyalists would tolerate the erosion of their position of privilege. Even optimum Loyalist tolerance would not permit equality because 'Equality is synonymous with national rights. Partition is a direct contradiction to that.' The SDLP's acceptance of the Anglo–Irish Agreement was the lynchpin of a British Government strategy aimed at stabilising the Six Counties in its own interests by introducing limited or symbolic reforms which attempted to make the Northern state more tolerable for a section of the nationalist community and to international opinion. The advantage of this from the British point of view was that it could claim to be part of the process of resolution when in fact cross-border security co-operation from Dublin actually ensured that there was no resolution of the national question:

> Since Sunningdale in 1973 the British have repeatedly attempted to establish an internal governmental arrangement involving Unionists and nationalists. Our struggle and strategy has been to close down each option open to the British until they have no other option but to withdraw. The SDLP – with the conditions of power-sharing and a variable 'Irish dimension' – have continually given the British succour and allowed them to believe that an internal arrangement may be possible, a belief that would be reinforced by an SDLP involvement in a devolved assembly.

> Sinn Féin is totally opposed to a power-sharing Stormont assembly and states that there cannot be a partitionist solution. Stormont is not a stepping stone to Irish unity. We believe that the SDLP gradualist theory is therefore invalid and seriously flawed.

> The claim that Britain is neutral ignores their role as a pawnbroker and guarantor of Unionist hegemony. It ignores the basic political fact of life that Unionist hegemony was created by the British, to maintain direct control over a part of Ireland and a major influence over the rest of it. Britain's continuing involvement in Ireland is based on strategic, economic and political interests.[58]

The SDLP's reply offered an alternative Nationalist interpretation of the Northern Ireland problem. Hume, in a letter to Adams, summarised the latter's analysis and the methods of the Republican Movement while putting forward the SDLP's arguments and proposals for a peaceful political alternative. Hume identified the basic method of the Republican Movement as the PIRA campaign. The price of that campaign was clear to everybody – lives had been lost; people had been maimed; young lives had been wasted in prison; untold damage had been done to the economy, destroying the future hopes of many young people and, therefore, diminishing Ireland. Hume argued that it was not an adequate answer to suggest that the British presence was the primary source of all problems, and therefore the cause of all violence. It was not enough to suggest, as Provisional spokesmen frequently did, that the cause of all the violence was the British presence in Ireland: 'All of us must take our own decisions and use our own methods for dealing with that presence. We must also take responsibility for those methods and for their consequences, particularly when such circumstances can be foreseen. The IRA must take responsibility for their methods, as they do, but also for the foreseeable consequences of those methods which have brought so much suffering to Irish people.' It was clear to the SDLP that there was little chance of those methods succeeding in the foreseeable future and achieving the stated objectives of the PIRA. Hume asked:

> Does anybody in Ireland, even among supporters of the IRA, believe that the present British Government will accede to the demands of the IRA made by force? Does that not mean that the whole country and the members and families of the IRA face at least another decade of what we have just been through with all the suffering and without any guarantees of achieving their objectives at the end of it?

> Is it not time for the IRA and the members of the Provisional Republican Movement to seriously reconsider the methods that they have chosen to achieve their objectives, or are they in danger of moving to a situation, or are they already in it, where the methods have become more sacred than the cause?

Even if the stated objectives of the PIRA were to be achieved in the manner in which they had been set out, the SDLP argued, they would not bring peace to Ireland but would lead to much greater chaos and to permanent division and conflict. The SDLP saw no difference between a British withdrawal from Ireland or a declaration of intent to do so within a given period: either option would create a political vacuum which experience showed would be immediately filled by force as each section of the community moved to secure its own position. This route was the route of maximum risk and it was a risk which the SDLP believed no group had the right to take unless they did so with the full authority of the Irish people. Hume predicted a Cyprus/Lebanon situation in which the British Army would become inactive and the 12,000 armed members of the RUC and 8,000 armed members of the UDR might simply identify with the Protestant community from which most of them came, becoming its military defenders. Hume also asked what would become of the Catholic community in such circumstances, particularly in those areas where they were most vulnerable. He offered an alternative:

> ... in our [the SDLP's] view the political road is the only one that will ensure that there is lasting peace in Ireland. For the SDLP, Ireland is first and foremost its people; the territory is secondary, since without people the territory isn't much different from any other piece of earth. The strategy is that the people of Ireland are deeply divided and have been deeply divided for centuries on some very fundamental matters.

But it is the Irish people who have the right to self-determination. It is the Irish people who have the right to inalienable sovereignty. It is the search for agreement among the Irish people on how to exercise these rights that is the real search for peace and stability in Ireland. It is a search that has never been seriously undertaken by the nationalist-republican tradition in Ireland and it is the real challenge facing us today if we have any belief in the future of the Irish people as a whole.

In practice this meant agreement between the people of the Unionist and Nationalist traditions on how to exercise self-determination. It was a search that could not be conducted by force. And, asked Hume, did anyone believe that if such agreement was reached any British Government could refuse to endorse it? Indeed, the current British Government had made it clear in an internationally binding agreement that if such agreement on the exercise of self-determination took the form of Irish unity they would endorse it. Hume enquired if it was not the clearest possible challenge to the Nationalist-Republican tradition to begin the task of building a new Ireland with their unionist fellow citizens. Hume argued that the father of Irish Republicanism, Wolfe Tone, had claimed that the method of breaking the link with England was by uniting the people of Ireland first, and that this challenge removed all justification for violence because Britain was now saying that she had no interest of her own in being in Ireland except to see agreement among the people who shared the island of Ireland.[59]

By this stage it was clear that an impasse had been reached over the role and intentions of the British Government. This was most clearly revealed at the point when Adams indicated his disbelief of the SDLP's analysis; he criticised Hume for 'incredulously' pronouncing that Britain had no self-interest in occupying Ireland.[60] The key issue for Sinn Féin was the right of the Irish nation to self-determination which it defined as a 'nation's exercise of the political freedom to determine its own economic, social and cultural development, without external influence and without partial or total disruption of the national unity or territorial integrity'. For Republicans the key questions were, firstly, how to get the British Government to recognise Irish national rights; and, secondly, to change its present policy to one of ending partition and the Union, within the context of Irish reunification and, having done so, how to secure the co-operation of a majority in the North to the means of implementing those rights.[61]

The SDLP countered this by rejecting Sinn Féin's 'simple' definition of national self-determination, describing it as a 'tendency to get hung up on abstract principles such as whether or not the British have a right to be in Ireland'. The Irish would argue that they had not; the British would always argue that they had. This endless argument simply led to a reinforcing of each position and no progress on the real problem. The SDLP felt that it was much better to deal with the realities than to have endless debate about ideological rectitude. Instead, the 'real question is how do we end the British presence in Ireland in a manner which leaves behind a stable and peaceful Ireland?' In reality: 'There is, therefore, nothing to stop British governments becoming pro-Irish unity in their policies. Our task is to persuade them to go in that direction and to use all their considerable influence and persuade the Unionist people that their best interests are served by a new Ireland; a new Ireland in which Unionist fears are accommodated to their own satisfaction and in which there is a new relationship with Britain.'[62]

The talks had revealed fundamentally different Nationalist interpretations of the Northern Ireland problem. Adams and Sinn Féin saw the British Government's strategic, economic and political interests in Ireland as the cause of the conflict. Hume, on the other hand, claimed that implicit in Article 1(c) of the Anglo-Irish Agreement was a declaration that the British had no interest of their own in staying in Ireland. In short, the SDLP leader was claiming that the British Government was already 'neutral in that it was no longer pro-Union. There is nothing, therefore, to stop the British government from becoming pro-Irish unity in their policies.' The SDLP's task was to persuade the British to move in that direction;[63] Article 1 of the Agreement, embodying the 'Unionist Veto', was now regarded by the SDLP as a 'natural veto' – a significant change in SDLP thinking – because Unionist agreement was essential if Irish unity was to be achieved.[64] In the SDLP's view, the British Government had made it clear that if the people of the unionist and nationalist traditions in Ireland reached agreement on the unity and independence of Ireland, then the British Government would legislate for it, facilitate it, and leave the people of Ireland, North and South, to govern themselves. In short, they were stating that Irish unity and independence was 'entirely a matter for those Irish people who want it, persuading those Irish people who don't'.

There were fundamental lines of departure between the SDLP and Sinn Féin on the issue of self-determination, Britain's role in Ireland and the question of violence. Whereas both parties – the Republicans were exploring a position which the SDLP had arrived at more than a decade before – wanted the British Government to become persuaders for a united Ireland, the factor of violence was crucial: it was clear, argued Hume, that the British Government had no other interest at stake in the exercise of self-determination 'except that violence or the threat of violence shall not succeed'. In this context the 'armed struggle' could only be a negative factor.[65]

But the British were not the only ones Hume had to persuade to change policy; he had also to persuade Republicans that violence was not the way to achieve a united Ireland. If he could, then the consequences would be profound. As one observer noted, Hume was 'trying to lead Mr Adams further down the constitutional road'. Ruairí Ó Brádaigh, now leading the breakaway Republican Sinn Féin organisation, recognised that the next stage in this process – 'Now that he (Mr Adams) has accepted the 26-county state with all that entails' – would involve Hume seeking to bring Adams 'further in accepting Westminster and Stormont and a constitutional role in the six counties as well as in the twenty-six'. Republican Sinn Féin observed that Adams and 'Leinster House Sinn Féin' were in the 'peculiar and illogical position of accepting constitutional politics south of the border and still supporting armed struggle in the North'.[66] Adams, of course, disputed such an analysis, and remained disdainful of both the SDLP and Republican Sinn Féin's analysis. However, Provisional Sinn Féin's thinking on one strategic point was becoming clearer: by themselves they could not move the British Government into the role of persuaders for a united Ireland. They needed allies from outside the Republican Movement. To secure these would involve a gradual reassessment of long-cherished positions. One compromise can often lead to a flood of compromises and not always of one's own choosing. Both constitutional Nationalists and Unionists were also to find that this was so.

Unionism in Retreat

The leadership of Unionism was caught unawares by the Anglo-Irish Agreement. This was partly its own fault and partly, as has been seen, a result of the long-term requirements of British crisis management in Northern Ireland. Unionism had remained unimaginative and unwilling to seriously evolve beyond the report of the Northern Ireland Constitutional Convention. Even the demise of the UUUC did not see Unionism develop an alternative strategy to the demand for the return of majority rule. In fact, Direct Rule suited many within the unionist community. As both the PIRA and British security forces began a low-level war of attrition, the lack of an immediate threat to Northern Ireland's position within the United Kingdom – such as the Council of Ireland – saw a corresponding decline in Loyalist paramilitary violence. Within the mainstream of Unionism, and the UUP in particular, there was growing support for Direct Rule. James Molyneaux had fallen under the spell of Enoch Powell, who advocated full integration with Great Britain. This effectively entailed the abandonment of full legislative devolution, although Molyneaux was careful not to antagonise the devolutionist wing of the party and lent towards supporting administrative devolution. Molyneaux was a Westminster man through and through. He practised as well as preached the 'long view', in which Unionism sought to build support by behind-the-scenes networking at Westminster. What Molyneaux, and for that matter Ian Paisley, did not see coming was the Anglo-Irish Agreement.

While Mrs Thatcher had stated in the House of Commons that the Intergovernmental Conference 'would have no executive authority either now or in the future,' Unionists were alarmed by Garret FitzGerald's claim in the Dáil that the Agreement was 'going beyond a consultative role but necessarily, because of the sovereignty issue, falling short of an executive role'.[67] What did this mean? The problem for Unionists was that with the Intergovernmental Conference discussions conducted in total secrecy, they could not know whether Thatcher or FitzGerald's description was the more accurate. Furthermore, the joint declaration on Northern Ireland's status was ambiguous. On the status of Northern Ireland, Article 1 of the Agreement stated that the two Governments:

- affirm that any change in the status of Northern Ireland would only come about with the consent of a majority of the people of Northern Ireland

- recognise that the present wish of a majority of the people of Northern Ireland is for no change in the status of Northern Ireland

- declare that, if in the future a majority of the people of Northern Ireland clearly wish for and formally consent to the establishment of a united Ireland, they will introduce and support in the respective Parliaments legislation to give effect to that wish.

But this did not actually define what Northern Ireland's constitutional status was. It did not mention that Northern Ireland was part of the United Kingdom. Therefore, the Irish Government could claim that Northern Ireland was still part of the Republic. This was confirmed when a court action taken by the McGimpsey brothers – both members of the UUP – saw the Irish Supreme Court confirm that the declaration in the Anglo-Irish Agreement was consistent with Articles 2 and 3 of the Irish Constitution. In fact the Court went much further than any previous legal decision when it decided that the Constitution imposed a 'constitutional imperative' on Irish Governments to pursue Irish unity as a policy objective. The fudging of Northern Ireland's status in the Agreement was also illustrated by the necessity of different preambles in the British and Irish Government versions of the Agreement texts. The Irish version could not recognise Northern Ireland as part of the United Kingdom. Consequently, in the British version, the preamble read:

> Agreement between the Government of the United Kingdom of Great Britain and Northern Ireland and the Government of the Republic of Ireland

whereas the preamble to the Irish version read:

> Agreement between the Government of Ireland and the Government of the United Kingdom[68]

Unionists reacted badly to the Agreement. They took to the streets. But, apart from the RUC, what could they attack? Unlike the power-sharing Executive, the Anglo-Irish Agreement had no tangible, institutional body to disrupt or boycott. At its heart was the Intergovernmental Conference between two sovereign governments. It did not need Unionist participation, in order to function.

And with the impotent Northern Ireland Assembly soon terminated by the British Government, Unionism had no platform and no strategy to get rid of the Agreement. In the aftermath of the Agreement, Unionism was rudderless and the SDLP was clearly in the political ascendancy. The fact that a British Government had imposed the Agreement against the wishes of the unionist community led Hume to predict that the 'loss of the Unionist veto', which he described as a 'boil being lanced', would force Unionists to agree to talks with the minority on the basis of equality. He stressed that he was prepared to talk with Unionists about devolution or any other subject that would bring about peace. But for the moment nobody on the Unionist side was listening. They were going through a process of confronting the British Parliament. Only when they learned that they could no longer do that would they realise the reality which could only come from genuine dialogue based on equality: 'The Anglo-Irish Agreement gives that equality for the first time.'[69]

Hume called for the Unionist leadership and its community to rethink some of its traditional attitudes. The SDLP leader argued that it was not with the Unionist objective that Nationalists had their quarrel; it was their method, which was to 'live apart from the people with whom they share a piece of earth. Their method is to hold all power in their own hands.' This was summed up in their political slogans: '"What we have we hold." "Not an inch." "Ulster says no." All negative, all defining the society in which they live as themselves alone.' If the leaders of the unionist tradition wanted to live in a society which was both stable and peaceful and which respected the integrity of their tradition then the way to do it was simple. This was to follow the way in which 'every democratic society in the world does so – respect and accommodate the differences and have the self-confidence to live in a genuine democracy'. This would be found when Unionists sat down with the political leaders with whom they shared a piece of earth and abandoned the sheer negativism of their past approaches.

Only a process would heal the division in Ireland. Hume saw the road ahead in three stages. The first stage was the creation of equality of treatment in the North for all people. The second, based on that equality, was the process of reconciliation, of breaking down the barriers that divided the people there. In practice that meant people working together in new institutions in the North and, by doing so over the years, building trust and replacing the distrust that disfigured them. This second stage would naturally evolve into the third stage, the development of new relationships within Ireland and between Ireland and Britain. This would bring the 'only unity that really matters, a unity born of the agreement on how we are to live together, the forms of such unity to evolve by agreement and out of mutual trust and respect'. Hume was adamant that using the Anglo-Irish process to by-pass Unionist consent was fully justified:

Firstly, because it is the framework of the problem. The relationships which are in conflict are not confined to the North, they are within Ireland and between Ireland and Britain. The framework of the problem, the British-Irish framework, should be the framework of the solution. Secondly, it is the framework of maximum consensus, since it is based on the consensus of the 59 million people of both islands, rather than the consent of one-and-a-half million of them [in Northern Ireland]. Thirdly, and because of that, it is the road of minimum risk. Every road towards an answer is fraught with risk. The road of minimum risk is the road based on the democratic consensus of the peoples of both islands.

He described the Anglo-Irish Agreement as a permanent Council of Ministers from Britain and Ireland. It was a decision-making process which was far fairer than any previous process. It was also ideal, firstly for tackling immediate grievances within the North and ensuring equality of citizenship; and secondly, for dealing with the wider relationships which had a direct bearing on the problem of the North. It was, in short, an opportunity to use the democratic process to the full in order to pursue the healing process. It removed the slightest justification for the use of violence in Ireland to achieve political objectives.[70]

Furthermore, Hume saw the Agreement as embodying the potential to draw both parts of the island together without the brake of the Unionist veto; he believed the Agreement was capable, 'without changing a word of it,' of major developments. There was nothing to stop future governments dealing with the wider relationships as they affected Northern Ireland; for example, 'there is nothing to stop the setting up of a common agricultural policy for Ireland ... or a common energy policy. And, indeed, the harmonisation of a whole lot of other measures; until they [the Governments] are face to face with the real divide in Ireland – the divide between Catholic and Protestant.' Hume did not see that any Protestant or Unionist had anything to fear from such a strategy, since they had to be part of that building process. The offer existed for the Unionists to remove a great deal of decision making from the Anglo-Irish Conference by entering into talks with the SDLP and agreeing on a means of administering Northern Ireland: 'If they wish to do so, they will find us ready and we would prefer that they would. If they don't, we won't worry unduly because the system of decision making that now exists is better than we have ever had.'

However, Hume qualified this robust statement by re-emphasising that the long-term peace and stability of the island would be best-served by Unionists entering into partnership with Nationalists.[71] By 1989, Hume accepted that the Unionists were ready for dialogue. The SDLP leader felt that Mrs Thatcher and the Anglo-Irish Agreement had done for Unionism what President Kennedy had done 'for the whites in Alabama. They knew that something had to be done, they knew they couldn't do it for themselves but, once it was done, in their own heart of hearts they were glad it was done and to go on from there.' Hume had once again changed his stance regarding the Republican Movement, adding that if Sinn Féin were to take part in such talks it would have to abandon its support for the PIRA: 'You can't expect anyone to sit around a table with somebody who reserves the right to pull a gun if he doesn't get his own way.'[72]

While Hume was wrong in the ability of the Anglo-Irish Agreement to act as a mechanism to circumvent Unionist opposition to the harmonisation of laws in Ireland – executive power remained with the British who did not want to antagonise Unionists any further – he was correct in his assessment that it was forcing some movement in Unionist circles. In 1987, the political representatives of the UDA, the Ulster Political Research Group, published *Common Sense*. Although it did not incorporate an Irish dimension it rejected pure majority rule. Instead, it proposed 'co-determination' between Ulster Catholics and Ulster Protestants who would form an 'agreed process of government for Northern Ireland'. In a Northern Ireland Assembly, seats on a series of committees would be allocated according to the proportional strength of the parties. Seats on an 'Executive Committee' would be also allocated on a proportional basis.[73] Although *Common Sense* rejected permanent, institutionalised power-sharing at cabinet level, the electoral and communal reality in Northern Ireland meant that this is what would effectively occur. Catholics were being offered a share in a united Northern Ireland. As one of its authors, John McMichael, explained, *Common Sense* dealt with four cardinal realities:

- Northern Ireland is at present an integral part of the United Kingdom and this position is not likely to change for the foreseeable future.

- We live in a deeply divided society with a large disgruntled and separatist minority which is not going to disappear nor be wished away.

- Unionists will not accept formal Irish government involvement in Northern Ireland proceedings nor agree to any political scheme which is believed to be the thin edge of the wedge towards a united Ireland.

- Ulster Catholics will not continue to be 'alienated' nor excluded from playing a full role in the affairs of Northern Ireland.[74]

None of the mainstream Unionist parties were prepared to go this far. But in 1988 the need for some form of dialogue was recognised by the UUP and DUP. Boycott and protest could not destroy the Agreement. The need for flexibility and negotiations was effectively conceded by Molyneaux and Paisley when they submitted 'Draft Proposals for a British-Irish Agreement' to the British Government. The aim was to formulate a new British-Irish

Agreement to supersede the Anglo-Irish Agreement. The UUP and the DUP now recognised that 'it is H[er] M[ajesty's] G[overnment] we have to convince; therefore the realities upon which these proposals are based are not necessarily those that unionists contend do exist but rather those that the government has demonstrated do exist.' The Unionists had effectively conceded that the rules of engagement had changed.

The Unionists offered to 'regulate and normalise' relations with the Republic of Ireland and to effect progress towards devolution in the Province which would enjoy widespread consent in the community. If the Irish Government would amend its Constitution, the Unionists offered to foster an improvement of relations with the Republic. For example, it would be open to the Republic to establish a Government Office in Northern Ireland as a point of contact no less adequate than that available through the Intergovernmental Conference's secretariat situated at Maryfield; a joint British-Irish Parliamentary Body would promote better understanding and improve relationships among Parliamentarians throughout the British Isles; there could be periodic contacts with Unionists forming part of a British team meeting Irish Ministers; there could be *ad hoc* meetings between Government Ministers in the Republic and appropriate Northern Ireland representatives; and an External Affairs Committee could be established, drawn from a Northern Ireland Assembly in proportion to party strengths, to supervise and oversee matters of mutual advantage and common interest between the Republic and Northern Ireland.

The Committee would also consider Northern Ireland's relationship with the rest of the United Kingdom and the EEC. Internally, the structure was based upon proportionality. Each party would have a role commensurate with its support in the community. The participation of minority representatives ensured their community interests were not threatened while the Unionist interests would be safeguarded by their majority in committees and ultimately in the Assembly.[75]

Much of this was still based on the proposals put forward during the Northern Ireland Constitutional Convention over a decade earlier. The demand for a majority rule cabinet had been dropped, but there appeared little evidence of advance beyond this. However, Unionists were politically impotent and desperate to get into some form of dialogue. They now wanted a face-saving suspension of the Agreement in order to engage in inter-party talks with the SDLP. The pressure was on them: if the talks failed the two Governments could simply re-activate the Agreement.

Unionists were forced to flesh out their proposals for North-South relations. David Trimble, a law lecturer and UUP member, pointed out that it was wrong to assume that all Unionists were negative on institutional North-South relationships. To illustrate this, he focused upon two schemes that involved an element of joint Belfast-Dublin authority. These were the Great Northern Railways Board, wound up in 1958, and the Foyle Fisheries Commission, which was established in 1952 after a High Court decision in the

Republic affected the ownership of fishing rights in a branch stream of the River Foyle in the Republic. The Unionist Government in Northern Ireland approached the Republic's authorities to try and achieve a solution. The result saw parallel legislation in both jurisdictions establishing the Foyles Fisheries Commission, which consisted of four members, two from the North and two from the South. After the previous fishing rights were bought out, these rights and the management were vested in the Commission.

This was an example of a cross-border body with executive power, established by separate legislation in the Dáil and the Northern Ireland Parliament. Trimble saw it as an instance where Northern Ireland and the Republic could engage in cross-border co-operation that recognised the separate jurisdictions, North and South. North-South co-operation on matters of mutual concern would present no difficulty. Problems arose, however, claimed Trimble, when co-operation was proposed for political reasons or when institutional relationships were proposed. For example, when formalised arrangements such as the Anglo-Irish Agreement were proposed, Unionists objected on two grounds:

> First they ... want to know what the ultimate object of the relationship is to be, and they will want to be sure in their own minds that the relationship will not be prejudicial to the continued existence of Northern Ireland. The second objection is closely related to the first. Unionists say they cannot enter into such relationships with a state that maintains a claim to sovereignty over them.

However, Trimble pointed out that the above example showed that Unionists were prepared to co-operate on an *ad hoc* basis, even with Articles 2 and 3 intact. If those claims were gone, argued Trimble, and there was a greater equality of esteem between Dublin and Belfast, then the situation would be different; or to 'put it another way, a certain level of trust is necessary before there can be a good relationship between the two parts of the island.' But trust was impossible while Dublin proclaimed the object of absorbing Northern Ireland into the Republic. Trimble quoted a UUP policy statement, from February 1986, which contained evidence of this, suggesting a willingness, subject to certain preconditions, that London and Dublin and a newly constituted Northern Ireland Government would agree a new British-Irish framework within which 'genuine friendship, co-operation and consultation may be developed and encouraged'.[76] Unionists, Trimble was suggesting, were prepared to consider institutional North-South arrangements in a form which previous Unionist Governments had done – but only if they knew the limits of the arrangements which had to be based on trust and constitutional recognition.

The Brooke-Mayhew Talks

The problem for Unionists of all persuasions remained how to end their community's political isolation. They had made the first moves following a series of 'talks about talks' with the British Government. As a result, London was able to persuade Charles Haughey's government to suspend the Inter-governmental Conference for a time. This face-saving exercise allowed the UUP and the DUP to enter negotiations. The talks would cover three 'strands'. Strand One was concerned with the internal government of the province; Strand Two its relationship with the Republic; and Strand Three relations between the UK and the Republic. All of this aptly demonstrated the influence of John Hume's analysis of the problem.

On 26 March 1991, the Secretary of State for Northern Ireland, Peter Brooke, announced talks on this basis. Speaking in the House of Commons, he repeated once more – for the benefit of nervous Unionists – that Northern Ireland's status as part of the UK could change only with the consent of a majority of its electorate. The guiding rule of the talks would be that nothing would be finally agreed in any strand until everything was agreed in the talks as a whole. If this substantial obstacle could be negotiated then any agreement would be submitted to people of Northern Ireland in a referendum.[77] After some initial optimism, and the declaration of a temporary ceasefire by Loyalist paramilitary groups at the end of April to help the process, the talks broke down in the summer. In July the Loyalist ceasefire ended.

Violence continued throughout 1991 and there were calls for Brooke's resignation in January 1992 following his appearance on a Dublin chat show immediately after the murder of seven Protestant workers by a PIRA bomb in County Tyrone. Although Prime Minister John Major rejected his offer of resignation, from then on Brooke was a lameduck Secretary of State. Nevertheless, Brooke's achievement was in getting Unionists and Nationalists to engage in substantial exchanges for the first time in 15 years. Another round of talks on Strand One began in March 1992. They resumed under the chairmanship of a new Secretary of State, Sir Patrick Mayhew. This time there were substantial exchanges between the parties – the UUP; the DUP; the SDLP; and the cross-community Alliance Party.

The SDLP was the first party to present detailed proposals for the internal government of Northern Ireland. Its strategy was driven by the concept of 'parity of esteem' for the nationalist community in Northern Ireland. This translated into absolute equality for Northern nationalists in all institutions established by agreement with Unionists. The SDLP did not regard the nationalist community as a minority within Northern Ireland: it was of equal status and entitled to equal rights with the unionist community. The SDLP observed how:

> The Nationalist community in Northern Ireland sees its identity as essentially Irish and part of the wider Irish family on the island of Ireland. Its vision and aspiration are the creation of a new and tolerant society that unites and accommodates all traditions in a New Ireland, where Nationalists and Unionists can co-exist in harmony and mutual respect.

The Unionist community, on the other hand, perceives itself as British. The majority of Unionists are also Protestant and, as such, are strengthened in their allegiance to the British Crown by the latter's essential Protestantism. Unionists generally also regard themselves as being Irish, although this does not include a willingness to live under all-Ireland institutions. However, many of them identify with Ireland and with various features of Irish life and their culture and way of life embrace much that is common to people throughout Ireland.[78]

Key elements of the SDLP proposals drew heavily from their 1972 proposals and those for joint authority expressed at the New Ireland Forum. Although the SDLP proposed the establishment of a Northern Ireland Assembly, this would effectively have a scrutinising and consultative role only. Real executive power would be located in a six-member Commission for Northern Ireland, in which there would be:

- three members directly elected – from a three-seat Northern Ireland Constituency

- one member each to be nominated separately by the British Government, the Irish Government and the European Community ...

The Chairmanship/Presidency of the Commission would be held by the elected Commissioner receiving the highest number of first preference votes. In terms of the Commission's principal powers and functions, it might:

- function as a normal Cabinet, with powers which include the initiation of legislation, with each Commissioner heading one of the six traditional Departments of Government in Northern Ireland, while exercising certain responsibilities collectively (e.g. security and judicial matters, civil, human and communal rights, fiscal and budgetary matters, European and external relations etc.)

  or

- exercise the same range of functions exclusively according to the principle of collective responsibility.[79]

The Unionist parties were taken aback by the SDLP's proposals. The SDLP proposal, they claimed, challenged Northern Ireland's status within the United Kingdom and ignored the Unionist identity. It was very unclear what Northern Ireland's constitutional status would be under the SDLP's proposals; the UUP had no knowledge of this type of arrangement being tried elsewhere in the world. Instead, it would achieve the objective of levering Northern Ireland out of the United Kingdom. The UUP had thought that the issue of Northern Ireland's status had been settled but these proposals appeared to re-open it. Not only was the Commission unaccountable to a Northern Ireland Assembly but the Northern Ireland electorate had no control over the appointment of Commissioners from outside the province. The appointment of a Commissioner by the British Government did nothing to meet Unionists' concerns about their own identity. Similarly, the DUP team expressed their 'sadness' with the SDLP. They were expecting Unionists to accept proposals which would mean that they would no longer be Unionists.

The Anglo-Irish Agreement had provoked a reaction; the consequences of this could be worse. The Commission was like a quango. It was difficult to conceive of appointed representatives at the highest level but unthinkable to contemplate appointments from outside Northern Ireland. The arrangements would be inherently unstable because the Northern Ireland electorate would have no role except to complain that appointees from outside Northern Ireland were in authority. The Northern Ireland electorate would not be responsible for the election of the three Commissioners from outside Northern Ireland and had no power to remove them. The Executive Commission was not representative of the community in Northern Ireland: the people of Great Britain, the Irish Republic and the European Community did not live in Northern Ireland; the two sides of the Northern Ireland community did. It seemed to the DUP that the SDLP believed that Unionists and Nationalists were incapable of addressing their own relationship and needed to be chaperoned by Britain, the Irish Republic and the EC.[80]

The SDLP rejected the Unionist criticisms. They denied that their proposals represented the removal of a British identity from those who felt it. They had proposed a system of government within a United Kingdom framework, and accepted that Northern Ireland could not be taken out of the United Kingdom without the consent of a majority there. But there were many within Northern Ireland who felt themselves to be Irish, and to belong to a body politic comprising the whole of the island of Ireland. Currently they were immersed in a wholly British framework, and the SDLP sought to reflect their sense of Irish identity as well as those with a British identity. The SDLP were content for Unionists to define their own relationship in terms of links to the rest of the United Kingdom, but reserved the right to do likewise to the rest of the island of Ireland.[81]

Thus the SDLP defined its Irish identity as being two-dimensional. This meant not only a link with the rest of the Irish nation outside Northern Ireland but also that nation, in its political embodiment the Irish State, having a legitimate concern and input in Northern Ireland matters, not least because what happened there had significant implications for them. This was not moving the goal posts; the issue had been there since the exchanges between the British and Irish Governments in the late 1960s and the early 1970s, culminating in the Sunningdale Agreement. Then the Irish Government had been involved in determining the process by which Northern Ireland was governed. The SDLP made it clear that it accepted the Unionist requirement to have the Unionist identity protected by membership of the United Kingdom. Its proposals had been represented as taking Northern Ireland out of the United Kingdom against the wishes of its people; it did not see this as the immediate effect. After all, the Anglo–Irish Agreement had already acknowledged the right of the Irish Government to be involved in the affairs of Northern Ireland.

Unionists refuted all of this. In particular, the DUP feared that the SDLP had now defined their Irish identity in a new way. Previously it had been simply the idea of kinship with an entity with which Northern nationalists were associated – the Irish Republic; the DUP appreciated that. But it had now also taken on a new meaning in which those with whom one shared an identity should have a political role. The DUP repudiated that approach; indeed it was contrary to the Anglo-Irish Agreement, which emphasised that in the event of devolution to Northern Ireland, Dublin would have no role in respect of devolved matters. The SDLP had opened up a new agenda, and this thinking had moved away from that of the other parties, not closer to them. The SDLP were breaking new ground. Whether or not it had always been part of the SDLP aspiration to involve the Irish Government in the internal affairs of Northern Ireland, it had never been part of the Sunningdale Agreement or the Anglo-Irish Agreement. Now it was said to be a central issue, and it presumably followed that, without it, the SDLP would not be able to agree anything. In the DUP view, there was no argument for the Republic itself being involved – unless that involvement was intended as a Trojan horse.[82]

If the Unionist parties were horrified by the ambitious nature of the SDLP's proposals, the latter was deeply disappointed by what was offered by their opponents. Both Molyneaux's UUP and Paisley's DUP proposed a Northern Ireland Assembly. But there would be no central cabinet made up of Unionists and Nationalists. Instead there would be a series of committees that would take over the running of the Northern Ireland Departments. Membership of the committees would also reflect the strength of the constitutional parties elected to the Assembly, with Chairmanships and Deputy Chairmanships allocated on a proportionate basis, called the D'Hondt Rule.[83] As the DUP explained, Unionists had taken a principled stand against executive power-sharing, and had secured electoral mandates on that point in the past. They recognised that future generations of politicians might have a different view and that institutions might develop, if all parties were content and the disagreement between them had diminished, into a more cabinet-style form of government.

At this point in time, however, the DUP had deliberately tabled proposals they believed the community could accept. The Protestant community had rejected executive power-sharing before, and no doubt would again if the same proposal was put before them. The DUP proposals did not rule out a coalition cabinet eventually, but it would need to be generated by agreement rather than be imposed. They accepted that a cabinet-type structure would be preferable to a committee one, but recognised that their preferred option – majority rule – would not be acceptable to the SDLP, and that the SDLP's would be equally unacceptable to them. The DUP offered an External Affairs Committee within the Assembly which did not preclude direct contact between committee chairmen and vice-chairmen and the respective ministers of the Republic of Ireland on matters of common concern. But any links between Northern Ireland Assembly chairmen and ministers in the Republic would be on an *ad hoc* basis.[84] There would no North-South institutional link separate from the Assembly.

The SDLP found all this a 'severe disappointment'. The Unionist proposals contained nothing new and took no account of the need to accommodate different identities. The SDLP questioned whether the Unionists seriously believed their party could accept it. For example, the proposal that business in the Assembly's committees should be directed by majority voting was not one that endeared itself to the SDLP. They commented that those who saw themselves as Irish were not an ethnic minority, but an indigenous part of the population of Northern Ireland. They had not been accommodated in the Unionist proposals.[85] When the UUP countered that, in fact, 100 per cent of the Northern Ireland people could regard themselves as Irish if they so wished, the SDLP accepted this; the reference they had made was merely to those who saw themselves as Irish and not British, as opposed to others who saw themselves as both Irish and British.

While other parties had criticised their proposals for failing to reflect views other than their own, the UUP proposals failed to give any recognition to the Northern Nationalist identity and reflected the old majoritarian 'Ulster is British' approach.[86] It seemed that the impasse between it and the Unionist parties arose because while the SDLP accepted that Unionists saw themselves as part of a British nation within the UK, and accepted that Northern Ireland would remain part of the UK for the foreseeable future, the Unionists did not seem able to grasp the Nationalist need to identify themselves as part of the Irish nation. Any new institutions created would need to reflect the legitimate right of the Irish nation to some involvement in Northern Ireland.[87]

Given the gulf before the talks participants, a small Sub-Committee composed of the UUP, DUP, Alliance and the SDLP was established. The Sub-Committee came up with a compromise package in June 1992 combining elements of the Unionist and SDLP proposals. It suggested that there should be a single, unicameral Northern Ireland Assembly, elected by proportional representation with a separate election from a single Northern Ireland constituency to a panel of three people with significant consultative, monitoring, referral and representational functions. This excluded any election to the panel from jurisdictions outside Northern Ireland and terminated the SDLP's hope of Dublin-Belfast-London-Brussels joint authority. The institutions would have executive and legislative responsibilities over at least as wide a range of subjects as the 1973 Assembly, with scope for further transfers if the arrangements proved stable and durable and there was agreement on how to exercise such powers. Executive responsibilities would be discharged through Northern Ireland Government Departments, the Heads of which would be drawn from the Assembly. The Secretary of State would remain accountable to Westminster for matters that were not transferred from London to Belfast.

The Assembly would exercise its powers through a system of departmental committees, with chairmanships, deputy chairmanships and memberships allocated broadly in proportion to party strengths in the Assembly. There would be no power-sharing cabinet; instead there would be non-departmental Committees which would include a Business Committee and a General Purposes Committee with co-ordinating functions. In order to protect minorities, all legislation could require the support of, at least, a majority of both the relevant committee and the full Assembly. Important legislation could require a weighted majority approval of 70 per cent. Other measures might be dealt with on the basis of majority decision unless, for example, they were contentious or a petition to that effect secured a certain threshold of say 30 per cent support in the Assembly. There would also be a Bill of Rights, which the Assembly could not amend.[88]

Crucially, while the pro-Union parties appeared satisfied with the Sub-Committee's Report, the SDLP delegation remained unconvinced. They did not believe that the overall solution to Northern Ireland's problems could be addressed simply by who wielded power in Northern Ireland. Therefore, the SDLP had reservations about the position that had been reached because the question of identities had not been adequately addressed. The SDLP represented one identity, whereas the Unionists represented the other. The SDLP believed that the allegiance of both identities to the institutions of government was essential if those institutions were to be stable. Currently that allegiance was not there because the identities issue had not been satisfactorily addressed. Strand Two was the forum in which the Unionist parties had said this issue would be addressed and Nationalist concerns met. Therefore, the SDLP believed discussions in Strand One had gone as far as they could, and it was now time to move to Strand Two. But the SDLP had reservations about the workability of the institutions proposed in Strand One. Effectively it was withholding its approval from the Sub-Committee Report.[89] However, the stance taken by the party allowed a window of opportunity to move the talks into Strand Two.

Mayhew: Strands Two and Three

At the beginning of July 1992, Sir Patrick Mayhew proposed that Strand Two and Strand Three should be launched. This meant the introduction of the Irish Government to proceedings. For the first time, the main representatives of constitutional Nationalism and Unionism negotiated on the future relations between the Republic of Ireland and Northern Ireland. Strand Two formally commenced on 6 July under the chairmanship of the former Governor-General of Australia, Sir Ninian Stephens, at Lancaster House in London. It began, and effectively remained bogged down, in a discussion of constitutional issues. The Irish Government and the DUP took the two most hardline positions.

Charles Haughey's Fianna Fáil dominated coalition government suggested that it had no desire to change Articles 2 and 3. The Irish Government began negotiations with a robust defence of its Constitution and an attack on the Government of Ireland Act. The Irish denied that Articles 2 and 3 represented a territorial claim. Instead, they argued that the Constitution reflected the Nationalist assumption that the traditional historic and political entity encompassing the island of Ireland should remain the valid frame of reference for the collective exercise of the right of the Irish people to self-determination. The conflict was not about a territorial dispute between the British and Irish states. For example, the Irish Supreme Court had not deemed the Anglo-Irish Agreement as inconsistent with the Irish Constitution. That Agreement was not about land or territory, but about the wishes of the people. The Agreement set the problem firmly in the context of reconciling the conflicting rights of two communities with divergent views of the status of Northern Ireland, based on different identities and aspirations. To cast the issue in primarily territorial terms, as the Unionists did, was to devalue or miss the real focus of the problem. This was the failure to create political structures which could command broad consensus and general support, whether from within Northern Ireland or in the island as a whole. The Northern Ireland problem existed before the Irish Constitution. The provisions of the Irish Constitution reflected, rather than caused, the basic divisions of opinion between Nationalism and Unionism. Taking issue with the provisions of the Constitution could not be a substitute for addressing and resolving these basic divisions of opinion themselves.

Articles 2 and 3 were criticised as aggressive by Unionists, but this, argued the Irish, was to ignore the fact that the Constitution, as a whole, bound Ireland to the ideal of peace and friendly co-operation among nations and to the principle of the peaceful settlement of disputes. While rejecting unfounded criticism of the Irish Constitution, the Irish Government made it clear that it did not rule out constitutional change ensuing from the current negotiations. This would have to be passed by a referendum in the Republic. But, warned the Irish, their electorate would want to be reassured that any proposed constitutional amendment would reflect the wish to reconcile and acknowledge the rights and aspirations of both communities in Northern Ireland on a basis of their equal legitimacy. It could not be an attempt to resolve the conflict in favour of one side at the expense of the other.[90]

It followed from this analysis that new structures to address the problem must cater adequately for both sets of identities and allegiances, on terms each could identify with. The Irish Government believed, in the words of the New Ireland Forum Report, that 'Both of these identities must have equally satisfactory, secure and durable political, administrative, and symbolic expression and protection.' Since Northern Ireland was a divided society its fundamental problem, from its establishment down to the present day, had been disagreement not just about how Northern Ireland should be governed, but as to whether it should exist at all. The search for consensus in other areas, including on constitutional issues, had to begin with consensus on this critical point since the constitutional debate was merely a variation of the original disagreement.

The two communities in Northern Ireland were in strongly contrasting positions in terms of the political expression of their respective identities. The Government of Ireland Act affirmed that 'the supreme authority of the Parliament of the United Kingdom shall remain unaffected and undiminished over all persons, matters, and things in Northern Ireland.' The symbols of the state exclusively reflected the Unionist identity, to the point that they were routinely used as partisan symbols for party political purposes. The security forces manifested themselves in their badges and titles as upholders of the Union as well as guardians of the peace. This meant that the British identity of the unionist community was the dominant public reality at every level.

The position of the nationalist community in Northern Ireland was the obverse of this. Yet that community comprised a sufficiently large proportion of the population of Northern Ireland to warrant a hearing in its own right. Any attempt to relegate it to its previous role of subordinate minority was likely to prove less and less tenable. The essence of the nationalists' identity was that they were Irish and not British: they aspired to participate in a wider Irish political system no less strongly than unionists asserted the claim to have their British identity expressed in a British system. Internal structures would not cater adequately for the nationalist identity.

Therefore, from a nationalist perspective, the issue of devolution was not the central issue between the two communities. Neither, however, was it neutral terrain. Sharing in the local application of British jurisdiction in Northern Ireland was an affirmation of identity from a unionist representative. From a nationalist perspective it could imply endorsement of a constitutional arrangement which the nationalist community had never so far supported. The degree to which proposed devolved structures reflected the reality that a substantial percentage of the population in Northern Ireland persistently refused to define themselves as British would be an important factor in nationalist attitudes to them. However, no purely internal structures in Northern Ireland could hope to cater adequately for the nationalist identity. Exclusively internal structures, by definition, failed to reflect the wider Irish identity in which Northern nationalists claimed an active share. The Irish Government suggested that new institutions emerging from Strand Two might accomplish a three-fold purpose:

- They must provide meaningful expression for the aspirations of Northern nationalists.

- They must help to bridge divisions between the unionist and nationalist traditions in Ireland in an agreed framework.

- They must provide an institutional framework with executive functions for the development of practical North-South co-operation and co-ordination in all areas of mutual benefit.[91]

What precisely this meant was outlined by the SDLP: the establishment of a North-South Council/Council of Ministers as an expression of relationships between the people of the whole island. Such a Council would have responsibility for the overall development of relationships between both parts of the island. The membership of such an institutional North-South link would consist of the relevant Head of Department from Northern Ireland and his/her Ministerial counterpart from the South, depending on the issues under discussion.[92]

The Unionist response illustrated the ideological gulf between them and the Nationalists. On the Unionist side, the most uncompromising stance was taken by the DUP. As far as it was concerned the main issue in North-South relations was the Republic's territorial claim to Northern Ireland. There could be no peace between Northern Ireland and the Irish Republic until this 'illegal, criminal, and immoral claim' was given up. Unilaterally made, it had to be unilaterally withdrawn. Dublin had to recognise Ulster's right to self-determination. It had to be prepared to spell out Northern Ireland's status as an integral part of the United Kingdom both *de facto* and *de jure* – this was the primary pre-requisite for any future to the talks. If the Irish Republic was not prepared to make the necessary changes they should say so in plain language. Any changes in the Irish Constitution would have to

- eliminate the Republic's claim to Northern Ireland

- obtain recognition by the Republic of the 'people of Northern Ireland'

- obtain recognition from the Irish Republic of Northern Ireland's right to self-determination

- formalise the Irish Republic's acknowledgement of two traditions on the island.[93]

The DUP argued that the whole underlying aim of the Irish Republic, 'after you clear away all the peace jargon and pious Irish baloney and blarney,' was to wipe out Northern Ireland's existence and bring about a unitary state in some form or another. In other words it was a call to implement the New Ireland Forum Report. This was a purely Nationalist document, asserting Nationalist imperialism, while professing some sympathy for members of groups with other traditions. To the DUP, this verbal smoke-screen in reality meant

- that the 1920 Settlement should be set aside

- that there should be joint sovereignty by the Republic and the United Kingdom over Northern Ireland

- that, failing joint sovereignty, there should be joint authority with full involvement of the Republic in all Northern Ireland's affairs.[94]

The UUP, while identifying with the DUP's interpretation of the conflict as one between states, were prepared to be more constructive. They supported the goal of the Irish Government to 'connect structures'. Similar to the External Affairs Committee mentioned by the DUP in Strand One discussions, the UUP offered to establish an Inter-Irish Relations Committee within the Northern Ireland Assembly. This would facilitate business between the Belfast and Dublin administrations. The role of such a committee would be to provide a vehicle for dealing with areas of common interest and to facilitate better understanding between both Irish traditions and political entities in Ireland. The UUP outlined the case for cross-border co-operation in economic matters and listed areas where current co-operation might prove of genuine benefit to both Northern Ireland and the Irish Republic. An initial list of areas included the following: transport; energy; industrial development; skills and education; agriculture; and tourism. But the UUP emphasised that:

> These are not arguments for political integration which has always been decisively rejected by the overwhelming majority of the people of Northern Ireland. It is rather a case for the extension and formalisation of those good neighbourly relations which already exist. Of course, good neighbourly behaviour is unlikely to flourish so long as the Irish Republic retains a territorial claim or even a constitutional aspiration to control Northern Ireland. The removal of the harsh and irredentist claim over the people and territory of Northern Ireland will unlock the door to closer, mutually beneficial co-operation.[95]

The UUP envisaged the Inter-Irish Relations Committee of the Assembly operating within a wider Britannic framework. This was developed by David Trimble, now UUP MP for Upper Bann, for the Strand Three stage of the talks. Trimble argued that any North–South relationship would have to operate within the ambit of a Council of the British Isles. The Council would consist of the British and Irish Governments, plus representatives of regional administrations within the British Isles. Thus, the existing regional administrations of the Isle of Man and the Channel Islands, which were not part of the United Kingdom, would be invited to take part. Consideration would also be given to representation of the English regions, as well as devolved Scottish or Welsh administrations should these occur.

Trimble's concept reflected Unionist concern at what they considered a disproportionate emphasis on North–South relations. He believed that any agreement had to look to the totality of relations within the British Isles. For

Unionists, the interactions on an East/West axis between Northern Ireland and Great Britain were greater in relative and absolute terms than those on a North/South axis between Northern Ireland and the Republic. Appropriate cross-frontier relationships would be located within the Britannic umbrella, based on pragmatic considerations of mutual benefit and not on a political agenda. Such a relationship would not pose a threat to either jurisdiction and, unlike the present arrangements, would correspond to the 'real needs' of all the people. A Council of the British Isles would provide the necessary varied and flexible structure. Provision would be made for meetings at various levels, i.e. government only; governments plus representatives of some or all regional interests; meetings at regional level; and meetings at official levels.

The Council would not have, nor would it acquire, any direct executive function. It would be consultative only. It would be the place where mutual co-operation would be discussed and it could be the place where agreements on inter-governmental or inter-regional co-operation could be made. Matters discussed within the Council, whether at governmental, regional or official level, might result in a government or regional administration deciding to take action within its own area of responsibility. Such discussions might also result in agreement between two or more governments and/or regional administrations.

The implementation of these agreements, whether by means of legislation or administrative action, would be the responsibility of the particular governments or regional administrations that had entered into the agreement in question. It could, however, be appropriate to create agencies to deal with specific matters on an inter-governmental or inter-regional basis. Any such agency would be distinct from the Council and would be directly responsible to the governments or regional administrations that created it, thus ensuring that the Council remained solely a forum for discussion and agreement. The creation of an agency would not prevent further discussion of the matter within the Council.[96] Thus, for example, an agency – which could be a cross-border body with executive powers – could be established between a Northern Ireland administration and the Republic's government; between the Republic and a Scottish devolved government; or by combinations of all three.

Unfortunately, for the UUP, neither its proposals for an Inter-Irish Relations Committee of the Northern Ireland Assembly nor those for the Council of the British Isles were taken seriously by the Irish Government or the SDLP. In particular, a Council of the British Isles appeared unrealistic in the context of a Conservative Government opposed to any devolution within the United Kingdom – apart, that is, from such a possibility in Northern Ireland. Therefore, with the British and Irish Governments concluding that all that was going to be achieved in the process had been accomplished, the talks finally concluded in November 1992, once the decision had been reached to proceed with a meeting of the Anglo-Irish Conference.

In fact, the Brooke–Mayhew talks seemed to emphasise the gulf between the participants, rather than a meeting of minds. While Unionists had argued that a Bill of Rights and a regional assembly, based upon proportionality, was sufficient to guarantee Catholic Nationalist rights within a Northern Ireland framework, this, on its own, was rejected by Irish Nationalists. The SDLP would not accept majority rule within an Assembly or Committee structure; they were also opposed to any devolved administration which did not have executive power-sharing at cabinet level. Indeed this power-sharing at cabinet level would not be restricted to Northern Ireland but would include Irish, British and European appointees in the executive. Nationalists also wanted to see the establishment of a separate institutional North-South Council of Ministers. The remit of this body remained obscure but it was likely to have executive powers, and a similar dynamic to that in the Sunningdale Agreement.

At this stage the Irish Government appeared intent on defending Articles 2 and 3. Unionists, on the other hand, placed greater emphasis on the internal government of Northern Ireland, seeking majority decision-making powers in both an Assembly and the Committees established therein. In terms of North-South relations, both Unionist parties were offering a framework for *ad hoc* consultation between the Republic of Ireland and Northern Ireland – the DUP's External Relations Committee and the UUP's Inter-Irish Relations Committee. But both of these were committees of the Northern Ireland Assembly. As such they could not satisfy the Nationalist demand for a separate institutional dimension, external to an Assembly, for North-South relations. Future prospects for agreement looked bleak.

PART II

Building a Peace Process, 1990-1997

Sinn Féin and the British Government

At this stage, the inter-party talks process appeared to be the only show in town. It wasn't. In 1990 the British Government had begun its own initiative to woo Republicans away from violence. The key figure on the British side was Secretary of State Peter Brooke. His opening move was to state that it was 'difficult to envisage a military defeat of the IRA'.[1] The initial response of the Republican Movement to this was one of delight. According to Danny Morrison, the timing of Brooke's statement was 'extraordinary. Our information is that he said it quite consciously, quite deliberately, in a calculated fashion. Imagine the effect it must have had on the troops out in the street when they realise they are engaged in a campaign they cannot win. So, it's bound to be good for Republican morale.' From the Republican perspective, argued Morrison, the British Government had gone from a position in 1981, where Mrs Thatcher described the Hunger Strikes as the PIRA's 'Last Card', to a position where a Secretary of State 'says, "The IRA cannot be defeated." Where has Britain advanced in these last seven years? A guerrilla actually only has to [frustrate] the ability of the government to stabilise the situation in the government's interests. [For] A government to win [it] actually has to show it is winning and the British government cannot demonstrate that.'[2]

Morrison, the articulator of the armalite and ballot-box strategy, saw Brooke's statement as a sign of British weakness. However, the British did not need to militarily defeat the PIRA to win the war. This becomes clearer if one focuses on the aims of British policy. From the Republican perspective, the British remained in Ireland for imperialist motives. But the British Government perspective was radically different. And Brooke went out of his way to emphasise this in a speech, in November 1990, to his constituency association in Westminster. It was clearly aimed at the Republican Movement.

The theme of the speech was Britain's reason for staying in Northern Ireland. Brooke explained that the British Government remained in Northern Ireland as a result of the desire of the people there to remain within the British state. He acknowledged the aspiration to a united Ireland; that it was possible to take this position with integrity; and that it was acceptable to advocate it by all legitimate, peaceful and democratic means. What was not acceptable, and what totally lacked integrity, was the promotion of this view by the crude and brutal methods of violence and coercion. Brooke asked for what purpose did this killing continue; why, in particular, had a desire for Irish unity to be pursued in a way which could only deepen division? He observed that at the heart of this matter was the question of the so-called 'British presence' in a part of Ireland. As it was to remove this presence that Republican terrorism was said to be dedicated, Brooke examined what the British presence actually was. The Secretary of State identified four main aspects.

The first, and perhaps the most high-profile, was the presence and activity of British troops on the streets and in the countryside of Northern Ireland. Brooke emphasised that the British Government had no vested interest in maintaining these high force levels a day longer than was necessary; but this kind of military profile was 'made necessary by violence, will be maintained as long as there is violence, but will certainly be reduced when violence comes to an end. We have heard for so long about the "security forces" because others have created a security situation.' The second aspect of the British presence was Brooke's own presence in Northern Ireland as Secretary of State. The third aspect of the British presence was simply the transfer from the common exchequer every year of very large sums of money to enable programmes well beyond the capacity of locally raised taxation to be carried out. This support was not given in furtherance of some strategic interest or in the expectation of some corresponding gain to the people of Great Britain; it sought no return other than the satisfaction of improving the conditions of life in Northern Ireland. This brought Brooke to the fourth and 'most significant' aspect of the British presence:

> Every time I hear that call for 'Brits out', it brings home to me the paramount reality that the heart and core of the British presence is not the British army or British ministers, but the reality of nearly a million people living in a part of the island of Ireland who are, and who certainly regard themselves as British. ... This 'Britishness' ... is not only a legal status; it is also a fact of life and a product of history.

Brooke argued that the Anglo-Irish Agreement similarly acknowledged the reality that the people of Northern Ireland had different views about the status of Northern Ireland. Against that background, Article 1 of that Agreement acknowledged that the status of Northern Ireland could only be determined by the people of Northern Ireland themselves. The question which arose, therefore, was whether the sense of Britishness, held by one million people, and their desire for no change in the status of Northern Ireland, could be reconciled with an Irish identity which would embrace them and to which they would freely consent. At present, a great number of these people clearly did not feel or wish themselves to be Irish in the sense Nationalists would like them to be, although they might feel Irish in other important respects. The obstacle to the development of a new and more inclusive Irish identity, if people wanted this, was not to be sought in Great Britain: 'Those who live here [Great Britain] would not bar the way, if, at some future time, that were to be the wish of the people of Northern Ireland themselves. ... However, we will fully support our fellow-citizens while, by their own free and clearly-expressed wish, they remain our fellow-citizens. Partition is an acknowledgement of reality, not an assertion of national self-interest. The Border cannot simply be wished away.'

Brooke argued that no British Government stood in the way of constitutional and peaceful attempts by Irish Nationalists to persuade unionists that a change in Northern Ireland's status could take place without prejudice to the interests of the latter, reflecting their Protestantism and Britishness. He concluded that 'Violence is futile. Violence can never be allowed to succeed. It is, and will remain, the first priority of the government to defeat terrorism, from whichever side of the community it comes' – there was no acceptable level of violence. Brooke predicted that an Irish Republicanism seen to have finally renounced violence would be able, like other parties, to seek a role in the peaceful political life of the community. In Northern Ireland it was 'not the aspiration of a sovereign, united Ireland, against which we set our face, but its violent expression'. Brooke warned that:

> Only if violence is abandoned can a true reconciliation be achieved. There is a need for reconciliation at three levels – between the communities in Northern Ireland, within Ireland, and between the peoples of both these islands. The terrorists constitute a major impediment on the road to peace and greater understanding and to new political institutions which adequately reflect everyone's interests.
>
> The British Government has no selfish strategic or economic interests in Northern Ireland: our role is to help, enable and encourage. Britain's purpose, as I have sought to describe it, is not to occupy, oppress or exploit, but to ensure democratic debate and free democratic choice. That is our way.[3]

The phrase referring to Britain's lack of a selfish strategic or economic interest in Ireland was the key phrase. It denied the rationale for the entire Provisional campaign. However, it was not a new claim. The difference this time was that the Republicans might be prepared to listen. Brooke was attempting to engage in an ideological debate with the Republicans. He was asking them to consider a broader view other than their own insular perspective. And this was to face the reality that it was not the British Government which barred the way to a united Ireland; it was one million British citizens who did not regard themselves as part of the Irish nation as defined by Republicans. But Brooke was also to point out that although the British Government had no selfish strategic or economic concerns – the undeclared implication of this was that Britain might have *unselfish* strategic concerns – this did not mean that the British Government was *politically* neutral in Northern Ireland. He emphasised that the present British Government remained the Conservative and Unionist Party, and that the Prime Minister, as leader of that party, 'has made clear that her [Margaret Thatcher's] views are supportive of the Union'.

On the question of the Union itself, the Conservative Party 'would wish very much to see Northern Ireland remain part of the Union'. Accordingly, the conclusion John Hume drew from his observation that the British Government was neutral, and that it was now up to Nationalists to get Britain to join the ranks of the persuaders, 'would be a false analysis if it was thought that the British government was part of the process of seeking to exercise that element of persuasion'. Brooke was 'not part of the process'. Inducing consent was 'not part of [his] strategy'.[4]

It still remained unclear as what the thinking was within Republican circles. To tease this out, Brooke now took his initiative a stage further by authorising a private back-channel to the Republican Movement. This began while Margaret Thatcher was still Prime Minister and continued when John Major succeeded her in late 1990. Perhaps the most significant factor in the whole initiative was the Provisional's eagerness to seize any opportunity to engage with the British. The contacts lasted three years. There were three distinct phases. In the first, which lasted from 1990 until February 1991, the British Government courted the Republicans, sending nineteen messages while Sinn Féin only sent one in response. In the second phase, between February and November 1993, the pace quickened with an average of a message a week passing between the British and Sinn Féin, where the possibility of 'delegate' meetings were explored. A third, short, phase followed before the back-channel was closed in November 1993.

Contact with the Republicans was conducted through a British Government 'representative'. This was a member of the security services who had been in touch with the Republicans in earlier periods of tension. In January 1992, messages were passed back and forth concerning what Sinn Féin were now calling the Irish Peace Initiative. The Republicans considered these contacts to be between the political representatives of the Republican Movement – Sinn Féin – and the British Government; as far as the British were concerned they were in contact with the PIRA – Sinn Féin and the PIRA were one entity. The British, according to Martin McGuinness, kept Sinn Féin informed of the progress of what was now the Mayhew talks process. For example they passed on to the Republicans, in October 1992, a detailed internal Government report and assessment of the discussions. None of the talks participants had seen this. It was followed, in December 1992 and January 1993, by meetings between the Republican contact and the British representative.

Republicans claimed that they were unenthusiastic until the British representative indicated that a face-to-face meeting between the British Government and Sinn Féin was possible, and began to discuss the logistics of such a meeting. According to the Republican account of a meeting with the representative, in February 1993, the latter emphasised that 'Events [violent activity] on the ground will bring an enormous influence to bear. The IRA needs to provide the space to turn the possibility of meetings into a reality. A suspension [of violence] is all that is being required of them. The British believed that two or three weeks was a sufficient period to convince republicans [that the IRA campaign was unnecessary]. There would be an intensive round of talks.'[5]

The role of the British representative, and whether or not he exceeded his authority, became a matter of some controversy. The representative appeared to suggest that a mere suspension of violence would allow Sinn Féin entry into dialogue with the British. However, as one shall see, this was at variance with both the public and private positions set out by the British Government. What was actually on offer could be seen in public with set-piece statements and speeches from British ministers. In February 1992, during a speech delivered at Coleraine, Sir Patrick Mayhew challenged the Republican Movement to end paramilitary violence. This, he suggested, would have profound consequences for the maintenance of law and order, and for the administration of justice in Northern Ireland. It would allow the British Army to return to its garrison role as in the rest of the United Kingdom.

Mayhew claimed that it was the Republicans who had so far excluded themselves from discussions, by their devotion to the armed struggle. If their cause did have a serious political purpose to it then the Republican Movement should 'renounce unequivocally the use and threat of violence, and demonstrate over a sufficient period that its renunciation is real'.[6] Sinn Féin had received advance copies of the speech. There was no indication that the British required anything other than a permanent ending of violence. This remained the central platform of British policy towards the Republican Movement – a permanent and demonstrable end to their violence.

When news of the contacts seeped into the public domain, Mayhew described the Republican allegations that it was the British who initiated the exchange of messages as 'entirely false'. The Secretary of State claimed that the first message which signalled a move to substantial exchanges between the parties was received by the British on 22 February 1993 and originated from the PIRA.[7] According to Mayhew an oral message from Martin McGuinness had stated, 'The conflict is over but we need your advice on how to bring it to a close. We wish to have an unannounced ceasefire in order to hold dialogue leading to peace. We cannot announce such a move as it will lead to confusion for the volunteers because the press will misinterpret it as surrender. We cannot meet [the] Secretary of State's public renunciation of violence, but it would be given privately as long as we were sure that we were not being tricked.' Mayhew defended the contacts by stating that the Government had a duty to respond to that message.[8]

While the Republicans strenuously denied that they sent any such message, it does appear from the exchanges that the British thought that they were *replying* to something significant. The chaos factor between the two sides would appear to be the informal nature of the contacts. In their 'reply' to the Republicans, the British Government acknowledged that it understood and appreciated the seriousness of what had been said. They emphasised, 'We wish to take it seriously and at face value.' The British attitude to the Provisionals would be influenced by events on the ground – violence; in view of the importance of the message it was not possible to give a substantive response immediately.[9] The Republicans welcomed the possibility of a meeting and offered two representatives, Martin McGuinness and Gerry Kelly, for an exploratory meeting.[10] The British replied that they wished to take seriously what had developed, and were preparing a considered and substantive response. However, in the light of continuing violence, the British felt unable to do so. The British insisted, 'There must be some evidence of consistency between word and deed.'[11] This meant a reduction in violence at the very least.

This fixation on PIRA violence obscured what was a significant shift in the position of the Republican Movement. In 1992, Sinn Féin published *Towards a Lasting Peace in Ireland*, which was their analysis of how the logjam in the North might be broken. *Towards a Lasting Peace* again placed the onus on the two Governments, but particularly the British Government, to work to secure change. Crucially, it appeared to shift the Republican Movement's strategy towards that of the SDLP. It called on the British Government to 'join the persuaders', and to use its influence to convince unionists that their future did not lie within the Union. It also called on the Dublin Government to persuade the British that partition had failed; to persuade unionists of the benefits of reunification; and to persuade the international community that it should support a 'peace process' in Ireland.[12] The unseen influence of John Hume was revealed in this document.

Just as significant was a speech in June 1992, by a senior Sinn Féin figure, Jim Gibney, at the Wolfe Tone commemoration in Bodenstown. The timing and the place of delivery indicated its importance. Gibney admitted that Republicans now realised the need for a 'sustained period of peace' before a British withdrawal. Implicit in this was the suggestion that Irish unity would not necessarily be a rapid occurrence.[13] Republicans now wanted the British Government to become persuaders for a united Ireland. If the Church of England was once described as the Tory party at prayer, Sinn Féin were effectively becoming the SDLP at war. Slowly, almost imperceptibly, the Republican position was undergoing an evolution in policy. It was very doubtful that the Republican Movement had any idea of just how far it would be nudged from its shibboleths.

For the moment, the Republican-British contacts continued. On 19 March 1993, the British Government sent a key document to the Provisionals which could not be misinterpreted by anyone. Employing Republican phraseology, the British accepted that all of those involved shared a responsibility to work to end the conflict and that 'No one has a monopoly of suffering. There is a need for a healing process.' The British were anxious that there should be no deception nor any misunderstandings. They also thought it essential that both sides had a clear and realistic understanding of what it was possible to achieve, so that neither side could in future claim that it had been tricked. Given this, the British position was that 'any dialogue could only follow a halt to violent activity. It is understood that in the first instance this would have to be unannounced. If violence had genuinely been brought to an end, whether or not that fact had been announced, then a progressive entry into dialogue between the British and the Republican Movement could take place.' It had to be understood, though, that once a halt to activity became public, the British Government would have to defend its entry into dialogue. Crucially, it would do so by pointing out that its agreement to exploratory dialogue – this did not mean immediate or full negotiations – concerning the possibility of an inclusive process had been given because, and only because, it had received a *private insurance that organised violence had been brought to an end*. The British Government made it clear that it had:

> ... no desire to inhibit or impede legitimate constitutional expression of any political opinion ... and wants to see included in this process all main parties which have sufficiently shown they genuinely do not espouse violence. It has no blueprint. It wants an agreed accommodation, not an imposed settlement, arrived at through an inclusive process in which the parties are free agents ... [but] The ... Government does not have, and will not adopt, any prior objective of 'ending partition'. The British Government cannot enter a talks process, or expect others to do so, with the purpose of achieving a predetermined outcome, whether the 'ending of partition' or anything else. It has accepted that the eventual outcome of such a process could be a united Ireland, but only on the basis of the consent of the people of Northern Ireland. Should this be the eventual outcome of a peaceful democratic process, the British Government would bring forward legislation to implement the will of the people. ... But unless the people of Northern Ireland come to express such a view, the British Government will continue to uphold the Union, seeking to ensure the good governance of Northern Ireland, in the interests of all its people, within the totality of relationships in these islands.[14]

Four days later a further meeting took place between the British representative and the Sinn Féin representatives Martin McGuinness and Gerry Kelly. According to the Republicans the message conveyed by the representative at this meeting was much more encouraging to the Republicans: 'The final solution is union [i.e. a united Ireland]. The historical train – Europe – determines that. We are committed to Europe. Unionists will have to change. This island will be as one.'[15] If true this message has to be placed in context. There is no evidence that this represented British Government policy. In fact, from official British messages three points were made crystal clear to the Republican Movement – firstly, violence had to end for good; secondly, the British required at least a private assurance that this was so; and thirdly the

British would not become persuaders for Irish unity. The British representative may have been telling Republicans what they wanted to hear. What is significant is that they appeared willing to believe it. This was not evidence of the Republican Movement negotiating from a position of strength. Furthermore, there is some doubt as to the authenticity of the Republican version of events. Prime Minister John Major later described the Republican claims that the British only required a two-week PIRA suspension of violence and references to the 'island will be as one' as a 'self-interested piece of Republican propaganda' and a 'tissue of lies' designed by Gerry Adams and Martin McGuinness to 'cover themselves'.[16]

In fact, the penny still had to drop for the Republicans regarding violence. Their reaction was one of anger to the British position. In their next message to the British Government, they pointed out that everyone in the conflict shared the responsibility to bring about a real and lasting peace in Ireland, and emphasised that they were not reluctant to face up to their responsibility in this. However, the Republicans argued, the British Government 'clearly has the power and the major responsibility to initiate the necessary process'. Pre-conditions, by which the Republican Movement meant the British insistence on a permanent ending of violence, represented an obstacle to peace. For the Republican Movement the route to peace in Ireland was to be found in the 'restoration to the Irish people of our right to national self-determination – in the free exercise of this right without impediment of any kind'. British sovereignty over the Six Counties, as with all of Ireland before partition, 'is the inherent cause of political instability and conflict'.

The Republican Movement drew confidence from the emerging political and economic imperatives both within Ireland and the broader context of greater European political union which supported the logic of Irish unity. It was their view, therefore, that the British Government 'should play a crucial and constructive role in persuading the unionist community to reach an accommodation with the rest of the Irish people'. Furthermore, the Republican Movement complained to the British Government that 'Your disavowal of any prior objective is contradicted by commitment to uphold the unionist veto. The consequence of upholding the veto is, in effect, to set as your objective the maintenance of partition and the six-county statelet. And, consequently, the maintenance of the primary source of the conflict.'[17]

By now it was clear that these contacts were going nowhere. This particular line of communication was closed in November 1993, although it had been effectively exhausted by the summer of that year. The British would not budge from their insistence that there had to be a permanent end to violence and that this had to be demonstrated. The British adherence to the principle of consent and the refusal to become a persuader for Irish unity were fixed principles. Furthermore, the Republican Movement was left in no doubt that British policy required a permanent end to the armed struggle. But it was also clear that the Republicans were unprepared to offer anything more than a temporary ceasefire: the dual electoral-military strategy was to continue. Having achieved no movement from the British, the Republican Movement focused its hopes closer to home.

Hume-Adams

Despite the failure of the SDLP-Sinn Féin talks in 1988, John Hume had never given up on the belief that the Republican Movement could be persuaded to end its armed struggle. Contact between Hume and Gerry Adams had continued. The Irish Government were also brought into the process. Hume developed the idea that a joint declaration, made by the British and Irish Governments, could persuade the Republicans to end their campaign of violence. This could be achieved by convincing Republicans that their traditional foe – the British Government – was no longer a barrier to their hopes of a united Ireland. In October 1991, Hume wrote *A Strategy for Peace and Justice in Ireland*, the prototype for the Downing Street Declaration of 1993.[18] A second draft, drawn up by Hume, the then Taoiseach Charles Haughey and Dublin officials, refined the SDLP leader's earlier draft. The new draft envisaged a British Prime Minister reiterating, on behalf of the British Government, that it had 'no selfish, strategic, political or economic interest in Northern Ireland'. It also called for the Taoiseach to accept that the 'exercise of the democratic right of self-determination by the people of Ireland as a whole cannot in practice be achieved except with the agreement and the consent of the people of Northern Ireland'.[19] Discreet contacts established with Sinn Féin meant that the project began to take on a rather more serious character.

The British Government was soon notified of progress on this initiative. It was in December 1991 that Haughey first put to John Major a suggestion for a joint declaration by the two Governments, designed to set out principles for an eventual settlement in a way which would tempt the Provisionals away from violence. Major remained un-committed but was prepared to examine the proposal's merits. In January 1992, Irish officials passed on a text for a declaration; in February a different version, apparently from Sinn Féin, was passed on to the NIO. The British Government, said Major, found that 'it did not take us long to consider these texts. They were utterly one-sided, so heavily skewed towards the presumption of a united Ireland that they had no merit as a basis for negotiation. They were little more than an invitation to the British Government to sell out the majority in the North.' The Prime Minister was surprised that experienced politicians, such as Hume and Haughey, should have 'lent themselves to such an unrealistic approach'.[20]

Nevertheless they did – primarily because they were Nationalists seeking a Nationalist solution to the conflict and because they needed such an outcome if they were to convince the PIRA to end its armed struggle. So, when the Republicans came up with another version for a joint declaration, it had the support of John Hume. This version remained the basis of his talks with Gerry Adams. It became known as the 'Hume-Adams' document. The crucial section relating to self-determination read:

The British Prime Minister reiterates, on behalf of the British Government, that they have no selfish, strategic, political or economic interest in Northern Ireland, and that their sole interest is to see peace, stability and reconciliation established by agreement amongst the people who inhabit the island. The British Government accepts the principle that the Irish people have a right collectively to self-determination, and that the exercise of this right could take the form of agreed independent structures for the island as a whole. They affirm their readiness to introduce the measures to give legislative effect on their side to this right (within a specified period to be agreed) and allowing sufficient time for the building of consent and the beginning of a process of national reconciliation. The British Government will use all its influence and energy to win the consent of a majority in Northern Ireland for these measures. They acknowledge that it is the will of a majority of the people of Britain to see the people of Ireland live together in unity and harmony, with respect for their diverse traditions, independent, but with the full recognition of the special links and the unique relationship which exists between the peoples of Britain and Ireland.[21]

This version contained all of the main Republican demands – that there would be a declaration of British withdrawal within a time period to be agreed; that the desired outcome of negotiations was an independent Ireland; and that the British Government would adopt the role of persuaders for a united Ireland. The document as it stood would have no chance of being accepted by the British Government. But by now, 1993, Albert Reynolds was the new Fianna Fáil leader and Taoiseach in Dublin. Reynolds was a pragmatic politician, without the baggage and doctrinaire nationalism of Haughey. Reynolds warned the Republican Movement that he would be unable to move the British on the subject of a time-frame or the question of persuasion. Subsequently, he claimed that he was of the view that 'we are simply not going to persuade the Unionists to do anything; they're going to have to make up their own minds.' The Taoiseach's instinct told him that the British would find the document unacceptable; furthermore he considered it unbalanced – 'it was a nationalist document, and there was no balance whatsoever in it in relation to the Unionist position.'[22]

Despite this subsequent claim, Reynolds joined Hume in trying to pressurise the British into becoming persuaders for a united Ireland and argued that they should 'deliver' the Unionists. John Major resisted this pressure. He regarded the Hume-Reynolds approach as 'unrealistic and undemocratic', and believed that it undermined the principle of consent. Major was conscious that a settlement which did not enjoy genuine consent would have stood no chance of working. The Prime Minister was aware that the unionist community could have made Northern Ireland ungovernable and that 'we would have replaced one problem with a far bigger one.' Major felt that London had to constantly remind Dublin that there were two sides to the conflict.[23]

Whatever private doubts Reynolds may have had, he nevertheless presented a version of the text on a 'take it or leave it' basis to the British. The Taoiseach told Sir Robin Butler, the British Cabinet Secretary, that the draft declaration was a breakthrough, and a basis for a 'lasting cessation of violence'. He claimed that the Provisionals had accepted consent and the separate self-determination of Northern Ireland. Two days later, Hume produced yet another draft complaining that Reynolds did not understand the complexities of this text. After studying the rival texts, Major and the British concluded that far from being a breakthrough, they still showed 'little comprehension' of what might be acceptable to the British Government, let alone the Unionists. The word 'consent' appeared, but was swamped by the phrase 'self-determination by the people of Ireland as a whole'. The text also required that the British Government would become a persuader for a united Ireland. It was, in Major's words, 'simply ... not a starter'. To have any chance of gaining Unionist agreement, Major thought it essential to take James Molyneaux into his confidence. The UUP leader was sceptical and questioned the ability of the PIRA leadership to deliver a complete end to violence without factions breaking away. He also pointed to elements of the text which were unbalanced and needed drastic alteration.[24]

But at this stage the priority for constitutional Nationalism was clearly to persuade the Republican Movement that more progress towards a united Ireland could be made through the political process and the abandonment of the armed struggle. Hume was completely focused on what was required for ending Republican violence, not on what was required for reaching agreement with Unionism. On 24 April 1993, he and Gerry Adams released a joint statement which declared:

> We accept that the Irish people as a whole have a right to national self-determination. This is a view shared by a majority of the people of this island, though not by all its people.

> The exercise of self-determination is a matter for agreement between the people of Ireland. It is the search for that agreement and the means of achieving it on which we will be concentrating.

> We are mindful that not all the people of Ireland share that view or agree on how to give meaningful expression to it. Indeed we cannot disguise the different views held by our own parties.

As leaders of their respective parties, Hume and Adams concurred that they saw the task of reaching agreement on a peaceful and democratic accord for all on the island as their primary challenge. Both also recognised that such a new agreement was only achievable and viable if it could earn and enjoy the allegiance of the different traditions on the island, by accommodating diversity and providing for national reconciliation.[25] According to Adams, the basic principles underpinning Hume-Adams were as follows:

- The Irish people as a whole have the right to national self-determination.

- An internal [Northern Ireland] settlement is not a solution.

- The exercise of self-determination is a matter for agreement between the people of Ireland.

- The consent and allegiance of unionists are essential ingredients if a lasting peace is to be established.

- The unionists cannot have a veto over British policy.

- The British government must join the persuaders.

- The London and Dublin governments have the major responsibility to secure political progress.[26]

Many of the points now adopted by Sinn Féin were, in fact, borrowed from a much older SDLP analysis. It was Hume, more than a decade earlier, who had argued that the consent of unionists was essential to a lasting peace – but not to the extent of a veto on British policy. It was the SDLP in 1972, and Hume in his 1988 talks with Sinn Féin, who argued that the British Government should persuade unionists that their future lay in a united Ireland. It had taken key elements of the Republican Movement a generation of armed struggle to reach this same position. Where, of course, Hume and Adams departed was on how to define national self-determination. For Hume it remained the divided *people* of the island of Ireland; for Adams the divided *territory* of the island of Ireland.

By this stage it seemed that another factor – though it should not be overestimated – was influential in shaping some minds in Sinn Féin. By the early 1990s it was becoming obvious to some senior Republicans that the armed struggle was undermining the very idea of Irish unity. In particular the killing of locally recruited members of the security forces in Northern Ireland, which usually meant Protestant members of the community, shattered the Republican ideal of uniting Protestant, Catholic and dissenter. Once again, this had been pointed out by Hume to Adams in 1988. The perception which existed in the unionist community was that the PIRA attacks against members of the RUC and the UDR was a sectarian murder campaign. Republicans disputed this. However, it is difficult to argue that it is necessary to liberate an oppressed nation by killing people who claim not to belong to that nation. For Republicans, unionists stubbornly adhered to a false consciousness that they were British. In 1991, Sinn Féin's Mitchel McLaughlin was prepared to admit that the armed struggle might be having some negative effects on the struggle for Irish unity. He revealed that, in a document presented by a Protestant academic to a Sinn Féin conference, the author had presented Republicans with three interpretations of the PIRA's armed struggle held by Protestants:

- Republicans are evil terrorists who do not believe in law and order, but seek to undermine the stability of society.

- Republicans are actively hostile to Protestants. In this regard the killings of policemen increase the resistance of the Protestant community.

- Republicans do not care about Protestants. Accidental killings are seen as avoidable. [PIRA] Apologies cause anger because the possibility of an accident should have been foreseen.[27]

Some of the Sinn Féin leadership, such as McLaughlin, had come to the conclusion that 'if we are ever to have real and lasting peace on this island, there must be a rapprochement with the Unionist community in the North'. Unionist agreement was essential to a durable and democratic settlement. McLaughlin described John Hume's call for a healing process, in which Britain would join the ranks of persuaders for Irish unity, as a similar concept to Sinn Féin's 'Process of National Reconciliation'. McLaughlin also defined what Republicans meant by the consent of unionists. It revealed that the Republican definition had, in fact, showed no evolution at all:

> Unionists are a substantial minority on the island of Ireland. It should never be disputed that Unionist agreement is not only desirable but vital if we are to have lasting peace and stability in Ireland. The Unionist community must be encouraged to recognise that their future lies in a newly negotiated Ireland, in which their power and influence will have a legitimate determining effect. Such a national agreement is unattainable within the context of Partition which denies the Irish people their right to self-determination. ... Britain created the Unionist veto and Britain created the 'consent' misnomer. Because Britain has the power to remove the veto, it holds the key to the resolution of this problem. Britain has the responsibility to change this contrived and historically divisive policy. Sinn Féin believes that by ending the constitutional guarantee and the 'veto', Britain can at long last break the political log-jam in Ireland by instituting a new realism and determination to enter into inclusive dialogue.

What in effect had changed was the realisation that a post-partition Ireland, through the granting of the Irish people's right to self-determination, 'will not solve overnight a history of conflict'.[28] Violence was having the opposite effect to unifying the Irish nation. In the long term a period of national reconciliation would be required to heal the wounds of conflict within the Irish nation. Forcing some Republicans to realise this, because of the PIRA's inability to kill mainland British soldiers, was the long-term impact of Ulsterisation.

The Downing Street Declaration

'Hume-Adams', as the secret negotiations became known, had angered and alarmed Unionists and Loyalists who denounced the talks as evidence of a 'pan-nationalist front'. The subtle difference between Hume's and Adams's definition of national self-determination was lost in the waves of outrage which greeted the alliance of constitutional and violent Nationalism. Amid increasing violence, particularly Loyalist, on 23 October 1993, a PIRA bomb exploded on the Shankill Road, Belfast. Ten people were killed and 57 were injured; nine of the dead were Protestant shoppers, the tenth one of the PIRA bombers. The UFF retaliated, on 30 October, when gunmen entered the Rising Sun bar in Greysteel, County Londonderry, shooting dead seven Catholics and one Protestant. By the end of October 1993, a total of 27 people were killed, the highest number for a single month since October 1976.

By this stage, John Major had come to believe that the process was on the brink of collapse and would indeed have broken down but for the Shankill and Greysteel atrocities. The former outrage allowed the Irish Government to seize the initiative away from Hume-Adams. Labour's Dick Spring, the Irish Minister for Foreign Affairs, issued a set of six principles, emphasising the principle of consent and the renunciation of violence; this initiative was noted by Unionists. During a European Council meeting in Brussels, Major and Reynolds agreed to sideline Hume-Adams and drive the process forward themselves.[29]

The outcome of inter-governmental discussions was the Joint Declaration, or Downing Street Declaration, in December 1993. In the Declaration, the British Government, in an effort to remove the main Republican justification for violence, namely British imperialism in Ireland, formally declared that it had 'no selfish strategic or economic interest in Northern Ireland'. It was significant that the British did not renounce a political interest in Northern Ireland remaining part of the Union. They did add, however, that their primary interest was to see 'peace, stability and reconciliation established by agreement among all the people who inhabit the island'. The British would not be persuaders for Irish unity but would, instead, 'encourage, facilitate and enable' the achievement of an agreement over a period of time, through a process of dialogue and co-operation, based upon 'full respect for the rights and identities of both traditions in Ireland'. The British Government accepted that such an agreement might take the form of a united Ireland, but crucially stated that:

> The British Government agree that it is for the people of the island of Ireland alone, by agreement between the two parts respectively, to exercise the right of self-determination on the basis of consent, freely and concurrently given, North and South, to bring about a united Ireland, if that is their wish.

The British Government thus rejected the Republican demand that the unit of self-determination should be the island of Ireland as a single territorial unit; concurrent referenda, in Northern Ireland and the Republic of Ireland, still permitted Northern Ireland to self-determine its constitutional future. Northern Ireland alone would consent, or not consent, to a change in its constitutional status, regardless of how the rest of the island voted. This, of course adopted John Hume's concept of the people of Ireland acting collectively which could be interpreted by Nationalists as an act of Irish national self-determination. Unionists could also claim that it recognised the self-determination of Northern Ireland alone.

For the Irish Government, the Taoiseach, Albert Reynolds, agreed that it would be wrong to attempt to impose a united Ireland in the 'absence of the freely given consent of a majority of the people of Northern Ireland'. He accepted, on behalf of the Irish Government, that the 'democratic right of self-determination by the people of Ireland as a whole must be achieved and exercised with and subject to the agreement and consent of a majority of the people of Northern Ireland.' This recognised that the unionist community, as the majority in Northern Ireland, effectively had a veto on unity. The Taoiseach committed his Government to an examination of any elements in the democratic life and organisation of the Irish state that could be represented to the Irish Government, in political talks, as a real and substantial threat to the unionist way of life and ethos, or which could be represented as not being fully consistent with a modern democratic and pluralist society. The Taoiseach then confirmed for the first time that, in the event of an overall political settlement, the Irish Government would, not could, put forward and support proposals for changing the Irish Constitution which would fully represent the principle of consent in Northern Ireland.

Both Governments offered an opening for Sinn Féin's participation in negotiations. But only democratically mandated parties which established a commitment to 'exclusively peaceful methods and which have shown that they abide by the democratic process, are free to participate fully in democratic politics and to join in dialogue in due course between the governments and the political parties on the way ahead'. As a sweetener for this, the Taoiseach suggested that democratic parties could consult together in a Forum for Peace and Reconciliation.[30]

The importance of the Downing Street Declaration was that it represented a common set of principles for the British and Irish Governments in their dealings with Northern Ireland. Its significance was that it marked an end to any Republican hopes that the principle of consent would be on their terms. The Declaration enshrined the Unionist veto. It also marked the point at which constitutional Nationalism in Ireland finally embraced the principle of consent on Unionist terms and abandoned previous hopes of manoeuvring the British into becoming persuaders for a united Ireland.

Although the substance of the Declaration was welcome for many Unionists, for example in the matter of consent, this was partly masked by the document's language, which was distinctly Nationalist, as in its rhetoric describing Irish self-determination. The British Government realised that it was the unionist community in Northern Ireland which now required most reassurance. The whole process appeared to be geared towards appeasing Nationalism and enticing Republicans in from the cold. Therefore John Major moved to reassure the unionist community that the Joint Declaration involved no sell-out of their rights as British citizens. Firstly, he explained, paragraph 2 of the Declaration expressly reaffirmed the British Government's statutory constitutional guarantee to Northern Ireland – that for so long as a majority of the people of Northern Ireland wished to remain a part of the United Kingdom, the British Government would uphold their right to do so: 'That pledge is rock solid.' This, said Major, was explicitly set out in paragraph 4 which reaffirmed that the British Government would uphold the democratic wish of a greater number of the people of Northern Ireland on the issue of whether they preferred to support the Union or a sovereign united Ireland.

Later in the paragraph, the British Government agreed that it was for the people of the island of Ireland alone, by agreement between the two parts respectively, to exercise their right of self-determination on the basis of consent, North and South, to bring about a united Ireland, if that was their wish. 'This', said Major, 'is a crucial sentence, and one about which there has been much misleading speculation. So let me repeat that it says that a move to a united Ireland can only take place "by agreement between the two parts respectively" and "on the basis of consent, freely and concurrently given, North and South". This fully protects the position of the majority in Northern Ireland, and means that change can only come about with their consent.'

Major also placed great emphasis on paragraph 10 in which both Governments reiterated that the achievement of peace had to involve a permanent end to the use of, and support for, paramilitary violence. In these circumstances democratically mandated parties which established a commitment to exclusively peaceful methods and which had shown that they abided by democratic processes, were free to participate in democratic politics and dialogue. The Prime Minister said: 'Let me make it plain on behalf of the British Government what that undertaking means. If there is a permanent end to violence and if Sinn Féin commit themselves to the democratic process, then we will enter into preliminary exploratory dialogue with them within three months. But, first, they must end violence for good'. In summary, the Prime Minister made it clear what was in the Declaration and what was not. What was in the Declaration was:

- A renewed commitment by the British government to Northern Ireland's constitutional guarantee

- An acknowledgement by the Taoiseach that a united Ireland could only be brought about with the consent of a majority of the people of Northern Ireland

- A confirmation that if Sinn Féin renounce violence, they would be able to participate in future democratic discussions.

What was *not* in the declaration was:

- Any suggestion that the British government should join the ranks of the persuaders of the 'value' or 'legitimacy' of a united Ireland

- Any suggestion that the future status of Northern Ireland should be decided by a single act of self-determination by the people of Ireland as a whole

- Any timetable for constitutional change

- Any arrangements for joint authority over Northern Ireland.

'In sum, the declaration provides that it is – and must be – for the people of Northern Ireland to determine their own future.'[31]

There appeared to be a consensus between the British and the Irish Governments that peace would entail the dismantling of terrorist armouries and organisations. Both sides agreed that a cessation of violence would involve the paramilitaries handing over their arms. Dick Spring told the Dáil: 'We are talking about a permanent cessation of violence and we are talking about the handing up of arms with the insistence that it would not be a case of "We are on a temporary cessation of violence to see what the political process offers." I think there would be no equivocation in relation to our determination in that regard, in fact the determination of both governments in that regard.'[32]

Unsurprisingly, Sinn Féin was not enamoured to the Declaration. As Gerry Adams observed, the Declaration did not meet the Republican Movement's demands on the question of consent, or on the role of the British Government as a persuader for a united Ireland. Sinn Féin, while accepting that Britain no longer had any selfish, economic or strategic interest in staying in Ireland, were not satisfied that the British Government did not state that it had no remaining political interest in Ireland. Sinn Féin believed that the British remained politically committed to the Union, and saw the weakening of the link with Northern Ireland as potentially the first stage in the disintegration of the United Kingdom.[33]

Adams also asked, 'Why is the Unionist veto reiterated repeatedly in the Downing Street Declaration? Why is the Government of Ireland Act not mentioned even once? This is the act of the English Parliament that claims British jurisdiction over this part of Ireland. The British hold the power to keep the Unionists locked in a negative mindset forever, or abandon them to their fate, or persuade them along the road to an agreement with the rest of the people of Ireland. British ministers have stated repeatedly over the past few weeks that they will not join the ranks of the persuaders. Why not?' He concluded that any scrutiny would have to include the following:

- Is the Declaration evidence of a real political will to build a genuine peace process, or is it the best that could be put together by two governments conscious of the popularity of the quest for peace but unwilling at this stage to deal in a real way with the core issues?

• Is this as far as the British government will go?

• Is it as far as Dublin wanted them to go?

• Does the Declaration contain any evidence of a dynamic to move everyone significantly in the direction of peace?

• How does it match up to the initiative launched by John Hume and Gerry Adams?

• Will the IRA's positive and open attitude to Hume/Adams apply also to the Downing Street Declaration?

Adams conceded that there was Nationalist rhetoric in the document, but he was forced to ask, 'Have the British merely conceded the wording of certain irresistible concepts, and then, by qualification, rendered them meaningless?' He complained that the Declaration 'does not set any timetable for a united Ireland. It does not commit the people of Northern Ireland to join a united Ireland against their wishes, and it does not establish any arrangement for joint authority.'[34]

In July 1994, after buying time with calls for clarification, Sinn Féin formally rejected the Declaration. At a national delegate conference in Letterkenny, County Donegal, Adams described the Declaration as a 'step' in the Peace Process. Sinn Féin were now looking forward to the next steps. These would have to deal in a fundamental way with the 'core constitutional issues as well as the secondary issues'.[35] Just what one of the next steps was became clear a month later. On 31 August 1993, following a briefing from Adams, the PIRA issued a statement announcing a ceasefire. Recognising the 'potential of the current situation and in order to enhance the democratic peace process', and underlining their commitment to its success, the leadership of the PIRA decided to call a 'complete cessation of military operations'. The PIRA believed that an opportunity to create a 'just and lasting settlement has been created. ... We note that the Downing Street Declaration is not a solution. ... A solution will only be found as a result of inclusive negotiations. Others, not least the British government, have a duty to face up to their responsibilities.'[36]

Why at this point had the PIRA declared a ceasefire? The key factor influencing the Republican Movement was probably the belief that there would never be a better chance to construct a pan-Nationalist alliance from Belfast to Dublin and to Washington which would be too powerful for the British to resist. None of this meant a compromise by the Republican Movement on its fundamental principle concerning the use of violence, the principle of national self-determination, and the new goal of engineering the British Government into a position of being a persuader for a united Ireland; rather, a new front in the struggle was being opened. A briefing paper circulated by the Republican leadership in the summer of 1994 emphasised that its goal had not changed: it remained a 32-county democratic socialist republic. But a new strategy, 'TUAS' – originally interpreted by a number of journalists as the Totally Unarmed Strategy but later revised to the Tactical Use of Armed Struggle – argued that the main strategic objective for Republicans was to construct an Irish Nationalist consensus with international support. This should aim for:

- the strongest possible political consensus between the Dublin government, Sinn Féin and the SDLP

- a common position on practical measures moving Republicans towards their goal

- a common nationalist position

- an international dimension (mostly USA and EU) in aid of the consensus.

These strategic objectives had come from prolonged debate but were based on a straightforward logic: 'that republicans at this time and on their own do not have the strength to achieve the end goal'. The struggle needed strengthening; most obviously from the other Nationalist constituencies led by the SDLP, the Dublin Government and the emerging Irish-American lobby around the new American President, Bill Clinton. The aim of any such consensus was to create a dynamic which could:

- affect the international and domestic perception of the republican position, i.e. one that was reasonable

- develop a Northern nationalist consensus on the basis of constitutional change

- develop an Irish national consensus on the same basis

- develop Irish-America as a significant player in support of the above

- develop a broader and deeper Irish nationalist consensus at grassroots level

- develop and mobilise an anti-imperialist Irish peace movement

- expose the British and Unionists as the intransigent parties

- heighten the contradiction between British unionism and Ulster loyalism

- •   assist the development of whatever potential exists in Britain to create a mood/climate/party/movement for peace

- •   maintain the political cohesion and organisational integrity of Sinn Féin so as to remain an effective political force.

As the Downing Street Declaration did not hold a solution, Republicans were not prepared to wait around for the British to change, but 'as always' they were prepared to force their hand. After prolonged discussion and assessment, the Republican leadership concluded that 'if it could get agreement with the Dublin government, the SDLP and the Irish-American lobby on basic republican principles which would be enough to create the dynamic that would considerably advance the struggle, then it would be prepared to use the TUAS option.' The Republican leadership therefore attempted to reach such a consensus on a set of principles which could be briefly summarised as follows:

- • Partition has failed.
- • Structures must be changed.
- • There can be no internal settlement within the Six Counties.
- • British rule breaches the principle of NSD (national self-determination).
- • The Irish as a whole have the right to NSD without external impediment.
- • It is up to the Dublin/London governments with all parties to bring about NSD in the shortest time possible.
- • The unionists have no veto over discussions involved or their outcome.
- • A solution requires political and constitutional change.
- • An agreed united and independent Ireland needs the allegiance of varied traditions to be viable.

Contact with the other parties involved had been in that context. There were of course differences of opinion on how a number of these principles were interpreted or applied. In particular these concerned how British rule breached the principle of 'NSD'; the absolute right of the Irish to 'NSD' without external impediment; interpretations of what 'veto' and 'consent' meant; and the 'issue of timescales'. Nevertheless, differences aside, the Republican leadership believed that there was common ground to create a significant momentum which would considerably advance the struggle at this time. A number of substantial contributory factors were put forward to indicate that this was the right time for such an initiative:

- – Hume is the only SDLP person on the horizon strong enough to face the challenge.
- – Dublin's coalition [Fianna Fáil–Labour Government] is the strongest government in 25 years or more.
- – Reynolds has no historical baggage to hinder him and knows how popular such a consensus would be among the grassroots.

- There is potentially a very powerful Irish-American lobby not in hock to any particular party in Ireland or Britain.
- Clinton is perhaps the first US President in decades to be substantially influenced by such a lobby.
- At this time the British government is the least popular in the EU with other EU members.

This, argued the Republican Movement, was the first time in 25 years that all the major Irish Nationalist parties were 'rowing in roughly the same direction. These combined circumstances are unlikely to gel again in the foreseeable future.'[37]

The PIRA's cessation, however, was not enough for Sinn Féin to gain immediate, and unconditional, entry into all-party talks with the British Government and the Unionist parties. From the Republican Movement's perspective, the PIRA should not have to declare that the war was over – in fact, as far as it was concerned, Sinn Féin had a right to be represented at all-party negotiations on its electoral mandate alone. Therefore, the PIRA cessation was a concession, their compromise. But was the PIRA cessation permanent? The Irish Government thought so. However, the British Government was sceptical of the PIRA's sincerity, since its ceasefire statement did not refer to a permanent cessation. Despite Sinn Féin's complaints of new British 'preconditions' to prevent their entry into all-party talks, the British position – as during its secret contacts with the Republican Movement – remained the same: an end to violence had to be permanent, not tactical. It was the refusal of the PIRA to declare that its war was over which led to the call for decommissioning.

As the Peace Process stalled month after month on the issue of the permanence of the cessation, Sir Patrick Mayhew, in Washington on 7 March 1995, outlined a three-point plan for decommissioning, i.e. the disposal of terrorist weapons which would allow Sinn Féin to join all-party talks. These were: a 'willingness to disarm progressively'; agreement on the method of decommissioning terrorist weaponry; and a start to the process of decommissioning as a 'tangible confidence-building measure'.[38] The British and Unionist argument was that if the PIRA cessation was permanent, then Republicans no longer needed their weapons of war. In contrast, the Irish Government, along with the SDLP, continued to take an optimistic view of the permanency of the PIRA's cessation. Republicans were uneasy with a recent change of government in the Republic. There was a new Taoiseach, and a new coalition government. John Bruton of Fine Gael was the new Taoiseach. But from a Republican point of view he was tainted with the image of being sympathetic to Unionists. With the political demise of Reynolds, Dick Spring, having been accused of Unionist sympathies in the past, now took on the mantle of advocate for the Republican perspective. Spring argued, 'The crucial point is that the guns are silent'.[39] Spring and the Irish Government, fearing that the decommissioning impasse would break the PIRA cessation, had now retreated from their publicly stated view that paramilitary disarmament was a crucial part of the Peace Process.

Unionist Reactions

For Nationalists and Republicans the 'Peace Process' was evolving slowly. Many were convinced that the Conservative Government's slim Parliamentary majority, and its dependence on periodic Ulster Unionist support to secure House of Commons majorities on controversial European legislation, was slowing down the momentum of the Process. But the relationship between the British Government and the UUP turned out to be of limited value for James Molyneaux. This was partly because Molyneaux overplayed the significance of the relationship. It cost him the leadership of his party.

Central to this Parliamentary 'understanding' was an expectation from the Ulster Unionists that they would continue to have direct access to the Prime Minister – something they had not had with regard to Margaret Thatcher in the run up to the Anglo-Irish Agreement. The UUP also expected initial discussions between the Government and themselves to focus on the creation of a Select Committee which would ultimately lead to the end of Orders-in-Council for Northern Ireland legislation. Senior Unionists were also commenting, both publicly and privately, that the Secretary of State was to look afresh at the powers and functions of Northern Ireland's District Councils.[40]

Molyneaux had, in effect, offered John Major's Conservative Government a similar relationship to that which had developed between the UUP and James Callaghan's minority Labour Government in the late 1970s. The UUP leader emphasised that he was not holding the current Government to ransom with a shopping list of demands. However, he expected the Anglo-Irish Agreement to 'wither', and the Conservative Party's relatively new regional presence in Northern Ireland – whose organisation there was seen as a potential electoral threat to the UUP in certain districts – to collapse. Commenting on the viability of the Anglo-Irish Agreement, Molyneaux now compared it to the Sunningdale Agreement, which was '[registered] somewhere in the United Nations, with a little layer of dust on it,' and he suggested that the Anglo-Irish Agreement had become just as meaningless with its 'mumbo-jumbo' communiqués and 'poppycock' assurances on security.[41] He thought it 'unthinkable that they [the British Government] can proceed with the Mayhew talks type of operation, and hope to cobble together something ...[such as] high powered devolution'.

Never one for the 'high wire', Molyneaux confirmed that the UUP would not be going back into the three-stranded talks which he found 'quite unthinkable and unworkable'. Molyneaux was confident that he would be able to make good his promise to his party that he would leave Northern Ireland in better shape than he found it when he became UUP leader, by winning regional government, a select committee and the end of the Orders-in-Council system.[42] He believed that the Prime Minister was not preparing to produce 'some magical blueprint'. The process which was now happening was one of continuing discussions between the British Government and the political parties. This was a kind of 'constructive operation rather than some dramatic presentation of a paper'.[43]

Molyneaux was also confident that something resembling the Strand One model structure of 1992, involving a reinstatement of durable and accountable democracy, could be acceptable to the British Government. He was further convinced that the trust between the main Northern Ireland parties thus achieved would enable them to 'reach out the hand of friendship to the sovereign Irish nation on our southern frontier. Our ambition would be to develop co-operation on matters of mutual interest and common concern.'[44] Molyneaux, in March 1993, had issued an invitation to all constitutional parties, groups and individuals to assist in designing a *Blueprint for Stability*. According to the UUP leader, the heads of agreement, which could arise out of this process, were as follows:

- Stability and reassurance – keys to the defeat of all terrorism
- Co-operation between constitutional parties essential for economic recovery
- Informal discussions between parties and Her Majesty's Ministers
- Early start on restoring accountability within existing legislation
- Removal of any remaining obstacles through amending legislation
- Need to safeguard interests of all sections of the law-abiding community.[45]

The UUP leader believed that the steady integration of Northern Ireland into the British state was the best way to secure the Union. Furthermore, the best strategy for achieving this was by building alliances at Westminster. By the early 1990s Molyneaux had come to the conclusion that the 'real truth' for the opponents of Unionism was 'terrifying', because of the 'obvious shift' in British Government and Parliamentary attitudes away from sympathy to Nationalism. This had resulted from an overdue recognition of the justice of the Unionist cause; from a discovery that 'we were right and they [Nationalists] were wrong'; from a realisation that Roman Catholicism was not synonymous with Nationalism; and, above all, a conclusion that Unionism and Nationalism owed allegiance to two different states. British ministers had become aware of the difficulty in linking their comparatively stable political system with a permanently unsuitable system in Dublin which had its instability guaranteed by proportional representation (PR).[46]

To a certain degree Molyneaux was correct. For a generation of British politicians their experience of Northern Ireland was the cutting edge of PIRA terrorism – colleagues and constituents murdered, British cities bombed. The memories of civil rights and any zeal for reforming Northern Ireland were lost in the aftermath of violence. Indeed, following the Anglo–Irish Agreement, there was a growing sense that the constitutional scales had tilted too much towards the Nationalists. Unionists were now the underdogs.

There was, of course, another Unionist view, which saw all aspects of the Peace Process as a sell-out to a pan-Nationalist front. This reflected a not insubstantial proportion of the unionist electorate that felt itself disenfranchised. It was powerfully articulated by Ian Paisley's DUP. For example, within minutes of the Downing Street Declaration being issued, Paisley warned of a Protestant backlash following 'this dark hour of treachery'. After arriving at Downing Street, Paisley delivered a letter to the Prime Minister recalling the old anti-Home Rule slogan that 'if England drives us forth, we will not fall alone'. Paisley accused John Major of 'dirty deeds' by speaking to the PIRA behind the backs of the British Army and the RUC. Addressing the media, the DUP leader read out his letter:

> The people of Northern Ireland are deeply shocked that before the la[te]st victim of the IRA murder campaign has been buried, you (Mr Major) have been making a deal to get them to the conference table. As you and your Secretary of State lied about your communication with the IRA men of blood, so you have deceived the Ulster people in your talks with Dublin.

According to Paisley, the Declaration signed by Major and Reynolds – the 'Dublin liar' – also involved the PIRA and so could not be solely between the two men. 'It is a tripartite agreement between Reynolds, the IRA and you [Major]. You have sold Ulster to buy off the fiendish republican scum ...' The letter claimed that the British Government had consulted the Irish Government but had not consulted the people of Ulster: 'You have given the Prime Minister of a foreign and alien power joint jurisdiction with yourself over part of Her majesty's dominions.' Paisley also accused the Prime Minister of failing to secure the removal of Articles 2 and 3. 'The self-determination you offer the Ulster people is the self-determination of a chained slave and the consent you offer is the consent of a battered child.' Paisley claimed that the PIRA had got 50 per cent of what it wanted, and the danger was that 'when we have the process under this document, they (will) get the other 50 per cent'. The Prime Minister's proposal for exploratory talks with Sinn Féin within three months of a cessation of violence was a 'disgraceful statement'.[47]

Paisley had of course been prominent in destroying the Sunningdale Agreement. Then he, and other anti-Faulkner Unionists, had the support of the Loyalist paramilitaries. Things were a little different this time. The sense among sections of Unionism that Republicans were on the defensive was now shared by the Loyalist paramilitaries. The UFF and UVF support for the Peace Process was the decisive difference from 1974. It robbed extreme Unionism of a cutting edge. On 13 October 1994, the Combined Loyalist Military Command (CLMC), consisting of the leaderships of the UDA/UFF, UVF and Red Hand Commando paramilitary organisations, followed the PIRA and declared a ceasefire. The CLMC explained that the permanency of their ceasefire would be dependent upon the continued cessation of 'all nationalist/republican violence. The sole responsibility for a return to war lies with them'. Crucially, the CLMC claimed that 'THE UNION IS SAFE.'[48]

The CLMC's ceasefire was based on a belief that the PIRA ceasefire was dictated from a position of weakness. In December 1993, the CLMC had set out its basic principles, making it clear it would not tolerate any change in the constitutional status of Northern Ireland within the United Kingdom, and that while cross-border co-operation could be explored it should not take any institutional shape in terms of joint authority over Northern Ireland by the British or Irish Governments. The CLMC listed its basic principles as follows:

1   There must be no diminution of Northern Ireland's position as an integral part of the United Kingdom whose paramount responsibility is the moral and physical well-being of all its citizens.

2   There must be no dilution of the democratic procedure through which the rights of self-determination of the people of Northern Ireland are guaranteed.

3   We defend the right of anyone or group to seek constitutional change by democratic, legitimate and peaceful means.

4   We recognise and respect the rights and aspirations of all who abide by the law regardless of religious, cultural, national or political inclinations.

5   We are dedicated to a written constitution and bill of rights for Northern Ireland wherein would be enshrined stringent safeguards for individuals, associations and minorities.

6   Structures should be devised whereby elected representatives, North and South, could work together to explore and exploit co-operation between both parts of Ireland which would not interfere with either's internal jurisdiction.[49]

Since the Anglo-Irish Agreement, Loyalist violence had steadily increased. The period from 1990 to the ceasefires of 1994 saw a major upsurge in Loyalist violence. In the eight years from 1978 to 1985 Loyalists were responsible for an average of 8.5 deaths a year. After the signing of the Anglo-Irish Agreement the average went up to 18.6 per year for 1986-90. In 1991 Loyalists killed 40 people, in 1992, 39, and 44 in the first eleven months of 1993. Much of this increase in activity came from the Ulster Defence Association under the cover name of the Ulster Freedom Fighters.[50] Many of their later victims were Republicans or their relatives. The UFF, in particular, believed it had contributed to the PIRA ceasefire by bringing the war home to Republicans.

Similarly, despite the PIRA ceasefire, James Molyneaux also appeared in a confident mood. He continued to advocate a 'modest Northern Ireland assembly' which would be given full powers of administration as a 'stepping stone to higher things. And that body should be allowed to decide, at its own free will, what the nature of the relationship with the Irish Republic should be.'[51] If Unionists were in an executive at Stormont, 'we would enter into discussions with the appropriate ministers in the Irish government, and co-operate with them on matters of common interest. ... There isn't any point in attempting to design joint structures North and South when you haven't even thought about, never mind secured agreement on, never mind established, the other end of the bridge in Northern Ireland, namely an assembly in Northern Ireland.' In essence, Molyneaux was explaining that the UUP wanted a Northern Ireland Assembly first; only then, at some unspecified juncture in the future, would Unionists work a cross-border relationship with the Republic.

Molyneaux also found himself puzzled as to what Sinn Féin thought it was getting out of the Peace Process. They were not being offered anything that was not available at the time of the assembly established in 1982, he maintained. 'The puzzle for me since the end of August [1994] is, will they not be inclined to say, so what? We're already in the democratic process. We have councillors elected and serving. All you're saying is we can stand for election as in [the 1982 Northern Ireland] Assembly. So what's the big deal?' Sinn Féin could not have been promised anything more, believed Molyneaux. No government could deliver on it. Sinn Féin, he suggested, should read the Joint Declaration. 'I haven't worked out who's being conned. Their feeling that the clock will start ticking and that in a matter of weeks they will be sitting around a table with everyone else – it will not happen.'[52]

In sharp contrast to Ian Paisley, Molyneaux dismissed any suggestion that Northern Ireland's constitutional position within the United Kingdom was under threat: 'There is no possibility of us being betrayed.' While accepting that he had at one stage been similarly confident that the Anglo-Irish Agreement would not become a reality, he insisted that his confidence on this occasion was based on more solid foundations. Molyneaux explained that 'The contrast [with the run-up to the Anglo–Irish Agreement] is that no party leader at that time was told by Margaret Thatcher what she intended doing about anything; she would never have consulted us about anything'. But 'On this occasion, I have the advantage of having been consulted about recent developments.'[53] At his party's annual conference, in 1994, Molyneaux felt confident enough to tell the assembled delegates that 'we are seeing the beginning of the end of terrorism in this land.' He described the past 25 years as a battle of wills. 'And the will of the greater number of solid law–abiding citizens has prevailed. In short, democracy has finally won. That was always inevitable. Those who refused to be unnerved and were capable of taking the long view knew it would come and saw it coming.'[54]

The Frameworks Documents

But Molyneaux had been lulled into a false sense of security regarding the dimensions of British policy. This was not so much that the British had deceived him, but because the dimensions of British policy had changed. With the continuing impasse over decommissioning, reviving the three-strand process with the possibility of using this as an entry vehicle for Republicans into the political process became a priority. The British and Irish Governments entered into discussions to produce a joint framework document for discussion. The political landscape had changed.

Within the UUP, doubts began to fester over Molyneaux's political judgement. Disconcerting rumours and leaks concerning the contents of the joint framework document began to seep out. The UUP MP, John Taylor, accepted that there was scope for cross-border co-operation in areas such as transport, agriculture and fisheries, but he maintained that any such North-South 'committees' should be 'created by democratic institutions in the Dáil and Stormont, and answerable to them'. 'The key issue is authority,' explained UUP party officer, Reg Empey. 'If they [the Governments] genuinely want cross-Border co-operation it has to be in the context of politicians in the North and South'. Empey, fearing 'constitutional change by the front door,' said that an acceptable form of co-operation, such as the Foyle Fisheries Commission – the North-South executive body established by Northern Ireland and Irish Governments – was not analogous to the kind of arrangements Dublin and the SDLP appeared to be seeking.[55]

Molyneaux now warned that any framework document would cause instability and chaos if it proposed the setting up of some form of supervisory body which would oversee the functions of elected politicians in Northern Ireland. While admitting that he had no direct knowledge of the document's contents, the UUP leader claimed that there were indications that it would advance such a proposal, which would constitute joint authority 'in a very blatant fashion'. He believed that there was going to be at least one supervisory body 'to ensure that we all behave ourselves if we're given any authority here in Northern Ireland'. His comments drew a sharp rebuke from the DUP, which accused Molyneaux and the UUP of having betrayed the people of Northern Ireland: 'They told the unionist people that the Union was safe. Now they see it is not, but do not have the courage to apologise for their stupidity and woeful incompetence.'[56]

Following a meeting between UUP MPs and the Prime Minister, on 15 February 1995, the former – Willie Ross, Martin Smyth and David Trimble – wrote to John Major expressing their disappointment that the discussion had done nothing to dispel their fears. The UUP had already informed the British Government that it would not support any proposal which 'envisages the establishment by the two governments of statutory North-South institutions or bodies to discharge or oversee a range of executive functions on matters which they decide will be administrated uniformly through the island. It is our view that any North-South co-operation must be established by agreement between, and derive their authority from, the Northern Ireland Assembly and the Dáil'. The three MPs emphasised:

We are unionists. We wish to maintain the union between Northern

Ireland and the rest of the United Kingdom. We wish to repair the damage done to that union by the ill-considered Anglo-Irish Agreement of 1985. The creation of all-Ireland political institutions with governmental powers to treat Ireland as one unit for any matter is the antithesis of unionism. Co-operation and even cross-Border bodies, properly defined, are one thing; all-Ireland bodies are quite another matter. And no amount of tinkering with the Irish constitution can make such a contradiction of unionism palatable ... we must point out that a framework document containing the proposals which we have indicated is completely unacceptable and would not provide a basis for political progress, and we will have to advise our party accordingly. While we remain willing to discuss our own reasonable proposals, we would not be able to enter into talks on the basis of an agenda which we regard to be a one-sided nationalist agenda. ... It is a matter of profound regret to us that what might be a good chance of resolving our troubles is being destroyed by nationalist greed and intransigence.[57]

In an attempt to placate the UUP MPs, John Major wrote to them, on 17 February 1995, to reassure them that 'parties will be entirely at liberty to propose alternative ideas if they so wish'. He also suggested that there would be similarities between the British Government's own proposals for the creation of a Northern Ireland Assembly and ideas put forward by the UUP in their *Blueprint* document.[58] Major did not see the forthcoming proposals as a threat to the Unionists' position since they were merely proposals to be discussed.

With the Peace Process stalled over decommissioning, the British and Irish Governments were desperate to inject some momentum. In February 1995, the two Governments published their long-awaited joint discussion documents. *Frameworks for the Future. Part I*, was solely a British Government proposal which borrowed heavily from the Strand One segment of the Mayhew talks. It suggested a uni-chamber Northern Ireland Assembly of 90 members elected by PR. All-party committees were to oversee the work of Northern Ireland Departments, while the Assembly would be overseen by a directly elected panel of three individuals. But it was *Part II*, referring to North-South relationships, which caught most attention. Both Governments envisaged regular and frequent meetings of a North/South body:

- to discharge the functions agreed for it in relation to a range of matters designated for treatment on an all-Ireland or cross-border basis

- to oversee the work of subsidiary bodies.

The two Governments agreed that legislation in the sovereign Parliaments should designate those functions which should, from the outset, be discharged or overseen by the North/South body. It would also be open to the North/South body to recommend to respective administrations and legislatures in Northern Ireland and the Republic that new functions should be designated or discharged by it; and to recommend that matters already designated should be moved on the scale between consultation, harmonisation and executive action. It was envisaged that the North–South body's designated functions would fall into three broad categories:

Consultative: the North/South body would be a forum where the two sides would consult on any aspect of designated matters on which either side wished to hold consultations. Both sides would share a duty to exchange information and to consult about existing and future policy, though there would be no formal requirement that agreement would be reached or that policy would be harmonised or implemented jointly, but the development of mutual understanding or common or agreed positions would be the general goal.

Harmonising: in respect of these designated responsibilities there would be, in addition to the duty to exchange information and to consult on the formulation of policy, an obligation on both sides to use their best endeavours to reach agreement on a common policy and to make determined efforts to overcome any obstacles on the way of that objective, even though its implementation might be undertaken by the two administrations separately.

Executive: in the case of these designated responsibilities the North/South body would itself be directly responsible for the establishment of an agreed policy and for its implementation on a joint basis. It would, however, be open to the body, where appropriate, to agree that the implementation of the agreed policy would be undertaken either by existing bodies, acting in an agency capacity, whether jointly or separately, North and South, or by new bodies specifically created and mandated for this purpose.

The East–West structure which was suggested involved the maintenance of a standing Intergovernmental Conference, similar to that established by the Anglo–Irish Agreement. The Intergovernmental Conference would be a forum for the two Governments jointly to keep under review the workings of an Agreement. Paragraph 47 of the Joint Framework Document envisaged how:

In the event that devolved institutions in Northern Ireland ceased to operate, and direct rule from Westminster was reintroduced, the British Government agree that other arrangements would be made to implement the commitment to promote co-operation at all levels between the people, North and South, representing both traditions in Ireland, as agreed by the two Governments in the Joint Declaration, and to ensure that the co-operation that had been developed through the North/South body be maintained.[59]

All Unionist parties were forthright in their rejection of the contents of the Frameworks Documents, which were a return to the Council of Ireland in the Sunningdale Agreement. Unionists were fearful that they encompassed a process whereby an all-Ireland government could evolve by stealth without a formal transfer of sovereignty from the United Kingdom to the Republic of Ireland. Once again there was a North–South body with executive power, with the ability to take executive all-Ireland decisions like an all-Ireland government. This, Unionists feared, was an attempt to introduce joint Belfast-Dublin authority. But, even worse was paragraph 47 which appeared to envisage a new British-Irish Intergovernmental Conference as a mechanism to introduce London-Dublin joint authority over Northern Ireland if Unionists in the Northern Ireland Assembly refused to co-operate with the North–South body.

The UUP warned fellow unionists that 'great efforts will be made to persuade you that the benefits of a continuing ceasefire are a fair price to pay for the sacrifice of your British identity. A ceasefire with terrorists retaining their weapons and bombs is not peace ... we will not surrender our British heritage for peace at any price. These papers cannot be considered as a basis for discussion, only rejected in their entirety.' The Frameworks Documents were designed to 'trick the Ulster people into themselves ending the Union and their British identity'. The UUP claimed that the Documents would

> ... render the consent of a majority to any change [in Northern Ireland's status] as unnecessary. The 'harmonisation' of functions (which means making our systems of government here more like those in the Republic of Ireland and less like those in the rest of the United Kingdom) will lead first to joint authority between Belfast and Dublin, and ultimately to a united Ireland. Mr Major's assertion that the consent of a majority is a guarantee of Northern Ireland remaining within the United Kingdom is made meaningless.

Once again, pointed out the UUP, there was no specific mention of Dublin's illegal claim to Northern Ireland. This was coupled with the proposition for a paralysed and ineffective Northern Ireland Assembly. The complex interlocking mechanisms, weighted majorities and a veto by the three-man panel would mean that the proposed Assembly simply would not work. Instead, the North–South body would be an 'embryonic all-Ireland government'. As a result of the initial designation of executive, harmonising and consultative functions, together with its ability to 'have unlimited acquisition of further [executive] powers', the North–South body 'would be a third government in Ireland, and very quickly become an all-Ireland administration'. Under these circumstances effective power would shift from the powerless Assembly to the North–South body, and the Documents envisaged no limit to the functions which could be so transferred. But the real killer, as far as the UUP was concerned, was in paragraph 47 where, in the event of the Northern Ireland Assembly ceasing to operate, the two Governments would 'ensure that the functions of the North–South body continue to develop, whatever the will of the people'. Consequently, 'If the Assembly collapses, joint authority would be imposed by the two Governments.'[60]

The major political casualty of the fall-out from the Frameworks Documents was Molyneaux, who resigned as party leader in August 1995. Once again, as on the eve of the Anglo-Irish Agreement, his political judgement had been woefully exposed. Many Unionists blamed him for being too trusting of John Major. Molyneaux's cultivation of the impression that he had a special relationship with and access to the formulation of British policy was cruelly exposed by the Frameworks Documents. In a surprise result, the UUP chose David Trimble, MP for Upper Bann, over the more fancied John Taylor to succeed Molyneaux. Trimble, prominent in the Drumcree stand-off, was elected as the new party leader in September 1995. He was regarded as a hardliner and his election brought an almost audible collective groan from the British and Irish political establishment. Trimble's election represented the mounting concern among the unionist community at the evolution of the Peace Process.

For many unionists, the process seemed to be a battle of wills between the British Government on one side and a pan-Nationalist alliance of Sinn Féin, the SDLP and the Irish Government on the other. It appeared to them that their community had no input into the debate. And the Frameworks Documents looked suspiciously like the British Government buckling under Nationalist pressure. These fears had crystallised during the marching season, at the 'Siege of Drumcree', in July 1995, when a stand-off occurred, with Orangemen being initially prevented from marching through what they considered a traditional route which passed along the mainly nationalist Garvaghy Road in Portadown. Unionists felt that their political rights had been taken from them; now their cultural rights were being eroded. The widespread violence and civil disobedience during this, and later stand-offs, echoed the UWC Strike. It reminded the British Government that the Protestant population had the capacity to paralyse Northern Ireland; and that the unionist community was increasingly alienated and nervous. Such was the level of alienation that some observers were conscious that Drumcree was a warning of how close Northern Ireland was to the abyss.

Nationalists, on the other hand, approached the immediate future with some optimism. One of the authors of the second part of the Frameworks Documents was satisfied with its endeavours. From the Irish Government's point of view, the North-South body was designed to act as a balance for the Northern nationalist community; the unionist community, after all, had its identity enshrined in the Union itself, and any supervising role by the Governments should be interpreted as ensuring that Unionists did not destroy the Nationalist expression of their identity in the North-South body. The Taoiseach, John Bruton, explained that the Joint Framework Document – the British-Irish segment – set out the shared understanding between the Irish and British Governments on how to remove the causes of the conflict in Anglo-Irish relations and in relations within Northern Ireland. To assist in this process, Bruton announced that he was prepared to introduce and support changes in the Irish Constitution. Bruton committed the Irish Government:

- To remove any jurisdictional or territorial claim of legal right over the territory of Northern Ireland contrary to the wishes of the people of Northern Ireland

- To provide that the creation of a sovereign united Ireland could therefore only occur in circumstances where a majority of the people of Northern Ireland formally choose to be part of the united Ireland

- To maintain the existing birthright of everyone born in either jurisdiction in Ireland to be part, as of right, of the Irish nation.[61]

As a 'reassurance to unionists' and to their 'sense of Britishness', the Irish Government would ask the Irish electorate to change Articles 2 and 3. This was not actually mentioned in the Frameworks Documents, but for the first time an Irish Government had expressly committed itself to end the territorial claim as opposed to vague references to changing the Irish Constitution. In return, the Irish Government would also expect that 'as a reassurance to nationalists and their sense of Irishness, unionists will agree to structures to cater for the inter-connections within the island of Ireland.'[62]

Sinn Féin were pleased, if not ecstatic, by the second part of the Frameworks Documents. If was, after all, a step in the right direction, if not the ideal model. They now had something tangible to show their supporters after months of stagnation. In fact, as Sinn Féin told the Forum for Peace and Reconciliation in Dublin, they envisaged the proposals in the second part of the Frameworks Documents being taken a step further. Republicans wanted the immediate establishment of all-Ireland institutions as a step towards the removal of partition. To ensure accountability and public confidence, it was vital that these bodies should have 'democratic' rather than 'bureaucratic' mandates. From a Republican point of view democratic meant an all-Ireland basis. It also meant no Northern Ireland Assembly but the immediate establishment of all-Ireland institutions instead. The key to this was the attitude of the British Government.

The Frameworks Documents envisaged a situation where Unionists might refuse to participate in all-Ireland institutions. Unionism's refusal to countenance a constructive relationship with the rest of the people of Ireland rested on Britain's guarantee of their position. Here again, concluded Sinn Féin, was evidence of the absolute necessity for Britain to change its policy and to adopt a pro-active role, persuading the unionist community to engage meaningfully in the development of an agreed Ireland with the rest of the Irish people. By adopting a pro-active role, the British Government would avoid the implied threat in paragraph 47, 'that in the event of failure to agree, all-Ireland institutions will be imposed by the two governments'.[63]

As Sinn Féin's Jim Gibney explained, his party saw all-Ireland institutions as free-standing institutions: 'these institutions don't necessarily need to be linked currently to any State apparatus as such.' Sinn Féin identified a number of areas – job creation, tourism, culture, finance, trade and electricity – where the two Governments could immediately introduce all-Ireland institutions. There was 'absolutely no reason why they can't be put in place and functioning currently on an all-Ireland basis. There is absolutely no reason why they can't be put in place now outside of a context of negotiations about the constitutional future of this country.' Sinn Féin did not see the need for any institution in Northern Ireland from which executive power could be mandated upwards to an all-Ireland institution. Sinn Féin was 'opposed to the emergence of a new Stormont administration'. It wanted the removal of partition. Therefore 'it is within the powers currently of the Irish Government and the British Government in advance of all-party peace talks, to put in place institutions which have an all-Ireland character to them, and to ensure that those bodies indeed would be representative of people who are elected, people who currently have a democratic mandate at the level of councillor or at the level of MPs' drawn from all over the island of Ireland.[64] The British and Irish Governments, argued Sinn Féin, should impose all-Ireland structures immediately, by-passing the Unionist veto. There was no need for a Northern Ireland Assembly at all.

The End of the PIRA Ceasefire

But overshadowing the Peace Process was the continuing impasse on decommissioning. The PIRA still refused to declare that its cessation was permanent. The British Government and Unionists still insisted that the PIRA disarm to demonstrate that their terrorist campaign was over. Sinn Féin still claimed that decommissioning was an attempt to force the PIRA into a humiliating surrender. They also still claimed that decommissioning was a new precondition imposed by the British. But, as has been made clear, decommissioning was not only established British policy, but an Irish Government objective as well. For example, in addition to Dick Spring's demands in the Dáil for decommissioning, Albert Reynolds had, in 1993, warned Gerry Adams that once public confidence in peace had been established every effort would have to be made to deal expeditiously with illegal arms and equipment. John Major was actually careful not to demand the surrender of terrorist weapons to the British Government.

In fact, an Anglo-Irish working group had been set up to explore how decommissioning could occur. It reported in February 1995 that decommissioning could get under way, starting with a 'worthwhile quantity of arms'. This would be encouraged by parallel progress in security matters and prisoner releases. The demand was for a token gesture of decommissioning at this stage in return for entry into talks. But this was scuppered by Dick Spring who publicly called it a 'formula for disaster'.

The raising of exploratory talks between British officials and Sinn Féin to a ministerial level saw no movement from Sinn Féin on decommissioning. Nor did an eagerly accepted invitation to the White House based on an assurance by Gerry Adams that he would 'discuss decommissioning seriously' if talks were raised to ministerial level. Sinn Féin later denied any such undertaking. This led to an infuriated President Clinton assuring John Major that the Americans would continue to say that Sinn Féin had to address decommissioning and discuss it sooner rather than later. Instead, in talks with British ministers, Sinn Féin quoted Spring's warnings on decommissioning being a disaster and demanded the demilitarisation of British security forces in Northern Ireland. In an attempt to circumvent this, the two Governments turned to an idea suggested by the UUP's security spokesman, Ken Maginnis. This was for an international commission on decommissioning.[65]

While the British pushed for a 'twin track' approach – parallel movement on decommissioning and political progress – the PIRA unnerved the Irish Government by warning them that if this went ahead there would be 'bodies in the streets'. While Taoiseach John Bruton appeared in favour of such a policy, the main opposition to it, from within the Irish Government, came from Dick Spring. Both Bruton and Major were attracted by a suggestion from David Trimble for an elected body, in which Unionists could engage with Sinn Féin without decommissioning having taken place, but Spring and John Hume were opposed – the latter calling it a 'back-door Stormont'. The SDLP leader now joined with Sinn Féin in demanding immediate all-party talks.[66]

Despite Spring's doubts, the British and Irish Governments did establish an international body, chaired by a former US Senator, George Mitchell, to look into the decommissioning issue. Also comprising the body was General John de Chasterlain, a Canadian army officer, and Harri Holkeri, a former prime minister of Finland.[67] The Mitchell Report delivered its findings in January 1996. It concluded that paramilitary organisations would not decommission any arms before the establishment of all-party talks. But it added that some decommissioning should take place during all-party talks, rather than before, as was the British view. The Mitchell Report recognised that any decommissioning would have to be voluntarily undertaken by paramilitary groups. It suggested that those involved in all-party negotiations affirm their commitment to a number of fundamental principles of democracy and non-violence. These, which became known as the six 'Mitchell Principles', were commitments by participants:

- to democratic and exclusively peaceful means of resolving political issues

- to the total disarmament of all paramilitary organisations

- to agree that such disarmament must be verifiable to the satisfaction of an independent commission

– to renounce for themselves, and to oppose any effort by others, to use force, or threaten to use force, to influence the course or the outcome of all-party negotiations

– to agree to abide by the terms of any agreement reached in all-party negotiations and to resort to democratic and exclusively peaceful methods in trying to alter any aspect of that outcome with which they may disagree

– to urge that 'punishment' killings and beatings stop and take effective steps to prevent such actions.

Among a number of possible confidence-building measures, the Report noted that an elective process could make such a contribution 'if it were broadly acceptable with an appropriate mandate and within the three-strand structure'.[68] When the Report was published the British Government focused on the suggestion for an elective process. This had been David Trimble's idea and was suggested to the Mitchell commission as a confidence-building measure for the unionist community. However, all shades of Nationalism, North and South, saw it as yet another delaying tactic by a British Government dependent on Unionist votes in the House of Commons. Most importantly, the PIRA drew the same conclusion. On 4 February 1996, the PIRA detonated a massive bomb near Canary Wharf, in London. Two men were killed, over 100 were injured, and more than £85 million worth of damage was caused. The PIRA blamed the British Government for the ending of its ceasefire, claiming Republicans had risen to the challenge created by its cessation, but that time and again selfish party and sectional interests had been placed before the rights of the people of Ireland.[69]

In the aftermath of the Canary Wharf bombing it seemed that the British and Irish Governments literally fell over themselves to make preparations for all-party talks. But it was virtually forgotten that the British Government had accepted, not rejected, the Mitchell Report. It followed from this that there was an opening for Sinn Féin to enter talks. In their Joint Communiqué of 28 February 1996, John Major and John Bruton confirmed that all-party negotiations would be convened on 10 June 1996. This was plainly aimed at appeasing Sinn Féin's demand for such a date. However, both Governments were also agreed that the resumption of ministerial contact with Sinn Féin and its participation in negotiations required the unequivocal restoration of the PIRA ceasefire of 1994. In accepting the Mitchell Report, the British had dropped their demand for actual decommissioning to commence before or during talks. Instead, the communiqué recognised that 'confidence-building measures' would be necessary, and that all participants would need to make clear, at the beginning of the discussions, their total and absolute commitment to the principles of democracy and non-violence as set out in the Report of the International Body. They would 'also need to address, at that stage, its [the Report's] proposals on decommissioning'.[70]

To satisfy the UUP, the Northern Ireland (Entry to Negotiations) Act 1996 provided for elections to a Northern Ireland Forum for Political Dialogue from which delegates to talks would be drawn. The elections for the forum/talks involved a complex party list based on constituency lists and a regional list.[71] This was specifically designed to ensure that minority parties associated with the Loyalist paramilitaries could be elected to the Forum. These were the Ulster Democratic Party, associated with the UDA/UFF, whose main spokespersons were the late John McMichael's son Gary, David Adams and John White; and the Progressive Unionist Party, associated with the UVF, whose main spokespersons were David Ervine and Hugh Smyth. Other parties elected to the Forum included the Women's Coalition, the Alliance Party and the Labour Party.

The structure and format of the talks was to be similar to that in 1991-1992: Plenary; Strand One; Strand Two; Strand Three; and a Business Committee. As before, the negotiations were to proceed on the principle that 'nothing will finally be agreed in any format until everything is agreed in the negotiations as a whole.' The British would chair Strand One of the negotiations and the British and Irish would jointly chair Strand Three. From the International Body, Senator George Mitchell, General John de Chasterlain and Prime Minister Harri Holkeri would chair the various aspects of the negotiations which required independent chairmanship. In particular, Mitchell and Holkeri would be joint chairs of Strand Two.

The negotiations were to operate on the basis of consensus. If there was no unanimity on a particular proposition, the Chairman might propose that negotiations proceed on the basis that the proposition had been approved by 'sufficient consensus'. This meant that a proposition would be deemed to have sufficient consensus when it was supported by a separate majority of the Unionist parties and a separate majority of the Nationalist parties which also constituted a majority of all the participating political parties. With the exception of Strand One, both Governments would also have to endorse the particular proposition for it to be deemed to have sufficient consensus.[72]

Outside the talks process, the Republican Movement continued to conclude that no progress was possible in the Peace Process as long as John Major remained Prime Minister and John Bruton Taoiseach. Therefore the conditions for the restoration of a PIRA ceasefire did not exist. This resulted in a return to murder and bombing, most spectacularly the devastation of Manchester's city centre where over 200 people were injured. The first part of the Republican equation appeared to be solved when, on 1 May 1997, the Labour Party won a landslide victory in the British General Election. Tony Blair became the first Labour prime minister since 1979. But this also opened an opportunity for the UUP.

The election of David Trimble as leader of the UUP signalled a fundamental departure in Unionist strategy. The new man possessed a very different personality and intellect to Molyneaux. Often seen as hot-headed and uneasy in social situations, Trimble was perceived as a hardliner. But there was another side to Trimble. He had also been, in his more youthful days, a member of Bill Craig's Vanguard Party and had supported his leader's plan for a voluntary coalition with the SDLP in 1976. After Vanguard ended its party political role in 1978, Trimble joined the UUP and consistently advocated the case for the return of devolved government to Northern Ireland. In the early 1990s, he succeeded the late Harold McCusker as MP for Upper Bann. Trimble, like the Republicans, had come to regard John Major's Government as a barrier to political progress; on this occasion because he believed that the Conservatives were wedded to the Frameworks Documents.[73]

As has been seen, as early as 1988, Trimble had indicated his willingness, as a Unionist, to consider cross-border implementation bodies with executive powers, as previous Unionist Governments had done – so long as the need for such mechanisms was based on practical co-operation and their authority and accountability was devolved from the respective North-South jurisdictions. Furthermore, Trimble had identified that the status of Northern Ireland as a part of the United Kingdom did not rest on Section 75 of the Government of Ireland Act 1920, but on the Act of Union 1800. Consequently, Sinn Féin's demand for a repeal of the Government of Ireland Act, and taken up by the Irish Government as an exchange for amending Articles 2 and 3, was seen by Trimble as of no threat to the constitutional position of Northern Ireland so long as the Act of Union remained untouched. In 1992, his idea for a Council of the British Isles had seemed fanciful – the United Kingdom remained less a unitary state than a union state; the election of the Labour Government in 1997, committed to Scottish and Welsh devolution, promised to transform the future constitutional make-up of Great Britain. Furthermore, the unexpected by-product of the Frameworks Documents was to propel Trimble and these ideas for a new Unionism to the forefront of Northern Ireland politics.

While Trimble would not accept a central North-South body as set out in the Frameworks Documents – with executive power itself – he was prepared to accept such a body if it was consultative. His idea of a consultative role for a North-South body would mirror those that he had set out for his Council of the British Isles. This could answer the SDLP's demand for an institutional expression of their Irishness without being an embryonic all-Ireland government and a threat to the Union. In was, in effect, taking the UUP's idea of a consultative Inter-Irish Relations Committee of the Northern Ireland Assembly from 1992 – which was also reflected in the DUP's proposed External Relations Committee for the Assembly – and giving it an institutional identity outside the Assembly but with authority and ministers emanating from the Assembly. It was also very similar to Brian Faulkner's consultative North-South Inter-Governmental Council of over 20 years earlier, which he had been forced to abandon in favour of the executive Council of Ireland. Crucial to Trimble's strategy was his relationship with the new British Prime Minister and whether the Irish Government were prepared to accept this model of a North-South body.

A week after being elected, Tony Blair's first official visit outside London was to Belfast. There he laid out the Labour Government's intentions towards

Northern Ireland. His aim was to reassure the unionist community and present an ultimatum to the Republican Movement. His message was 'simple. I am committed to Northern Ireland. I am committed to the principle of consent. My agenda is not a united Ireland.' Blair went on to say: 'Northern Ireland is a part of the United Kingdom, alongside England, Scotland and Wales. The Union binds the four parts of the United Kingdom together. I believe in the United Kingdom. I value the Union. I want to see a Union which reflects and accommodates diversity.' Blair was against a rigid, centralist approach, considering this the surest way to weaken the Union. The proposals the Labour Government were making, for devolution to Scotland, Wales and the English regions, were designed to bring government closer to the people. That would renew and strengthen the Union. The Prime Minister supported this approach for Northern Ireland also, with some form of devolution and cross-border arrangements which acknowledged the importance of relationships within the island of Ireland. Blair took the opportunity to make one thing 'absolutely clear':

> Northern Ireland is a part of the United Kingdom because that is the wish of a majority of the people who live here. It will remain part of the United Kingdom for as long as that remains the case. This principle of consent is and will be at the heart of my Government's policies on Northern Ireland. It is the key principle.

> It means that there can be absolutely no possibility of a change in the status of Northern Ireland as a part of the United Kingdom without the clear and formal consent of a majority of the people of Northern Ireland. Any settlement must be negotiated [by the Northern Ireland political parties], not imposed; it must be endorsed by the people of Northern Ireland in a referendum; and it must be endorsed by the British Parliament.

> Of course, those who wish to see a united Ireland without coercion can argue for it, not least in the talks. If they succeeded, we would certainly respect that. But none of us in this hall today, even the youngest, is likely to see Northern Ireland as anything but a part of the United Kingdom. That is the reality, because the consent principle is now almost universally accepted. ... So fears of betrayal are simply misplaced. Unionists have nothing to fear from a new Labour government. A political settlement is not a slippery slope to a united Ireland. The government will not be persuaders for unity.

Having re-emphasised the 'triple lock system' set out by the Conservatives – 'Parties, People and Parliament' – the Prime Minister explained that the Labour Government was fully committed to the approach set out in the Downing Street Declaration. Blair believed that the Joint Framework Document set out a reasonable basis for future negotiation. However, he recognised a fundamental problem. The truth, concluded Blair, was that there was no confidence on either side about the motives and intentions of the other. Each party often seemed utterly convinced of the duplicity of all the others. What gave these suspicions their uniquely corrosive character, on both sides, was the current prominence of violence in the equation. Violence had no place in a democratic society, whatever the motivation of those practising it. Terrorism, whether Republican, or so-called Loyalist, was contemptible and unacceptable. Blair asked:

What today is the aim of IRA violence?

– Is it a united Ireland? Violence will not bring a united Ireland closer, because now all the parties in Northern Ireland ... and the parties in the Republic [with the exception of Sinn Féin] ... agree that consent is the basic principle.

– Is it to defend the nationalist community? It is hard to see, to put it no higher, how killing people and damaging the Province's economy and local services helps the nationalist community from any point of view.

– Is it to force a way into talks? This is manifestly absurd, since the only obstacle to Sinn Féin joining the talks is the absence of a credible and lasting end to violence.

– Do they hope a loyalist backlash or a security crackdown would justify their violence and lead to communal trouble where republican aims might have more chance of flourishing?

Such an approach would be the height of cynicism. I hope the Loyalists will not fall for it. The Government certainly won't. Any shred of justification they might have claimed for violence has long since disappeared.

The Prime Minister also concluded that not only did violence achieve nothing, 'There is nothing it *can* achieve, save death, destruction and the corruption of more young lives.' Blair, in pointing out that multi-party talks had been established, saw that Sinn Féin had missed every single opportunity to declare a ceasefire and join the process. The Prime Minister offered Sinn Féin a place at the talks table on certain conditions: 'I want the talks process to include Sinn Féin. The opportunity is still there to be taken. If there is an unequivocal ceasefire words and deeds must match and there must be no doubt of a commitment to peaceful methods and the democratic process.' He also warned Sinn Féin and the PIRA that they faced a choice between negotiations and violence; violence was the failed path of the past and he urged them to choose negotiations once and for all; but 'If they do not, the talks cannot wait for them but must and will move on.'[74]

The second part of the Republican strategy had revolved around the election of a more Nationalist government in the Republic of Ireland. This seemed to have occurred soon after Blair's election with the return to power of a Fianna Fáil dominated coalition government. Bertie Ahern had replaced Albert Reynolds as the leader of Fianna Fáil; now he succeeded John Bruton as Taoiseach. But, as with Blair, an analysis of Fianna Fáil and Ahern's aims in any negotiation was liable to as much comfort to moderate Unionism as to Republicans. There was evidence that there was new thinking at the heart of Fianna Fáil, the home of traditional Nationalist thinking in the Republic. In a speech to the Irish Association, in February 1995, Ahern attempted to reassure Unionists that:

> North-South institutions with executive powers are a fundamentally different concept from joint authority. Joint authority, which Fianna Fáil have never advocated or regarded as a realistic possibility, is essentially joint rule over Northern Ireland by the Irish and British Governments. North-South institutions relate not just to the North, but to North and South equally. They mean North and South working together freely in their common interest, on the basis of a democratic mandate. Even if Government institutions in the North were to break down, there is no question of resorting to joint authority, but equally it does not necessarily mean that all functioning North-South co-operation would break down. The Lough Foyle Fisheries Commission continued in existence after Stormont was abolished, and no one has seriously suggested that that is a manifestation of joint authority.

Ahern emphasised that the Republic of Ireland was not asking Unionists to give an inch on their rights, on their birthright, on their traditions, or on their right to safeguard their future in any new dispensation. What they were asking was that they accord the same rights to Nationalists, recognising that they too valued their birthright, their traditions, and the promise of a future that was better than the past. Ahern warned that Northern Ireland would only work as a political entity if there was a spirit of give and take, if there was genuine partnership: 'It cannot operate on a one-party or one-tradition hegemony. Consent is a two-way process'. The Northern nationalist community were incorporated within Northern Ireland against their will and had been subjected in the past to both discrimination and coercion. Unionists now had to ask themselves: 'Do they want to win the consent of Nationalists for the political and constitutional arrangements that they wish to preserve in Northern Ireland, or do they believe deep down that even reasonable Nationalist wishes are profoundly subversive, and can or should simply be ignored, as they were for 50 years under Stormont?' Ahern claimed:

> Irish Nationalism has changed. Irredentism is dead. I know of almost no one who believes it is feasible or desirable to attempt to incorporate

Northern Ireland into the Republic or into a united Ireland against the will of a majority there, either by force or coercion. Ireland is, for the vast majority of us, one nation, which is divided, because its two traditions have by and large chosen up till now to live under two different jurisdictions. In my view we have to leave behind us the territorial claims, if that is the correct description, of the Irish and British States, and vest its future exclusively in the hands of its people, North and South, in keeping with the principles set out in the Joint Declaration. In keeping with our principles, it is the people of Ireland who are sovereign, not the State, be it British or Irish.

If negotiations were to be successful, then all parties had to be included. It was not only a question of full Sinn Féin participation. Ways had to be found of allowing the small Loyalist parties – associated with paramilitary organisations – to take part at the conference table. In Ahern's view it would be premature to attempt to insist at this stage on the decommissioning of weapons being dealt with first, even though it remained an important issue. Confidence in peace and mutual trust needed to be further built up through negotiation, before a permanent disposal of weapons became a real possibility, either for Loyalists or Republicans.[75]

For Trimble, Ahern appeared to open a door to move away from the Frameworks Documents. There was a feeling, among key elements of the UUP, that Ahern might be a different proposition to previous Taoisigh. Ahern, a former finance minister who had negotiated tough bargains with employers and unions, was thought by some Unionists as a man realistic enough to spot a deal when he saw one. Ahern, from his perspective, had to keep a number of different interests on board. As the Taoiseach told Trimble and John Taylor at a private dinner, in February 1998, sometimes, in order to secure an agreement, it was necessary to make a deal with the 'big unions' and pretend to the 'small unions' that no deal had yet been made. Some wags within the UUP team wondered precisely who the Taoiseach actually meant by the 'big unions'.[76]

Multi-Party Talks

So, when in July 1997, the PIRA declared another cessation of their armed struggle, the omens for achieving its goal of building on the Frameworks Documents and moving the British into the position of persuaders for a united Ireland were not as positive as they may have thought. Fianna Fáil was now wedded to Hume's definition of national self-determination, which included the consent of the people of Northern Ireland to any change in that region's constitutional status; and had retreated from Haughey's position on a unitary state and, apparently, previous Irish government positions on joint authority. The new British Government and Blair's personal intervention, which had seen the abandonment of his party's formal commitment to Irish unity by consent, appeared to set the Northern Ireland question in a Britannic model with regard to the issue of devolution.

But it was also clear that both new Governments wanted Sinn Féin in all-party talks. The prize of drawing the Republicans away from armed struggle remained alluring. Without them the talks were a political process but not a Peace Process. So, when, once again, the PIRA cessation did not mention anything about its duration, the Governments overlooked this for the time being. Instead, Sinn Féin had been assured that if they followed all other talks participants and signed up to the six Mitchell Principles, concerning democracy and non-violence, then they would be admitted to the talks. They were also assured that the talks would have a definite deadline – May 1998. The issue of decommissioning was fudged. As set out in the Mitchell Report, paramilitaries were encouraged to engage in decommissioning in parallel with negotiations, but this was to be entirely voluntary. Few, particularly the Unionist parties, expected this to happen.

But Sinn Féin did not have it all their own way. They were joining an already-established talks process. Sufficient consensus was at its core. This meant that a potential constitutional agreement could be hammered out between the SDLP and the UUP and Sinn Féin could not veto it. Furthermore, while Sinn Féin claimed to be at the talks because of its electoral mandate, the other talks participants saw Sinn Féin as inextricably linked to the PIRA. The ambiguities of the Republican commitment to non-violence became clear in *An Phoblacht*, during an interview with a 'spokesperson for the IRA leadership'. The interview included the following passage:

> *An Phoblacht*: Sinn Féin have affirmed the Mitchell principles. Do you have a view on that and what of your own view on the Mitchell principles themselves?

> *IRA*: Sinn Féin is a political party with a very substantial mandate. What they do is a matter for them. But I think all Republicans should understand them as they do what they believe is right and necessary to bring about a lasting peace. Sinn Féin's stated commitment is to secure a peace settlement which both removes the causes of conflict and takes all the guns, British, Republican, Unionist, Nationalist and Loyalist, out of Irish politics. The Sinn Féin position actually goes beyond the Mitchell principles. Their affirmation of these principles is therefore quite compatible with their position.

> As to the IRA's attitude to the Mitchell principles *per se*, well, the IRA would have problems with sections of the Mitchell principles. But then the IRA is not a participant in these talks.[77]

Unionists were outraged by the interview, which they saw as a clear violation of the Mitchell Principles. But David Trimble was reassured by the words of the Prime Minister. Tony Blair was scathing of the PIRA's pronouncement and pointed out that 'No one should be naïve about the IRA and Sinn Féin. The two are inextricably linked. One cannot claim to be acting independently from the other.'[78] This was a fundamental point for Trimble, since it meant that the British Government regarded Sinn Féin and the PIRA as two sides of the same coin, whatever Sinn Féin's protests. This also allowed the UUP leader some breathing space. The UUP's 110-member ruling executive authorised the leadership, in Trimble's words, to 'take whatever decisions and what course of action it considers appropriate in response to the current situation'.[79] However, the fundamental question for Unionism was: what to do once Sinn Féin was admitted to the talks. With the DUP and the smaller United Kingdom Unionist Party, led by Robert McCartney, set to boycott the talks, the UUP had a difficult decision to make: to join the boycott or present the Unionist case from within the talks process.

The UUP had little room for manoeuvre. The Governments were determined to have Sinn Féin in. The moment of truth came for the UUP with the procedural motion launching full negotiations on 15 September 1997. This saw the talks Plenary welcome the decision of the British and Irish Governments to appoint General John de Chastelain as Chairman of an Independent Commission on Decommissioning. The talks Plenary also agreed that the resolution of the decommissioning issue was an 'indispensable part of the process of negotiation, alongside other confidence-building measures'. The procedural motion supported the views of the British and Irish Governments, as set out in a joint statement by the Prime Minister and the Taoiseach, of the same day, on consent and on the decommissioning of some paramilitary arms during the negotiations.[80]

In this Joint Statement, the Prime Minister and the Taoiseach confirmed that 'Consent will be a guiding principle for them in the negotiations, from which no outcome is of course excluded or predetermined.' Both Governments re-affirmed that the aim of the negotiations was to achieve a 'new and lasting agreement, addressing the totality of relationships, which commands the consent of both Unionists and Nationalists'. Both Governments confirmed that they remained totally committed to the implementation of the Mitchell Report in all its aspects, and they looked to all parties to work constructively and in good faith with them on this basis. They recognised that successful decommissioning would depend on the co-operation of the paramilitary organisations themselves and could not in practice be imposed on them as a precondition for successful negotiation or as an absolute obligation. But both Governments 'would like to see the decommissioning of some paramilitary arms during negotiations, as progress is made in the political talks, and believe this could be a major contribution to confidence-building and momentum towards agreement'.[81]

This, of course, completely undermined the UUP's demand for prior PIRA decommissioning. Now, as Gerry Adams signed up to the Mitchell Principles on behalf of Sinn Féin, speculation surrounded the intentions of the UUP, and whether they would attend or withdraw from the talks. There was opposition to participation from many within the party, including MPs Willie Ross and Willie Thompson. But key elements within the UUP leadership were convinced that Republicans wanted them to withdraw, to by-pass Unionism and conclude a deal with the British Government. In August, six weeks before substantive talks were due to begin, Jeffrey Donaldson, the UUP MP for Lagan Valley, recalled an interview given by Gerry Adams in an American magazine prior to the latest PIRA ceasefire. Adams had said: 'I think if the IRA called a cessation tomorrow it would just put the unionists and the British on the wrong foot. What would the unionists do? They would be exposed as dunderheads and come across as the parties unwilling to make a deal.' To Donaldson it was clear that 'Sinn Féin/IRA' hoped to deliberately wrongfoot Unionists and to 'see us run away from the talks process, thus incurring the wrath of the watching world'.

Donaldson was convinced that Sinn Féin/IRA wanted to bypass Unionists and do a deal with the British Government because Republicans saw the conflict as being one between the British Government and the 'Irish people. They cannot cope with the reality of one million unionists who regard themselves as British in every respect.' Nor, in Donaldson's view, could they cope with the reality of the principle of consent which required that Northern Ireland's future be determined with reference to the wishes of these one million British unionists. Running away from the talks enabled Sinn Féin/IRA to avoid these realities and played right into their hands. To suggest, as other Unionists were doing, that the process would come to a halt if Unionists were absent, 'flies in the face of reality and past experience'. Unionists only had to look back to the Anglo–Irish Agreement to see how their own Government had joined with the Irish Government and was 'more than capable of imposing so-called solutions against our will. Is the best way to defend and promote the cause of the Union to abandon the playing field and leave our goals wide open for our opponents to score time after time and win the game?' If the process was flawed and needed to be changed then it could not be changed through absentionism.[82]

It was now clear that the UUP were to remain within the talks; as its leader stated, he was 'determined one way or another that the unionist voice will be heard'. Reg Empey emphasised that all was not well in the Republican camp and that it was facing serious problems. He argued that the PIRA's statement was 'partly aimed at least in quelling internal dissent' and that 'they are in fact taking the first faltering steps towards acceptance of partition.' Empey felt that while there were difficulties within Unionism, Republicans 'have even greater difficulties when you see and hear mothers of former dead hunger strikers coming out and saying "my son died for nothing".' Unionism should be focused on the difficulties within Republicanism 'instead of focusing on our own navels'.[83]

The DUP responded with a scathing attack on the UUP's 'indecision and dithering'. Deputy Leader Peter Robinson claimed that the attitude of Trimble and his party 'spells peril for the Union'. Robinson argued that given the direction of the talks process and the fact that all Unionists agreed that there was no possibility of a Unionist outcome, the talks should be abandoned and replaced by a 'fair process that allows a unionist outcome. Ulster requires a united approach from its unionist leaders.' The process, he claimed, was now 'irredeemably tilted' in favour of the pan-Nationalist front, and the proposals in the Frameworks Documents for a united Ireland were the pre-determined outcome of the process. Robinson added that the 'internationally-recognised principle of consent will not govern the process. The definition has been altered to make it meaningless.'[84]

But for Trimble, the overriding objective for the UUP was that the 'Unionist voice' should be heard and the 'Union ... defended'. It then became a consideration as to how that would be achieved and 'here I'm afraid we do differ from Dr Paisley; we don't think we're going to achieve that by avoiding issues, even when they're unwelcome issues. Now we did not welcome Sinn Féin into these talks, we didn't invite them in; others did. ... But while that situation obtains I don't think we should shirk our responsibilities. So we have that overriding objective.' For Trimble there was 'far too much emphasis on Sinn Féin in this. Sinn Féin are marginal to the process, bear that in mind.' The process involved two governments and a maximum of ten parties. Meetings in plenary within the same room were limited and of a formal character; they did not involve negotiation between the UUP and Sinn Féin. As meetings in a bilateral/trilateral format were at the option of the parties, the rules of sufficient consensus meant that the SDLP's support for a particular proposition alone would constitute sufficient consensus for a decision as that party represented a majority of Nationalists at the talks, and representatives of nationalists in Northern Ireland. Therefore, 'It's not necessary for Sinn Féin to agree to anything, nor does Sinn Féin have a veto, unlike Unionists, because assent by our Party is essential to any proposition and in fact in terms of the operation of the talks we have a veto. Sinn Féin does not. So Sinn Féin's participation is not essential.'

The question then arose as to where the Irish Government or the SDLP stood: 'Are they going to shield Sinn Féin; are they going to help them and continue their alliance with them; or are they prepared to join with us in trying to build a better Northern Ireland for everybody here?' This was the crucial question. Up until this point, according to Trimble, the SDLP had been able to avoid the question; but in the coming weeks and months that question would be unavoidable and one of the reasons why the UUP had continued in the process was the possibility that it might be feasible for the SDLP and the UUP to have serious discussions. Trimble added, 'now I could understand why in the past the SDLP were reluctant to do so, because John Hume wanted to see Sinn Féin involved in the process and you can understand the political and electoral considerations that may have led him to put that as a priority. Now that has been achieved he [Hume] ... has a very important strategic decision to take which will be more influential, more important in terms of the progress of the talks than the entry of Sinn Féin.'[85]

But, if Unionism had its divisions, it was slowly becoming apparent that

Republicans had theirs also. As preparations for the opening of the talks continued, a car bomb exploded in Markethill, a predominantly Protestant village in County Armagh. The key question was whether the bomb was the work of disaffected Republicans or had been officially sanctioned by the Provisionals with the aim of pressurising the UUP out of the talks. The security forces initially laid the blame for the bomb at the door of the Continuity Army Council of the IRA, or simply the Continuity IRA, which was alleged to be the paramilitary wing of the splinter political group, Republican Sinn Féin. Republican Sinn Féin denied this relationship. Nevertheless, the CIRA and Republican Sinn Féin shared a common analysis of the talks process. The former had come to the conclusion that the only way forward for Republicanism was the continuation of the armed struggle, and had pledged to continue its campaign until the 'British make a declaration of intent to withdraw and all political prisoners are released'. The CIRA was opposed to the talks, which it concluded would only result in a new Stormont with cross-border bodies.[86]

Further pressure on Provisional Sinn Féin stemmed from the establishment of the 32-County Sovereignty Committee in December 1997. It aimed to 'uphold the 1919 Declaration of Independence' from Britain and opposed any settlement emerging from the talks which fell short of Irish unity. Its main spokesperson was Bernadette Sands-McKevitt, the sister of the dead hunger striker Bobby Sands. As vice-chairwoman of the 32-County Sovereignty Committee, she called on Sinn Féin to withdraw from the Stormont talks immediately. Sands-McKevitt believed that the talks could not secure Republican goals, arguing, 'Gerry Adams and Martin McGuinness can stand up, wrap the green flag around themselves and sing A Nation Once Again at the top of their voices but it will do no good.' Any settlement which failed to end partition was anti-Republican. Sands-McKevitt concluded: 'Bobby did not die for cross-Border bodies with executive powers. He did not die for nationalists to be equal British citizens within the Northern Ireland state.'[87] Some of those within the PIRA who shared this analysis, such as the PIRA's former Quarter Master General, led a steady trickle of defections to a new splinter Republican group following a PIRA Convention held in Gweedore, County Donegal, in October.[88] These defections were to lead to the formation of the Real IRA and the worst single atrocity of the Troubles.

But for the moment at least politics dominated the proceedings – not that this amounted to much. From the opening sessions of the talks until the end of the year, no constructive progress was made. The talks were dominated by rhetoric. Media interest was heightened by the much anticipated meeting between Tony Blair and Gerry Adams, on 14 October 1997, in Belfast. This was the first meeting between a British Prime Minister and the leadership of Sinn Féin since Lloyd George met with Arthur Griffith and Michael Collins in 1921. Adams commented, 'I hope we do better than we did the last time'. David Trimble, however, was dismissive. He described the Blair-

Adams handshake as not of 'earth-shattering importance'; he added: 'Sinn Féin are only bit players. They're a small group, a minority of a minority.'[89]

If anything the dominant theme of the talks remained distrust. In the absence of a declaration that the PIRA cessation was permanent, or any actual decommissioning, the UUP believed that the Republican Movement was engaged in a tactical suspension of the armed struggle. At the beginning of the talks, on 23 September, the UUP indicted Sinn Féin for breaching the Mitchell Principles. The UUP attempted to (a) establish the link between individual delegates for Sinn Féin – such as Gerry Adams and Martin McGuinness – and the PIRA; and (b) establish that Sinn Féin was already committed to frustrating the objectives of the talks.[90] The procedure to be followed if a party had to be expelled from the talks was set out in Rule 29 of the Rules of Procedure for Negotiations. This stated that participants were no longer entitled to participate if they 'have demonstrably dishonoured the principles of democracy and non-violence' as set forth in the Mitchell Report. It was on this basis that the British and Irish Governments threw out the UUP indictment.

However, Sinn Féin was not pleased when the Governments stated that 'they will expect the Republican Movement as a whole to honour the commitment to the Mitchell principles affirmed by Sinn Féin'. In particular, the Governments found it hard to conceive of circumstances where, after a group with a clear link to any party in negotiations had used force or threatened to use force to influence the course or the outcome of the all-party negotiations, the relevant party could be allowed to remain within the talks.[91]

But this did not reassure the UUP with reference to Sinn Féin's 'tactical' participation in the talks. This seemed to be confirmed once again in November, at a Republican function, in Cullyhanna in south Armagh. There, Francie Molloy, a Sinn Féin councillor and talks delegate, told his audience that if the process failed, Republicans could 'simply go back to what we know best'. Trimble seized on the comment as evidence 'which seemed to indicate that the ceasefire was regarded by the republican movement as temporary'.[92]

The talks also took a dramatic turn when Ulster Unionist concerns were heightened by the comments of the new Irish Foreign Minister, David Andrews. In November, when asked for his understanding of a cross-border body, Andrews replied that it would be 'not unlike a government'. The phrase 'not unlike a government' produced the first real crisis in the talks. Reg Empey of the UUP pointed out that 'government' was one of the 'magic words' as far as Unionists were concerned.[93] The UUP were astonished at Andrews's timing, coming as it did on the morning of a DUP conference. Ian Paisley immediately seized on the comments to warn that the proposed North-South body would deal a 'mortal blow' to the Union and leave Unionists in a permanent minority in matters relating to Northern Ireland: 'Fifty per cent of the membership of such a body would be from the Irish

Republic. At least a third of the representatives from Northern Ireland would be republican-orientated, leaving the unionists always in a minority. That is going to be the body which, if a Northern Ireland assembly fails to operate in the way Dublin wants it to operate, can be abolished and that all-Ireland body take over its duties and responsibilities.'[94] Despite these warnings the talks produced no great excitement, even among the unionist community. The talks were stuck in neutral.

PART III

Endgame? Negotiations, December 1997–March 1998

Heads of Agreement

The end of 1997 and the beginning of 1998 were marked by an upsurge in paramilitary violence. The most significant killing was that of Billy Wright at the Maze prison by INLA inmates. Wright was leader of the UVF splinter group, the Loyalist Volunteer Force which was violently opposed to the Peace Process. His murder led to an increase in retaliatory LVF murders of Catholics. Yet inside Castle Buildings at Stormont the talks were stalled. There was no detailed agenda for negotiations. For example, in Strand One there was no agreement that there would even be a Northern Ireland Assembly, let alone what its role and function should be. Both Governments now sought to add some much needed impetus to the talks, and they agreed an agenda for discussion. The one-page document, published on 12 January 1998, was entitled *Propositions on Heads of Agreement*.

The document had originated in Downing Street, before the Christmas recess when Tony Blair had become concerned with the lack of momentum in the talks. The intention was to reach agreement that there would be a Northern Ireland Assembly; that there would be a North-South Ministerial Council; that there would be a Council of the Isles to act as a forum for co-operation between the sovereign governments and devolved administrations of the British Isles; that there would be a new British-Irish Agreement to replace the Anglo-Irish Agreement; that representatives of a Northern Ireland administration would have an input into the established British-Irish intergovernmental conference; that the rights of both communities in Northern Ireland would be protected; and that there would be discussion of controversial issues such as prisoners, policing and decommissioning.

Blair's original draft was a Unionist-flavoured document with references to a 'constitutional understanding', based on a 'commitment' to the 'principle of consent' by the British and Irish Governments, and specifically mentioning changes to Articles 2 and 3. There would be a Northern Ireland Assembly, elected by proportional representation, and with a devolution of executive and legislative responsibility covering at least the six Northern Ireland Departments. There would be a 'replacement' of the Anglo-Irish Agreement with a new British-Irish Agreement to establish closer co-operation and enhanced relationships, embracing a 'Council of these islands to deal with the totality of relationships', to include the British and Irish Governments, the Northern Ireland administration and representatives of devolved institutions in the rest of the UK. There was also to be a 'Council for North/South co-operation' to bring together those with 'executive responsibilities' i.e. ministers, from a Northern Ireland administration and the Irish Government. Each was to remain accountable to, and act within the mandate of, the Northern Ireland Assembly and the Irish Parliament respectively. All decisions were to be by 'agreement between the two sides, North and South'. There was also to be the retention of standing intergovernmental machinery between the British and Irish Governments, 'covering issues of mutual interest, including but not limited to Northern Ireland'. Finally, provisions were to be made to safeguard the rights of both communities in Northern Ireland by addressing equality and justice issues.[1]

In response the Irish Government produced their own Propositions paper which was sent to the British and the UUP. The Irish sought to add a Nationalist balance to Blair's paper. The Irish wanted 'balanced constitutional change' added to the text, with specific reference to a 'new British Constitutional Act' replacing the Government of Ireland Act 1920. They preferred that democratically-elected institutions in Northern Ireland 'could', rather than would, include an Assembly. They also wanted provisions which explicitly stated that 'these institutions [would] operate on the basis of cross-community agreement, with checks and balances to protect the interests of both communities' and would 'deal with the issue of collective responsibility' – in other words a power-sharing cabinet. As for a new British-Irish Agreement, this would operate 'under' a British-Irish Intergovernmental Council, which would meet twice a year at Head of Government level, on the EU summit model, with representatives of a Northern Ireland administration and other UK devolved institutions. There would be a 'series of North-South Ministerial Councils' bringing together those with executive responsibility and a 'number of executive agencies to implement policies agreed by both sides in these Councils at an all-island level. The agencies will be accountable to the Councils and to the elected institutions in their respective jurisdictions and will act in accordance with the appropriate arrangements for collective responsibility. Policies to be implemented separately in other areas.' There would also be a series of British-Irish Councils at Secretary of State level, including the British and Irish Governments, the Northern Ireland administration and representatives of devolved UK institutions, and a standing intergovernmental machinery covering non-devolved issues for Northern Ireland, with which representatives of the Northern Ireland administration would be associated.

The Irish wanted to flesh out the sections relating to the provisions for the rights and safeguards of both communities and the addressing of equality and justice issues that could involve a Bill of Rights for Northern Ireland and arrangements for a special Standing Commission for monitoring and enforcing this. The Irish also proposed a series of measures to be taken to establish and consolidate a normal peaceful society which could involve an unspecified programme of action in regard to prisoners; a commitment on the part of the British Government to reduce troop levels and to dismantle special security installations; reform in the policing area; a commitment to the decommissioning of illegally held arms within a fixed time period following the reaching of agreement; and an examination of the pattern and extent of legally held weapons[2] – which had been predominantly issued to members of the unionist community.

The final Propositions paper was hammered out between Tony Blair, Bertie Ahern and David Trimble over the weekend of 10–11 January 1998. The significance of the document was that, although devoid of detail, it set out for the first time the outlines of an agreement. Many of the more controversial details which the Irish had wanted to include, particularly on matters of power-sharing and British commitments on security and prisoners, were either deleted or watered down in order to secure Trimble's agreement. Nevertheless the final document was an advance on the previous situation. At least there was now something to discuss. For the first time it was acknowledged that there would be a Northern Ireland Assembly; that there would be a North–South Council which would have a consultative role – there was no mention of executive powers for that body; that there would be 'suitable implementation bodies and mechanisms' – the term cross-border agencies was deleted – between Northern Ireland and the Republic; and, a surprise to outside observers, a British–Irish intergovernmental Council to include Scottish and Welsh participation. Added to this, as the Irish wanted, was a fleshing out of the references to the question of rights and safeguards and the normalisation of Northern Ireland society. The Propositions on Heads of Agreement document stated that negotiations would be concerned with:

> Balanced constitutional change, based on commitment to the principle of consent in all its aspects by both British and Irish Governments to include both changes to the Irish Constitution and to British constitutional legislation.
>
> Democratically elected institutions in Northern Ireland, to include a Northern Ireland Assembly, elected by a system of proportional representation, exercising devolved executive and legislative responsibility over at least the responsibilities of the six Northern Ireland departments, and with provisions to ensure that all sections of the community can participate and work together successfully in the operation of these institutions and that all sections of the community are protected.

A new British–Irish Agreement to replace the existing Anglo–Irish Agreement and help establish close co-operation and enhance relationships, embracing:

- An intergovernmental Council to deal with the totality of relationships, to include representatives of the British and Irish governments, the Northern Ireland administration and the devolved institutions in Scotland and Wales, with meetings twice a year at Summit level.

- A North/South Ministerial Council to bring together those with executive responsibilities in Northern Ireland and the Irish government in particular areas. Each side will consult, co-operate and take decisions on matters of mutual interest within the mandate of, and accountable to, the Northern Ireland Assembly and the Oireachtas [Irish Parliament] respectively. All decisions will be by agreement between the two sides, North and South.

- Suitable implementation bodies and mechanisms for policies agreed by the North/South Council in meaningful areas and at an all-Ireland level.

- Standing intergovernmental machinery between the Irish and British Governments, covering issues of mutual interest and including non-devolved issues for Northern Ireland, when representatives of the Northern Ireland Administration would be involved.

Provision to safeguard the rights of both communities in Northern Ireland, through arrangements for the comprehensive protection of fundamental human, civil, political, social, economic and cultural rights, including a Bill of Rights for Northern Ireland, supplementing the provisions of the European Convention [on Human Rights] and to achieve a full respect for the principles of equity of treatment and freedom from discrimination and the cultural identity and ethos of both communities. Appropriate steps are to be taken to ensure an equivalent level of protection in the Republic.

Effective and practical measures to establish and consolidate an acceptable peaceful society, dealing with issues such as prisoners, security in all its aspects, policing and decommissioning of weapons.[3]

Strand One

Heads of Agreement allowed detailed negotiations to begin. Strand One sought to negotiate an agreed form of internal government for Northern Ireland. This had also been the aim set for Strand One during the 1992 talks. However, in

1998 there were now a number of crucial differences. Firstly, the SDLP had been forced to lower their horizons and adopt a more realistic approach to the internal government of Northern Ireland. They did this by moving closer to the model outlined in the British Government's segment of the Frameworks Documents. Now the SDLP no longer seemed to be demanding that there should be direct Irish and European involvement in the internal government of Northern Ireland. This appeared to an abandonment of British-Irish joint authority in Strand One. Secondly, there was a new situation in the rest of the United Kingdom. The new Labour Government had initiated a process which would lead to devolved institutions in Scotland and Wales. It could be assumed that any devolved institution in Northern Ireland would have to fit into this general pattern.

While it appeared that this might signal a closing of the gap between the SDLP and the UUP, one fundamental breach remained. This concerned the very existence of a Northern Ireland executive itself. The SDLP insisted there should be an inclusive Northern Ireland cabinet composed of Nationalists and Unionists. The UUP remained committed to a series of committees within a Northern Ireland Assembly. The committees would be made inclusive by allocating their chairmanships and memberships broadly in proportion to the strengths of the parties in the Assembly. The UUP's proposals would allow Sinn Féin's participation in these, providing that party had renounced violence. A business committee, instead of a cabinet, would provide co-ordinating functions. The difference between these two models went to the heart of the Unionist-Nationalist divide in Northern Ireland. The UUP's proportionality model involved a low-level form of power-sharing; the SDLP's executive, or cabinet, form of power-sharing institutionalised Protestant-Catholic parity of esteem at the highest level of Northern Ireland's government.

This was the very form of government which Unionists like David Trimble, and his deputy, John Taylor, had rejected in 1974. Could this gap be now bridged? And what of Sinn Féin? They resolutely opposed an Assembly. It destroyed their hope of free-standing all-Ireland executive bodies. The Irish Government, however, remained optimistic. At a meeting on 31 March 1998, between the Ulster Unionists and the Irish Government, the former confirmed their scepticism regarding Sinn Féin's intentions. Sinn Féin, pointed out the UUP, had disagreed with every element in the talks so far and, consequently, the Ulster Unionists did not believe there would be peace. The best that the UUP could say for 'Sinn Féin/IRA' was that it would go back to violence in unfavourable circumstances. The Irish, however, were more confident. They argued that 'Adams and McGuinness' had to be brought into the Peace Process and that 'in the proper circumstances' they would sign up to an agreement and would be prepared to 'work the Assembly'.[4] What the proper circumstances were remained to be seen.

More immediately, the Propositions paper had thrown a huge spanner into Sinn Féin's strategy. Up to this point the only substantial proposal advanced by Sinn Féin during the talks was that for an all-Ireland state with a National Parliament and 15 regional councils. These would include the Gaeltacht region; South Connaught; North Connaught; West Ulster; East Ulster; Belfast; South Ulster; North Leinster; Midlands; Dublin; South Leinster; East Munster; West Munster; Cork; and North Munster.[5] This left many participants wondering just how serious Sinn Féin's participation in the talks would be. In fact, apart from the above, Sinn Féin put forward no tangible or constructive suggestions in any of the Strands. It was left to the SDLP to put forward proposals for the participation of, and the safeguarding of, the nationalist community in the internal governance of Northern Ireland.

Instead, the Republican Movement reacted with fury to the Propositions paper. This was the first indication that the Irish Government might break Nationalist ranks and compromise with Unionists in crucial areas. The PIRA declared that 'it did not regard the "Propositions on Heads of Agreement" document as a basis for a lasting peace settlement.' It was a 'pro-Unionist document and has created a crisis in the Peace Process.'[6] But without violence as a lever, what pressure could the Republican Movement apply? They were trapped between their origins in armed struggle and demonstrating their commitment to an unarmed strategy. As Gerry Adams admitted, when Sinn Féin became aware of the thrust of the document, 'we left both governments in no doubt about our opposition and our firm belief that it was a mistake. The governments chose to place the paper on the table.'[7]

The proposition that there should be a Northern Ireland Assembly also revealed an ideological schism within Northern Nationalism. Mitchel McLaughlin was explicit: 'Sinn Féin is opposed to an assembly.' He accepted that there were those who would accuse Sinn Féin of not engaging properly in Strand One, 'because we refuse to accept the inevitability of an assembly'. This was untrue, as Sinn Féin was prepared to fully debate the issue: 'But any presumption that an assembly in the North has nationalist support is in my view deeply flawed. It ignored the widespread hostility among nationalists and republicans to a revamped, unionist dominated Stormont, with the power to veto progress on the island of Ireland.' This was the 'nationalist "nightmare" – trapped in a state without our consent; abused, victimised and killed – [which] has not changed in 75 years'.[8] This provoked John Hume, who played little or no part in formal discussions at Castle Buildings, to break a self-imposed silence which he had virtually held since the beginning of the talks. He reminded Sinn Féin that the challenge in the talks was to build new political institutions together. The SDLP leader pointed out that the 'new beginning suggested by the three stranded agenda necessarily includes new institutions in the North as well as North-South institutions. The latter cannot be created without the former. A North-South Council could not exist without new institutions in the North [from] which its Northern membership would be drawn. By suggesting otherwise Sinn Féin is being deliberately obstructive or is failing to face reality.'[9]

This theme was also taken up by one of the SDLP's key negotiators, Seán

Farren, who claimed that Sinn Féin's opposition to an Assembly betrayed the hopes of the nationalist community for a just, workable accommodation with Unionists. Their suggestion that Unionists could never be trusted rejected the very goal set for all the parties in the talks, which was a new beginning to political relationships based on mutual respect. Farren argued that opposition to an Assembly, because unionists would be in a majority, deliberately ignored the fact that such an Assembly would have to operate on a 'power-sharing, consensual model'. A jointly controlled Assembly would also have to protect the rights and identities of both communities. Farren criticised Sinn Féin for raking over the abuses and injustices of the past, thus perpetuating a sense of grievance to the point where trust was more difficult to achieve:

> The abuses and injustices of unionist governments are well documented. Added to those abuses are the pain and tragedy of the past three decades which Sinn Féin does not highlight. Paramilitaries who killed and maimed Catholics and Protestants, unionists and nationalists, indulged in a vicious form of discrimination. Businesses destroyed by IRA and loyalist bombs deprived workers of their jobs and deterred new investment, another brutal form of discrimination. Selective reminders of the nightmare through which both our communities have lived contribute nothing to the search for a solution. If we are to learn from the past, it must be from the whole of the past, not just those parts that suit narrow, party interests.[10]

Tensions between the SDLP and Sinn Féin were heightened further when Seamus Mallon described it as 'absolutely wrong and dishonest' for the latter to claim that the new Assembly under discussion represented a return to Stormont. Mallon asked, 'Does anyone seriously imagine that the SDLP or the Irish Government would agree to the creation of a new Stormont? How daft can they get? They are totally misrepresenting the type of body which we are currently talking about.' Rather than being something which would work against Nationalists, what was on offer was the opportunity to create a body which would give Nationalists, for the first time, a share of executive power in Northern Ireland: 'It would be something absolutely new.'[11] Mallon observed, 'I think Sinn Féin have to face up to the fact there is a Strand One. ... That is the reality because there is going to be a global package in terms of an overall agreement.'[12]

The first hurdle was how to agree the functions of a Northern Ireland Assembly. The direct comparison was with the proposed devolved institutions in the rest of the United Kingdom. As the British Government explained to the participants, since May 1997 it had initiated a wide-ranging programme of decentralisation within Great Britain. This firmly located any Northern Ireland proposals in a British context. The new Labour Government, unlike its predecessor, was committed to revolutionising the internal government of the United Kingdom. The main proposals were: the establishment of a Parliament and Executive in Scotland; the establishment of a National Assembly for Wales;

the creation of an elected Mayor and Assembly for London; and a programme of decentralisation to the English regions. This programme started from the premise that the demand for more decentralised government varied considerably across Britain, and that the new arrangements should reflect these differing local aspirations. This had two consequences comprising:

-    a 'variable geometry' approach: rather than impose a uniform pattern across the country, there are differences from one area to another in the degree of autonomy to be exercised, in the institutions proposed, and in the timetable for decentralisation.

-    popular approval of the new arrangements: in each area where they are introduced, the new arrangements are to be submitted to a referendum.[13]

In the Northern Ireland context the amount of administrative and legislative power devolved to a Northern Ireland Assembly could be of crucial importance – and division – between the UUP and the SDLP: the more power devolved, the more influence a North–South body might have since its remit for cross-border activity would spring from the Assembly's functions. In order to draw out the areas of convergence and divergence among the parties the British Government, as Chair of Strand One, produced a synthesis paper early in March. It intended the paper to be used as the basis for further discussions, focusing on areas where there was an absence of consensus. This showed that all parties, except Sinn Féin, agreed that the administrative and executive functions of the six Northern Ireland Departments should be among the responsibilities of the devolved institution. All parties, apart from the UUP, and of course Sinn Féin, could see at least a limited legislative, or law-making, capability also.

There was a general desire for the powers of the new institution to ultimately include policing and the criminal justice system and perhaps security as well. There was universal importance attached to the introduction of statutory rights as a safeguard for all, and particularly as a way of protecting minority rights. Specific proposals, such as the use of a weighted – two-thirds – majority for decisions of the Assembly, once more highlighted the differences between the SDLP and the UUP. Virtually all parties, however, agreed that there should be a committee structure to scrutinise the business of each function taken over by the Assembly.

It was widely accepted that committees should be appointed on the basis of proportionality. There was, however, a difference in approach regarding the role of an executive. Some parties saw the committees, through their chairmen, as an executive whilst others saw a separation of powers, with the committees holding the executive to account through scrutiny. This difference of emphasis was also replicated by views on the issue of collective responsibility, with those envisaging a separate executive arguing that collective responsibility, in the form of a cabinet, was essential.[14]

For example, the SDLP proposed maximum executive, legislative and administrative power for the Assembly, with a cabinet open to all parties to participate in it, subject to an electoral threshold which would be a matter for clarification and negotiation. The executive would be responsible for conducting government business, while committees would provide a scrutinising role and perhaps a policy formulation role. In contrast, the UUP's proportional committee model envisaged no collective responsibility: there would be no cabinet as such. This basically summed up Unionism's traditional aversion to institutional power-sharing. Instead a Chief Executive would have a co-ordinating and representational role between the committees and a negotiating role with bodies outside Northern Ireland. The co-ordinating role of the Chief Executive would be the nearest thing to an executive.[15]

The UUP believed that they had responded to the concerns of Nationalists in Strand One institutions by proposing a devolution model which was fully proportional but had sacrificed some degree of efficiency in the interests of inclusivity for all sections of the community through their system of committees. They had also proposed that nationalist rights would be protected by the introduction of an easy and cheap method for citizens to bring legal action against the infringement of rights under the European Convention on Human Rights. In addition the European Framework on the Protection of National Minorities would provide further protection.[16]

The UUP was particularly conscious of the need for an Assembly to be 'boycott-proof'. The Ulster Unionists feared that Nationalists could destroy the Assembly by refusing to participate in it, while a North–South body would continue to function. As a possible solution to this problem, a member of the UUP's talks team, Peter King, suggested how, 'First of all a mechanism could be employed whereby you wouldn't be allowed to pick and choose which institution of the settlement you would serve in. If you wanted to serve on any North–South body you would have to serve in the Northern Ireland Assembly.' 'Secondly', said King, 'we do not see the need for the power to create primary legislation for Northern Ireland.' Northern Ireland was a 'small jurisdiction, a small province. We see the Northern Ireland Assembly operating within a framework of [primary] UK legislation passed at Westminster.' However, King pointed out that the UUP had not closed its mind to a legislative role for the Assembly – 'but we would have to be persuaded.' The UUP, explained King, were even prepared to contemplate Sinn Féin chairing one or more departments in accordance with its level of support, although suitable account would be taken of parties which were not committed to exclusively peaceful means. The Mitchell Principles could be 'imported' into the workings of the Assembly.[17]

The SDLP had serious reservations about the UUP model. It believed in the need for an executive element, in the form of a separate and formal cabinet, for representatives of both sections of the community, institutionalising parity of esteem at the very heart of government. It opposed a committee system without a cabinet because such a system, in their opinion, would be open to abuse as Unionist majorities within the committees could determine policy without any safeguards for Nationalists. Nor was the SDLP content to rely on the ECHR rather than on a comprehensive system of checks and balances to prevent discrimination. There would have to be significant safeguards including checks and balances at *all levels* which would require the support of a majority of representatives in each section of the community.[18] The SDLP advocated some form of sufficient consensus in the workings of the Assembly itself.[19]

In order to bring some coherence to this ongoing debate, Downing Street produced, on 29 March, a paper entitled *Democratic Institutions in Northern Ireland*. The section on Safeguards sought to ensure that all sections of the community could participate and work together in the operation of a Northern Ireland Assembly and that all sections of the community were 'protected', by making 'arrangements to ensure that key decisions are taken on a cross-community basis. This might require the support of a weighted majority voting' or a 'majority of both Unionist and Nationalist members of the Assembly'. There was also the consideration of a right of petition which could be exercised by a minority of the Assembly. This appeared to be leaning towards the SDLP's position of transferring sufficient consensus and weighted majorities into the workings of the Assembly.

As to the thorny question of an executive, the British suggested that there could be a Liaison Committee whose composition would be determined proportionally or by bringing together the Assembly Secretaries of the departmental committees. This leaned more towards the UUP's position. The duties of postholders were to be defined in a Code of Practice, and there would be sanctions which 'might include removal from office if [a] postholder, in failing to meet his responsibilities, loses the confidence of the Assembly, voting on a cross-community basis'.[20] Effectively, this meant Sinn Féin would be entitled to be Secretaries of Committees and members of the Liaison Committee. There was no mention of paramilitary related parties being barred from holding office if paramilitaries refused to engage in decommissioning.

David Trimble complained to Downing Street that this draft 'omits the need to exclude paramilitary related parties from the benefit of the proportionality principle'. He added that the UUP 'require assurances that the wrecking by nationalists of the Assembly will not leave the North–South body bereft of Unionists with our positions replaced by government nominees and proceeding apace'.[21] On the other hand, from the SDLP perspective, there was growing frustration with the UUP's position. Seamus Mallon felt that Nationalist requirements were not being met. He listed the Unionist gains thus far: the principle of consent was 'now almost unanimous in terms of the entire agreement', and Unionist requirements on Articles 2 and 3, and on East–West relations were being met. 'If you look at the balance as of now, nobody could realistically say that the requirements of nationalists are properly being met, and if they are not being met, then a settlement is going to be very difficult to reach.'[22]

On 31 March, the UUP and the SDLP engaged in a bi-lateral meeting in an attempt to bridge some of the gaps in Strand One. Reg Empey of the UUP articulated the concerns of the SDLP as he saw them. These were: no return to a pre-1972 type Stormont Parliament under the dominance of Unionists; and the requirement for Nationalists to be 'protected' at all levels of Northern Ireland's government. Empey asked the SDLP to explain why Nationalists felt so vulnerable. John Hume replied that there was a need to overcome Northern Ireland's serious communal divisions and thereby avoid the dangers of the past. Stability required both sections of the population to work and share power together. The UUP's committee system appeared, to the SDLP, to be a 'return to majority rule'; therefore there was a need for some form of 'Government' to 'evolve' from the d'Hondt system which allocated committee seats in a proportional manner. David Trimble interjected to argue that the UUP's model was actually doing this. Ministers would automatically come from a range of parties rather than as the subject of a political deal between a small number of them. But, pointed out Trimble, any agreement would only work if people were prepared to work together. D'Hondt and a Cabinet system were contradictory; surely, said Trimble, a Cabinet system on its own was a return to 'Stormont 2'. Hume reiterated that for the SDLP a committee system was majority rule in another form.

Empey tried to reassure the SDLP that the UUP were not seeking a majoritarian system. The UUP's concerns were, firstly, the potential for gridlock in the Assembly; secondly, that Unionist nominees on the North–South body would be replaced by London's nominees; and, thirdly, that there should be a meaningful role for the Assembly's backbenchers through the committee system. Trimble added that arrangements for committee secretaries to come together would be more like a 'liaison' rather than a 'collective': because secretaries meeting together 'doesn't mean collective responsibility'. Mark Durkan of the SDLP, while reassuring the UUP that his party also wanted the widest sharing of responsibility, believed that there would be less gridlock in the Nationalist model – with a Cabinet-style executive – than in the Unionists' looser co-ordinating system. Trimble, however, argued that weighted majorities, as proposed by the SDLP, could lead to deadlock. Durkan countered that the UUP model was a distribution of functions rather than a sharing of power.[23]

Despite these fundamental divisions there were a number of areas where the UUP and the SDLP were in agreement by 1 April. These were as follows:

1   D'Hondt [proportionate] system should be adopted for allocation of posts.

2   There should be Secretaries in charge of Committees.

3   There should be Committees of the Assembly.

4   There should be Secretaries/Chairmen of Committees.

5   The Secretaries should 'come together' as a liaison/collective.

6   Committees should play a leading role in policy formation as well as scrutiny.

7   The Secretary should be [the] Head of Department and present the Departmental Programme to the Committee.

8   The Assembly should have a legislative role.

9   Legislative proposals could come from the Committee, Secretary or floor of the Assembly.

10   Operations should be modelled closer to the European Parliament than to Westminster, i.e. Plenary, Committee meetings on individual days/weeks.

11   There should be 'sufficient inclusion' of small parties on Assembly representation ... [to] outside bodies.

12   Representatives to North-South body would be fulfilling the wishes of the Assembly.

13   After a period of time there would be a Review of Assembly workings, but it would be essential to avoid giving this a 'transition' start; Governments to be included in the all-party review.

There was no agreement of the formal position/title of Leaders of the first and second largest parties in the Assembly, i.e. Prime Minister, First Minister.[24]

The key issues remained that of a cabinet-style executive and the level of safeguards Nationalists required. Guarantees for the minority's rights in the Assembly, in the form of the ECHR or proportionality, would not be enough for the SDLP. Nationalists would also have to have the right to veto all decisions of the Assembly. This, of course, would mean that Unionists could veto decisions they did not like. But, more fundamentally, it meant that power-sharing would be institutionalised, from the cabinet to the workings of the Assembly. The ghost of Unionist majority rule in Northern Ireland would be exorcised. As it turned out, the key to Strand One would lie in the lowering of Nationalist horizons in Strand Two.

Strands Two and Three

Strand Two was concerned with the relationships on the island of Ireland between Northern Ireland and the Republic of Ireland. It aimed to negotiate agreed institutions between the two parts of the island. Strand Two dominated the talks after the publication of the Heads of Agreement document, virtually to the exclusion of all other issues. Strand Three issues concerning the relationship between Ireland and the United Kingdom of Great Britain and

Northern Ireland, although technically the subject of discussion between the British and Irish Governments, were inevitably caught up in the North–South debate. Unionists emphasised the importance of the East-West relationship, while the Irish Government and the SDLP focused on the North–South relationship.

In an internal party memo, dated January 1998, David Trimble had described the UUP's principal concern in the talks as relating to the North–South axis where it 'has to be clear that any north–south forum will not have executive powers, will not be a "dynamic" body capable of evolving towards an All-Ireland state, and will be located within a British-Isles wide umbrella within which all relationships are on an equal basis with consistent procedures'. Trimble described private contacts with senior officials from the Irish Government, over Christmas and the New Year as 'promising'. Subject to an elucidation of how North–South matters would relate to other aspects, the Irish appeared receptive to the concept of a British-Irish Council. Interestingly, commented Trimble, they responded warmly to the suggestion that the umbrella be very flexible with a minimum of bureaucracy; the senior member of the Irish delegation had said that he always deleted the word 'secretariat' from any Irish draft on the matter.

The Irish described their concept of North–South co-operation as that of Southern and Northern 'ministers' meeting to discuss matters of mutual interest. If co-operation was agreed by the Northern and Southern representatives it would, if joint action was required, be carried forward by an appropriate vehicle established for that purpose. They made it 'extremely clear that they did not see the North–South forum itself exercising any executive powers'. An example given was that if it was agreed that the promotion of the island of Ireland as a tourist destination was desirable then an agency would be created for that purpose and the relevant aspects of the functions of the Irish and Northern Irish tourist boards would be transferred to it. Trimble listed a number of reservations concerning the above:

> ... co-operative action should be carried out through the most appropriate means and only through a cross-border agency if that was the most effective and economic method. We need to explore precisely what is meant by 'mandate'. The Irish are keen on prior mandate [to be given in advance to ministers in the North–South Council by the Northern Ireland Assembly]. We prefer the procedures to include subsequent ratification. In practice the two will be similar as the NI Assembly is unlikely to grant a mandate unless it has a pretty clear idea of what is proposed to be agreed [in the North–South Council]. It would be unacceptable if mandates were defined or could be manipulated to deny the Assembly control over decisions [in the Council] ... there is the question of just how the North–South formula will be located within the British-Irish umbrella. The Irish talked of a body with two pillars. We talked of viable geometry. We are certain that there must be equality:

that whatever happens East-West (North-West/North-East or South-West/South-East or any other variable) should be along similar lines with the same procedures and the same range of possible outcomes as North-South. ... Finally, the Irish desire to have, say half a dozen [North-South] co-operative ventures built into any agreement, irrespective of the circumstances, is trying to go too far too soon and, frankly, is not do-able politically.[25]

For Trimble and the UUP, the key aims were to prevent the North-South Council being anything other than consultative; to ensure that it would be the Northern Ireland Assembly which would control Northern Ireland representatives in the North-South Council; to ensure the North-South Council had the same remit as the British-Irish Council; and to ensure that it was the Assembly that decided what areas of North-South co-operation should be agreed with the Irish Parliament. Consequently, Trimble was delighted with the outcome of the Heads of Agreement document. As he explained, the UUP was seeking a 'settlement which recognises Northern Ireland's position as part of the United Kingdom, which enables everybody in Northern Ireland to be involved in real politics and provides for a sensible relationship with our neighbour to the south'. The UUP was 'not interested in some temporary transitional arrangement'. Trimble believed that Heads of Agreement recognised the Unionist requirement that the Anglo-Irish Agreement be replaced by a 'proper' British-Irish Agreement that embraced all the various inter-relationships within the British Isles through the creation of a 'council of these islands'. By bringing together representatives of all the devolved institutions and their governments, this would recognise both the diversity and unity that existed throughout the islands on so many matters.

Trimble acknowledged that some Nationalists were worried about the Council of the Islands, and that they feared it would be used to control or overrule their 'more narrow interests. But they are focusing on the wrong things.' The Council would be merely consultative. It would have no powers, but it would facilitate contact and co-operation. It was within this umbrella, in the UUP's view, that any North-South relationship should be located. Trimble considered that the Propositions paper supported this view, for it stated that this body was to 'deal with the totality of relationships'. The North-South relationship was a part of that totality and so, logically, it had to be comprehended within it. Furthermore, the proposed North-South Council would have to be 'merely consultative'. Heads of Agreement recognised this. It talked of a North-South Council where each side would consult, co-operate and take decisions on matters of mutual interest within the mandate of, and accountable to, the Northern Ireland Assembly and the Oireachtas respectively, with all decisions by agreement between the two sides, North and South. For Trimble it was 'obvious that such an arrangement is consultative and that the power lies, so far as Northern Ireland is concerned, with the Northern Ireland Assembly, for its authority is needed before there can be any agreement on co-operation'. To make matters certain, the document was explicit about the Northern veto over decisions in the Council.

Trimble declared that the North-South Council 'could not of itself have any executive power': nor, so far as he knew, was it ever suggested in the discussions prior to the publication of the Heads of Agreement that it should have. The question then arose as to how any scheme of co-operation could actually be carried out. It was no secret, noted Trimble, that the Irish Government wanted to see any such co-operation done through various quangos created for that purpose. Indeed, they wanted the term 'executive agencies' to appear in the Heads of Agreement, 'But it does not.' Instead, the paper referred to 'suitable implementation bodies and mechanisms for policies agreed'. As Trimble explained,

> Implementation bodies and mechanisms could mean anything, maybe the existing government departments in Northern Ireland or maybe some specially created quango. But it has to be 'suitable'. So this must be determined by purely pragmatic considerations.

> Moreover, this issue would only arise with regard to policies agreed and I would be amazed if the Northern Ireland Assembly agreed a policy without at the same time agreeing exactly how it is to be carried out. So, the assembly would have a veto also.

The Propositions paper, concluded Trimble, was only an outline. It set the agenda for detailed negotiations. Obviously, in those negotiations, Nationalists would be tempted to try and beef up the North-South dimension and marginalise the Council of the Islands:

> But I think this would be a mistake. The two can live together; indeed, they have to if we are to deal with the real world. The existence of both, in sensible forms, can provide reassurance to all sections of our community and free us to tackle the really important question of finding a way to live and work together here in the streets and fields of Northern Ireland.[26]

In essence, what Trimble was saying was that the UUP were not opposed to cross-border *bodies* with executive powers, such as the Foyle Fisheries Commission established by a former Unionist Government at Stormont, or as was practised across frontiers elsewhere in Europe, as long as it was the Northern Ireland Assembly that decided this was in the best interests of Northern Ireland. Accountability and the source of authority were the key points here. The UUP was opposed to a single, North-South *body* with executive powers, making decisions on its own and accountable to itself, for this would have all the trappings of a third government in Ireland.

However, Trimble's optimism was soon to be tempered by the reaction of the British and Irish Governments to Sinn Féin's rejection of Heads of

Agreement. Gerry Adams warned, 'We are obviously concerned that unionists may have succeeded [in diluting the Frameworks Documents]. The only way to ascertain whether that is true or not is if the governments put some flesh on the bones of what is proposed. The two governments' position had been that the North-South body would have executive powers. We want to know whether that continues to be their intention.'[27] The two Governments urgently tried to reassure Sinn Féin that, at this early stage in the talks, they had not departed from their commitment to a North-South body with executive powers. When the talks moved temporarily to London, the British and Irish Governments submitted a joint Strand Two paper on North-South structures, stating that they remained 'firmly committed' to the position 'set out in A New Framework for Agreement as their best assessment of where agreement might be found in the negotiations'. However, the paper also stated that both Governments 'of course accept that each of the parties may wish to contribute other ideas to the discussion, and would welcome such contributions. The final outcome depends on what can be agreed among the participants.'[28]

This last segment, suggesting that an alternative agreed by the parties might replace the Frameworks Documents, was not enough to pacify the UUP. The Ulster Unionists regarded this 'Structures' document as undermining the North-South position as set out in the Heads of Agreement document. The anger of the UUP was transmitted to the Prime Minister. When Tony Blair attended the talks, on 27 January, Reg Empey of the UUP described the new British-Irish document as an attempt to 'ram stuff down our throats'. The Prime Minister, however, emphasised that many people regarded the UUP as having an inside track to the talks process. The Propositions paper was an attempt to 'avoid saying yes or no to Frameworks'. While Empey acknowledged that Propositions was the 'first time we [Unionists] have been engaged and consulted in 15 years', Jeffrey Donaldson pointed out that there was a perception in Northern Ireland that the 'outcome is pre-determined'. The phrase in the Structures document referring to the Government's 'strong commitment' to the Frameworks Documents was seen as a 'response to IRA pressure and is a message to the Army Council'. Donaldson claimed that this made the talks appear 'pre-cooked – we cannot operate like this.'

The UUP anger was such that David Trimble now told Blair, 'This process is over; we are here to say no. The centre of gravity is not where I thought it was.' The Prime Minister attempted to reassure the UUP that the Propositions document was to allow people to express what they aspired to; he could not say that he rejected any previous paper, such as the Frameworks Documents.[29] It was only the following day, in a private meeting between Blair and Trimble at Downing Street, during which the Prime Minister reassured the UUP leader that he would be fully informed of any subsequent discussions between the British and Irish Governments, that the issue was defused.[30] From the UUP perspective the main problem between themselves and the British Government was the role played by the Secretary of State. Trimble and his team felt that Mo Mowlam consistently went back on her word to keep either them or Downing Street informed of discussions with the Irish.[31]

Still the question remained: could the gap in Strand Two be bridged? The gulf was enormous – between a consultative North–South Council advocated by Unionists and the executive body wanted by Nationalists. This was confirmed during Strand Two discussions at Castle Buildings, Stormont, where the Irish Government retracted its private comments to Trimble on the nature of the North–South body. Following the Structures document, the Irish Government reaffirmed its position that a North–South Council had to have 'real meaning' for the nationalist community in Northern Ireland. This, it made clear, meant a North–South Ministerial Council with executive powers. Although it would be accountable to Dáil Éireann and the Northern Ireland Assembly the North–South body should implement its own decisions.[32] While the Irish Government emphasised the precise form, the SDLP, on the other hand, emphasised the political requirement for such a Council. It was essential to the task of winning the agreement of Irish nationalists, North and South, to a political settlement. The SDLP described this as 'parity of allegiance'. It was, in effect, the means by which the rights of Irish nationalists to effective political, symbolic and administrative expression of their identity could be articulated. There was a fundamental political requirement for this to occur. The SDLP recalled past Unionist comments that this drive, for the promotion of Irish nationalist rights, was some sort of Nationalist plot to create unity in Ireland by subterfuge. If this were the case, the SDLP would not be publicly upholding the principle of consent.

The SDLP reminded Unionists that it was also important to remember that Nationalists who did not let off bombs were not, in some way, more wimpish in negotiations than those who did. This would be a dangerous mistake to make. The SDLP was fully committed to getting a core element such as the North–South Council in place if nationalists in general were going to support any agreement. There had to be clear institutionalised recognition of the need for nationalists to play a full part in any agreement. This would be through the North–South Council. The SDLP warned that it would also be wrong for others to make the mistake of believing that the talks could reach agreement without achieving this 'parity of allegiance'. But saying this did not mean that there was a plot concocted by the SDLP and the Irish Government to achieve Irish unity.

The SDLP explained that the need for an institutional expression of nationalist identity meant that this was a question of a political culture, not just the Irish language or Gaelic football. It was about one's own being, as a person and as a community, on a small island. It was about having recognition of one's political being in terms of political arrangements. It was clear from history that unless Nationalism could be part of an agreement there would not be one. The SDLP explained that the term 'rights' was usually understood to relate to individuals. But what was involved in Northern Ireland was a community's sense of itself, of its identity, allegiance and affiliation, which had been sundered and a recognition, however tenuous, that this affiliation required some expression. This was not a new idea: it went back to the Council of Ireland following partition, and had grown through Sunningdale, the Anglo-Irish Agreement, the Downing Street Declaration and the Frameworks Documents, to the current talks process.

The SDLP made it clear that this 'right' applied to both communities, albeit taking different forms of expression. On one side of the coin it was already expressed for the unionist community in the Union with Britain. On the other side of the same coin it did not, up to the present, have any expression for nationalists. This had been recognised by the British Government, the Irish Government, and more widely. Nationalists and Unionists were co-dependent in terms of the package as a whole and each component of it. The SDLP believed it could not sell an agreement to nationalists without a significant North-South element, but each Strand, including North-South arrangements, had to be able to command the allegiance of both communities. The Assembly could not be Stormont reborn, and North/South arrangements could not be a Trojan Horse for a united Ireland. Each element should be clearly and transparently recognisable for what it was. The SDLP accepted that any agreement that had a sniff of a united Ireland to it would have no chance at all.

The SDLP emphasised to the Unionists that Nationalism had advanced a great deal. Thirty years earlier no Nationalist party could have been at the current talks, speaking as the SDLP was doing, recognising the principle of consent and the difficulties of Unionism. 'Parity of esteem' was a divisive concept only if one made it so. Nationalist MPs went to Westminster and recognised the traditions and the system there so as to represent their constituents. They took the oath to the Queen, which was not easy for them, because they recognised that there were other rights than their own. Nationalists were asking for a similar recognition of their rights. If their basic right to an effective political and symbolic recognition of their identity and ethos was not even recognised, there was not going to be a solution. The recognition of the equal rights of both communities had to replace the tribalism that concerned itself with painting kerbstones red, white and blue or using the Irish language or Gaelic games as political weapons. The SDLP had been asked what it had meant by institutional arrangements to express this identity. It meant North-South institutions with executive powers, a North-South Council of Ministers with powers to make decisions and implementation bodies on an all-Ireland basis and practical underpinning structures such as a secretariat. This was no more than a statement of what was required for political Nationalism to even conceive of being part of a political settlement. Even to sell that and get it past a referendum would be difficult.[33]

Having attempted to reassure Unionists that a North-South body would not be a Trojan Horse, the Irish Government and the SDLP found Unionists outraged by the Strand Two discussion of 10 March. A storm broke within the talks, exposing the fundamental divisions between Unionist and Nationalist visions of a North-South body. The SDLP's comments, from Brid Rogers, produced sharp exchanges with all the Unionist parties. Usually, Mark Durkan and Seán Farren led the SDLP team. Rogers, speaking for the SDLP on this occasion, noted that all of the Unionist parties seemed prepared to accept North–South structures based on specific practical needs, but there seemed to be no recognition at all of the political requirements of Nationalists in this area. North–South arrangements could not be set in concrete. A settlement which precluded any further evolution could not be sold to nationalists. It was not enough to allow nationalists their aspirations so long as they could never hope to realise them. A structure which was just an add-on or an 'empty house', i.e. with no functions, would not be seen as creating a level playing field between Nationalists and Unionists. There could not be a North–South talking shop on one side placed against an Assembly and the Union on the other. The SDLP wanted structures that could bring people together, a settlement that was fair to both sides. This would allow Unionists the freedom to persuade Nationalists that the settlement achieved was the best arrangement forever more, and Nationalists to try to do the opposite.

The Unionists were alarmed by talk of a North–South body allowing Nationalists the potential to realise their aspirations. Why? Because the core aspiration of a Nationalist was a united Ireland. Thus Gary McMichael for the UDP stated that it was only prepared to see political structures which allowed for change through 'democratic structures' – in other words the Assembly. Once more, it seemed to the UDP, Nationalists saw the North–South institutions as the engine for political change. Unionists, on the other hand, saw these institutions as the embodiment of an agreement on North–South co-operation, and were very wary of an intention to devolve power to these structures which of themselves would confer power to Nationalists. The remarks by the SDLP underlined Unionists' suspicions. The UUP also warned that it could not live with the notion that North–South structures were only transitional arrangements. The UUP recalled references made in 1973 to the proposed Council of Ireland as the vehicle that would take unionists into a united Ireland. It regarded that particular point as one of the lessons of Sunningdale and if North–South structures were portrayed in this light again, then consensus for them would disappear.

Hugh Smyth of the PUP described the SDLP's remarks as very enlightening. The Loyalist party had been working, foolishly it now seemed, on the basis that North–South bodies could be of mutual benefit to both sides. But now it was being told there was something more, a political element. It appeared that there had to be a game plan that allowed Nationalists to move step by step towards a united Ireland. At least Sinn Féin had made it clear where they stood. The PUP would have nothing to do with a return to the old Stormont. It did not want anything more for unionists in the Shankill than for nationalists in Portadown. It wanted to demonstrate that nationalists were better off with an equal partnership in Northern Ireland. However, it would not enter into arrangements which gave one side a 'leg up', and would not allow people to think it was going south for meetings which were damaging to Unionist aspirations.

The UUP added that even if it was possible, no one present at the talks sought to deny Nationalists their aspirations. But Unionists were not going to agree to the establishment of structures that were an instalment in a process to realise that aspiration, against the democratic will in Northern Ireland. The UUP was concerned here about the need for consent being bypassed. Unionists would be undermining their own aspirations if they agreed to powerful, dynamic, executive all-Ireland bodies. Unionists did not have a level playing field now, with the Anglo-Irish Agreement in place. Nationalists had a special relationship with the Irish Government that Unionists did not have with the British Government. Nationalists were therefore in a win-win situation: if there was no agreement they reverted to the Anglo-Irish Agreement. There was a fundamental difference in that Nationalists saw the solution in terms of uniting the people on the island of Ireland, and the structures they proposed had the objective of achieving that.

The UUP saw its primary objective as uniting the people of Northern Ireland. The conflict was between the people of Northern Ireland, and that was where political change had to take place. No one could prescribe in advance where a settlement might lead, but the party could not agree to structures which undermined the reality that there was a democratic majority for remaining within the United Kingdom. It was not clear if parties could find sufficient ground on which to resolve that. The UDP was even more emphatic: there were not going to be North-South bodies that of themselves made change possible. Change would be possible, and facilitated, in a Northern Ireland Assembly. The UDP saw the Assembly not as a block to Nationalist aspirations, but as the level playing field in which anything would be possible provided it was pursued democratically. This would be open to anyone. Attitudes could change. A consensus needed to be developed about what was being created. But if North-South structures were seen or sold as the vehicle for political change, there was not going to be agreement.[34]

From this exchange it can be seen that Unionist suspicions of the Irish Government and the SDLP crystallised in one key area. The SDLP and the Irish argued that a North-South body was essential for any agreement to be acceptable to Nationalists. The body itself would have to have a meaningful and symbolic role. But to do this, suggested Unionists, the North-South body did not have to have executive powers. If it had executive powers it would be behaving like a third source of authority in Ireland over and above the Irish Parliament and the Northern Ireland Assembly. If a North-South body was merely to be an institutional expression of Nationalist identity why did it have to have executive powers – unless, of course, it was to be a transitional vehicle towards a united Ireland by stealth? The UUP emphasised that it accepted that Northern nationalists felt part of the Irish nation, and wanted an expression to be given to that. Possible levels at which to address this could be at the constitutional level in the Republic. It might be an institutional expression, with institutions on an all-Ireland basis. In this regard it had to be remembered that Unionists, unlike Nationalists, did not see the Irish nation as coterminous with the island of Ireland. Another level to address it could be within Northern Ireland, with a system of government which delivered equity of treatment, responsibility sharing and involvement at an equitable level in the administration. Underlining that would be the protection of group rights.

The UUP explained that Unionists had also moved considerably in their thinking. For example, the ultimate Unionist solution was full integration with Great Britain; the ultimate Nationalist solution was a united Ireland. People were trying to achieve a compromise, and this threw up differences between the two communities. There was a clash of needs and requirements, which were not mutually exclusive, although they did conflict. A way to accommodate these had to be found. It was important to recognise that Unionism had moved a long way. Unionism was no longer arguing for majority rule, or for total integration within the United Kingdom. Unionists were not opposing recognition of the validity of the Irish identity of Nationalists, or their sense of belonging to the Irish nation, or asking them simply to accept that they were British. It should also be recognised that Unionism was no longer a monolith. In fact, there were no longer two homogeneous blocs in the community, but a collection of different minorities. It was important that Nationalism recognised where Unionism had come from and how far it had moved – perhaps not as far as Nationalism would like, but there had to be compromise.

The UUP recognised the need for an agreement to get the support of a majority of nationalists in Northern Ireland. It was a question of finding a level that a majority in both traditions would support. The UUP was not at the talks to restore Unionist domination or to try and achieve a wholly British solution. It recognised it might not get everything it wanted, and might have to settle for something short of that; neither did it prejudice the right of the people to come back to the agreement at some point in the future and see if it could be improved on.[35]

For the Unionists a North–South Council had to be consultative only. The UUP suggested that the advantage of this for Nationalists could be that its areas for discussion might be unlimited. But it would have no power of itself. The Irish Parliament and the Northern Ireland Assembly would be the source of its authority. In other words, it would originate from those bodies. Executive, decision-making powers would not be devolved to the North–South Council by Dublin, London or even Belfast. North–South decision-making needed to occur within the mandate of those bodies to which the North–South structure was accountable – the Irish Parliament or Northern Ireland Assembly. There was no scope for taking decisions outside of this. There was no question of the North–South structure operating independently of the two parliamentary bodies that provided its basis; otherwise this would mean that a third body had been established. It could only handle matters by discussion but there could be no limit on the issues to be discussed. Such discussion could perhaps lead to a scheme of co-operation which would then be approved by a Northern Ireland Assembly and the Oireachtas and if there were any administrative consequences of such a scheme being adopted then this would have to be dealt with as a separate issue. There could, however, be no executive or delegated powers for such a Council.

This worried the SDLP. They were concerned that Unionists appeared to be suggesting all but a blank sheet for Strand Two while wanting an 'all singing all dancing' Strand One. In other words an Assembly would be established which took over the functions of the Northern Ireland Departments; but what would the North–South Council do if it had no functions at the outset? The SDLP warned that it was unlikely that an agreement could be struck on this basis. Were Unionists now saying that a North–South Council had no particular remit other than a calendar commitment? The North–South Council had to be given some sort of scope if it was going to mean anything. There simply could not be a settlement based on Strand One with a 'few knobs' attached.[36] It seemed to the SDLP that the UUP was suggesting that the North–South Council would have to start with an 'empty house', and that powers would only be transferred to it as and when the Assembly developed and evolved. This would cause immense problems for the SDLP, and would be unacceptable.[37]

As the SDLP pointed out, Nationalists could not accept an agreement on the basis of trusting Unionist goodwill. They required guarantees. In fact, none of the parties could be expected to agree on the basis of blind trust. Arrangements would have to be built in that took account of distrust. Trust was not enough: questions would be put to parties and they would have to answer them. The electorate would not be impressed by a referendum slogan of 'Trust the other side'. The impression given by the Unionist parties, with everything in Strand Two to be looked at later or left to an Assembly, obviously reinforced the SDLP's concerns. If Nationalists were to swallow an Assembly they were entitled to ask what was up front in an agreement for them. If Nationalists could say that an agreement was not ideal but it did make an allowance for them, to work both with unionists in Northern Ireland and with their fellow nationalists in the rest of Ireland, then they would be able to see what was in the agreement for them. However, if Strand Two was effectively on hold, it would be impossible to sell an agreement within the party, never mind on the streets.[38]

Added to this were Sinn Féin's concerns. In March 1998, Sinn Féin finally outlined what they were prepared to settle for. Gerry Adams explained that they wanted a Frameworks plus settlement: '... even the full implementation of the Framework Documents would present a huge challenge for us since we accept it only as a basis for discussion. Our party wants much greater change. We remain totally committed to our republican objectives and we will view any agreement in this phase as being part of a transitional process to Irish unity and independence.' The minimum transitional arrangements needed included:

> Powerful all-Ireland bodies, exercising significant and meaningful executive and harmonising powers alongside consultative functions, with direct responsibility for policy decisions and the implementation of

policy, with the range of functions to be discharged or overseen initially designated by the two governments, operating independently, immune from the veto of any proposed six county institutions, with no limit on the nature and extent of their functions, with the dynamic and ability to grow.[39]

The scale of the division between Unionists and Nationalists appeared unbridgeable. This became even clearer as the talks moved to bilateral meetings. In March, the UUP explained to the Irish Government that it distinguished between a central North–South body with executive powers and smaller implementation bodies with executive powers designated to cover a specific function. The UUP indicated that it envisaged 'THE cross-border body being the North–South Ministerial Council' and that implementation bodies would be separate from this. The North–South Council would be a co-operative body and therefore did not need to be a legal entity. The implementation bodies would be on the same basis as current co-operative bodies. The UUP stressed that 'we would not accept anything that looked like a Government.'

The Irish, however, indicated that they did not just want a discussion body and that what the UUP were proposing sounded like a series of quangos. They asked the Unionists how they saw these working in practice. The UUP explained that there would be a meeting of the North–South Ministerial Council; that a scheme of co-operation would be set; and that consideration would be given as to how to implement that scheme. This could occur, for example, by way of the creation of a quango, which would be accountable to the democratically elected bodies North and South, rather than to the North–South Ministerial Council. The UUP envisaged that implementation would be a variety of co-operative schemes and that the nature of co-operation and implementation would be judged on a case by case basis.

The UUP indicated that practical problems could be overcome, but that accountability could not be run through the Council. The UUP further indicated that implementation bodies could be executed through existing bodies; through purely cross-border bodies; or through all-island bodies. The gulf between the participants was dramatically illustrated when the UUP announced that it could think of only one example in the last category: tourist promotion. The Irish, on the other hand, indicated that they could think of 30 examples. They further indicated that a North–South Council without executive powers was a bridge too far for them, and that they could not accept mere *ad hoc* arrangements. The UUP warned that it was an 'absolute for us that there be no transfer of sovereignty' to the Council. Unless the lines of authority and accountability ran to elected bodies the Irish would be 'shooting themselves in the foot'. The Irish Government, however, indicated that the SDLP would have difficulty with the UUP's proposals and indeed had been alarmed by them. The UUP responded, 'we are at the limits of our supporters.' This was disputed by the Irish Government.[40]

Just how committed Nationalists were to a North–South body with executive power became apparent in an Irish Government memorandum on the legal basis of North–South institutions. The starting point for the Irish Government was the Frameworks Documents where the two Governments envisaged that legislation in the British and Irish Parliaments would 'designate those functions which should, from the outset, be discharged or overseen by the North–South body'. So far as the Irish Government was concerned the 'essential element is that the initial decision to establish the North–South body and the decision as to the functions to be conferred on it' would be one to be 'made by the two Governments'. This could be done in a number of ways, including the following:

- The Agreement could agree that the body would be established, leaving it to legislation in the two sovereign Parliaments to carry out the actual establishment.

- The Agreement could establish the body, and could agree on the remit of the body, leaving it to legislation to deal with matters of detail.

- The Agreement could actually establish the body and set out all the necessary details. (A variant of this would have the details set out in subsidiary agreements.)

The Irish Government did not see any major difference of principle between these procedures; rather a difference of degree. It was clear that the Agreement had to establish the body concerned, and at least in general terms agree what the remit of the body was to be. The Irish Government envisaged that there would be a number of subsidiary bodies to deal with particular issues, for example tourism and animal health. These were envisaged as bodies which would be implementing policy rather than making it. Crucially, the 'policy making function would be for the North–South body itself'. The area and competence of the North–South body and its subsidiary bodies 'would be agreed by the two Governments and contained in the agreement itself'. And, finally, it would be within the power of the North–South body, and subsidiary bodies, 'to make schemes, bye-laws or regulations, such as those that would normally be made by a minister of a semi-state body of statutory corporation'.[41] It would have executive power.

When David Trimble saw this memorandum he immediately warned Downing Street that the UUP could not accept these proposals. The UUP, he warned, could not accept functions being transferred from London and Dublin; could not accept that these functions would include policy making; could not agree that the North–South body's area of competence and that of any subsidiary bodies would be agreed by the two Governments and contained in any agreement; could not accept that the North–South body and subsidiary bodies would have powers to make decisions and make by-laws; and could not agree to any fall-back mechanisms in the event of deadlock. Trimble complained:

> Clearly the Irish see The Body as being a source of power in and of itself and effectively the government of Ireland in respect of matters transferred to it. This is at odds with what they [the Irish Government] were proposing to us in December [1997] and opposed to the model in Propositions on Heads of Agreement. It is clearly undo-able.[42]

Constitutional Issues

The negotiations relating to Constitutional Issues fared better. They sought to normalise relations between the Government of Ireland and the Government of the United Kingdom of Great Britain and Northern Ireland. These were primarily conducted between the British and Irish Governments and were concerned with proposed changes to Articles 2 and 3 of the Irish Constitution and with the repealing of the Government of Ireland Act 1920. The basic issue for the British and the Ulster Unionists was the Irish territorial claim to Northern Ireland contained in Articles 2 and 3. According to Irish law Northern Ireland was not part of the United Kingdom but part of Éire. In Irish versions of international agreements, such as the Anglo-Irish Agreement, the Irish Government would be described as the Government of Ireland and the British Government as the Government of the United Kingdom: it would be unconstitutional for an Irish government to recognise the existence of an entity called the United Kingdom of Great Britain *and* Northern Ireland in a legal document. Articles 2 and 3 merged the Irish nation with the Irish state. In Irish law everyone living on the island of Ireland was considered a part of the Irish nation. Irish law included Northern Ireland as part of the Irish state although Article 3 voluntarily restricted the exercise of the Irish Parliament's laws to the 26 counties of the Irish Free State formed in 1922.

Unionists bitterly resented the refusal of the Irish Constitution to recognise the legal existence of Northern Ireland as part of the United Kingdom and their communal right not to be part of the Irish nation. The aim of the UUP was to encourage the Irish Government to draw a distinction between the Irish nation, which would include nationalists throughout the island of Ireland but exclude Ulster unionists in Northern Ireland, and the boundaries of the Irish state. The Irish Government, for its part, wanted to protect the right of Irish nationalists in Northern Ireland to express their membership of the Irish nation. This was a major worry for Northern Nationalists.

The SDLP had highlighted its concerns at the opening of the talks. Here it stressed that it wished to be sure that any amendment to the Irish Constitution was part of an overall settlement which did not ignore the Northern nationalist identity and which commanded nationalist consent. Nationalists in the North, pointed out the SDLP, had always looked upon the Irish state as embodying their sense of nationality, and had always looked to Irish governments for support in pursuit of their right to express this national identity, and to fair treatment in Northern Ireland. While the SDLP accepted that there could be changes to the Constitution of Ireland designed to remove any perceived threats to the identity of the unionist community, it also expected that the right of the Northern nationalist community to be part of the Irish nation would be unimpaired and fully expressed.[43] Gerry Adams explained, in March 1998, that Sinn Féin were also nervous about any change in the Irish Constitution. However, Sinn Féin went further than the SDLP and expected an Irish government to uphold the constitutional imperative of pursuing Irish unity. No one, said Adams, had the right to negotiate away Irish nationality or Irish nationhood. In terms of constitutional change:

> The minimum nationalists want to see is fundamental constitutional and political change in British Jurisdiction, the Union of Ireland Act 1800 and related legislation such as the Government of Ireland Act 1920 and the N.I. Constitution Act 1973. They want to see balanced change in the Irish constitution so that in any Irish constitutional change, the definition of the Irish national territory should not be diluted – the constitutional imperative should remain – there must be no diminution of the rights of Irish citizens.

Furthermore, Adams argued, Irish citizens in the North should have the right to elect their representatives to the Irish Parliament and should have voting rights in Irish Presidential elections and referenda.[44] These were ambitious goals, which were based on the Republican strategy of securing an Irish Government-SDLP-Sinn Féin consensus. This would prove impossible to secure. However, both Sinn Féin and the Irish Government agreed on the desire to see the deletion of what they claimed was a British territorial claim to sovereignty in Ireland – Section 75 of the Government of Ireland Act 1920. As we shall see, the Irish Government's position was based upon a fundamental misunderstanding of British constitutional law. Section 75 *did not* contain a territorial claim to British sovereignty in Ireland. However, both Sinn Féin and the Irish Government thought that it did.

How could such a basic error occur? Put crudely the political leadership of the Irish Government and Sinn Féin were not scholars of British constitutional law. Nor were the Irish Government's legal advisors; they were experts in their own constitutional law. The Irish Government believed that an accommodation between the two traditions in Ireland would involve an agreed new approach to the traditional constitutional doctrines of the two Governments and the two main traditions. Any accommodation in regard to the constitutional expression of identity and allegiance would have to meet the requirements of both main traditions in a balanced and even-handed way. A 'balanced accommodation' could not reflect in any sense the pre-eminence of one tradition over the other – but rather must represent an 'honourable, balanced accommodation of the positions of both'.[45] Hence changes in Articles 2 and 3 in return for the repeal of the Government of Ireland Act 1920 and Section 75.

During one bilateral meeting between the Irish Government and the UUP, on 4 March 1998, the Taoiseach's special advisor on Northern Ireland, Dr Martin Mansergh, expounded his thoughts on the issue. He highlighted his belief that the Anglo-Irish Treaty of 1921 had superseded the Act of Union of 1800. From this perspective Section 75 was a reassertion of British sovereignty.[46] Mansergh believed that according to the terms of the 1921 Treaty, Northern Ireland had been incorporated into the Irish Free State in 1922. But the Northern Ireland Parliament also had the right to contract out of the Free State and back into the United Kingdom. This it duly did. Therefore, in Mansergh's view, the Anglo-Irish Treaty of 1921 and the Government of Ireland Act 1920 superseded the Act of Union and Section 75 was a reassertion of a British territorial claim to Northern Ireland. Deleting Section 75 would therefore end Britain's territorial claim to Northern Ireland.

But Mansergh, and consequently, Irish policy was wrong. In fact the Treaty was not the key reference point. British constitutional law is. To fully appreciate this complex argument we need to momentarily look at the Anglo-Irish Treaty. The constitutional lawyer Professor Brigid Hadfield explains how the Articles of Agreement for a Treaty, commonly called the 'Treaty', were given force of law in the United Kingdom by the Irish Free State (Agreement) Act 1922. Article 1 of the Articles of Agreement endowed 'Ireland' with the name of the Irish Free State. However, and crucially, Article 1's reference to 'Ireland' *did not* include Northern Ireland. According to British law the term 'Ireland' only referred to the twenty-six counties which seceded from the United Kingdom. Article 11 of the Treaty provided that 'the powers of the Parliament and the Government of the Irish Free State shall not be exercisable as respects Northern Ireland and the provisions of the Government of Ireland Act 1920, shall, so far as they relate to Northern Ireland, remain of full force and effect' unless the Parliament of Northern Ireland resolved otherwise, which it did not. Hence, the expression 'Ireland' in Article 1 is to be construed as *excluding* Northern Ireland, certainly in terms of United Kingdom law.[47]

Therefore, Northern Ireland never was part of the Irish Free State and could not contract out of it in 1922. Northern Ireland's status as part of the United Kingdom did not rest on Section 75 of the Government of Ireland Act 1920. Its status continued, unbroken and unaltered, from its incorporation within the United Kingdom in the Union with Ireland Act 1800. Furthermore, Section 75 was a *saving provision*, that is a section inserted for political purposes; it was not a declaration of British sovereignty in Ireland. British sovereignty was inherent in the Act as it was in all Acts of Parliament – the Westminster Parliament was sovereign over all persons and things in His Majesty's dominions. The new regional unit of Northern Ireland was part of the United Kingdom since 1801 because of the Act of Union, not the Government of Ireland Act in 1920. And it remained part of the United Kingdom because of the Act of Union. The importance of the above was this: in 1998 the whole basis of the Irish Government's policy towards constitutional issues was based on a fundamental misinterpretation of British constitutional law.

From the Irish perspective this must be considered a monumental error in their Anglo-Irish policy. It also gave the UUP an enormous advantage in negotiations. They were quite prepared to negotiate away the Government of Ireland Act 1920 – so long as there was no challenge to the title deeds of the Union. This meant the Act of Union. The UUP even dismissed the ideology of the Irish Government's negotiating position. David Trimble described the latter's demand for a 'balanced constitutional accommodation' as 'an intellectual absurdity', totally unacceptable to Ulster Unionists. Trimble explained:

> Northern Ireland is part of the United Kingdom, has been so since its creation on 1 January 1801, and has been part of the dominions of Her Majesty's predecessors since 1177. (The pre-1800 parliament, the parliament of 1921-72 and the assemblies of 1974 and 1982-86 were simply variations within the context of that sovereignty.)
>
> The issue in International Law is territorial sovereignty. And the question: which State has title? In the absence of agreed joint sovereignty, only one State can have title. This perforce must be the United Kingdom.

The UUP were confident that they held the moral high ground on this issue. Trimble believed that Ireland was almost certainly in breach of its international obligations. Irredentism was – or should be – the big issue between the United Kingdom and Irish Governments. He argued: 'No balanced constitutional accommodation is possible. Either the territorial claim – which goes deeper than Articles 2 and 3 of the Irish constitution – stays or goes.' The issue was for the Irish Government itself. But if the Irish Government was to take a real risk for peace by dropping its claim, Trimble asked, what could it expect in return? Realistically, the answer, other than a settlement in Northern Ireland, was 'very little'. But, such a settlement itself would be a significant prize full of historical compromise; it was in the interests of the Irish state to stretch itself to obtain that prize. Trimble argued: 'There is no major, or even symbolic, change to United Kingdom constitutional law, which could be made by way of response.'

This was because, in Trimble's opinion, Dublin, and in particular Martin Mansergh, 'has entirely misinterpreted Section 75 of the 1920 Government of Ireland Act as an equivalent United Kingdom claim to Northern Ireland. There is no such claim because it is not necessary.' The errors made by successive Irish Governments were 'so gross that it is difficult to believe any constitutional or international lawyer advised Albert Reynolds, John Bruton and now Bertie Ahern. Yet this idea of withdrawing claims simultaneously has been playing overtime in Irish intellectual and political debate for several years.' However, this did not mean that the United Kingdom Government and the Unionist parties could not accept political reforms for Northern Ireland which might be represented – erroneously and mischievously – by Dublin as a *quid pro quo*. Trimble concluded that give and take was the essence of negotiations but that 'there is no way that the end of the territorial claim on one side (which unionists would love to see), and some unspecified changes to United Kingdom statute law on the other, can be realistically and honestly represented as a balanced constitutional accommodation.'[48]

From an early stage in the talks, the UUP had knowledge of the Irish Government's position on Articles 2 and 3. It had been in December 1997 that representatives of the Irish Government had first given the UUP an indication of their proposed changes to Articles 2 and 3 during an oral presentation in Belfast. In an internal party memorandum David Trimble explained: '... our initial response was that the rewrite of Article 2 in terms of a nation to which people in the island were entitled to be members was on the right lines.' The UUP would prefer an equivalent statement in British legislation, although it was arguably already there in the Ireland Act 1949. There were, however, problematic aspects to the proposed rewrite of Article 3: namely a statement that an all-Ireland state would be an 'objective' of the Republic of Ireland.

The UUP considered that this would not lead to stability. It might lead to an Irish court again holding that the realisation of an all-Ireland state was a constitutional imperative, as it had done in the McGimpsey case following the Anglo-Irish Agreement. This was in any event, argued Trimble, inconsistent: 'How can the Irish Government sincerely say they wish co-operation while proclaiming the objective of eliminating Northern Ireland as an entity distinct from the Republic of Ireland?' Most Unionists would consider that the latter was the genuine intention and the former merely a devious means of pursuing the latter and would consequently reject any arrangements for co-operation, while still accepting that co-operation by itself could be desirable. It was also not clear that the assertion in Article 3 of a right to jurisdiction over Northern Ireland would be omitted: 'it should be,' commented Trimble. On the 'so-called "balanced"' changes in British law, the Irish asked for the deletion of Section 75 of the Government of Ireland Act 1920 and for the consent principle to be written into law in its 'positive' as well as its 'negative' aspects – these terms coming from the Irish point of view.[49]

However, Trimble remained worried that any proposed changes to Articles 2 and 3 would not expressly recognise the existence of Northern Ireland and would therefore fall short of the acknowledgement of 'legitimacy' as promised in the Frameworks Documents. The UUP had their own, rather ambitious, version of a new Article 3 for the Irish Constitution which would remove any ambiguity relating to a constitutional imperative for Irish unity. This read:

> The Irish nation's realisation in statehood remains the hope of those of Irish nationality in both parts of Ireland. The people accept that Ireland may be united only by the consent of the people of Éire, and of the people of Northern Ireland voting separately, and through peaceful means.[50]

But the Irish Government had its own problems in trying to reassure Northern Nationalists that their right to be part of the Irish nation and their ability to obtain Irish citizenship would not be lost by any changes to Articles 2 and 3. After receiving information concerning the contents of the Irish Government's proposed changes to Articles 2 and 3 at the end of March 1998, Sinn Féin's Northern chairman, Gerry Ó hÉara, described them as a 'disgrace'. Ó hÉara told a Republican gathering, 'We have a message here for Bertie Ahern: If you want to change Articles two and three, if you want to diminish our nationality at this point in our history ... come here and consult with us. Come here and ask for our consent. ... It's a disgrace and it's not going to be accepted and we are not going to take it lying down.'[51]

However, unlike the situation during the Mayhew talks of 1992, the Irish Government was already committed to changes to both Articles 2 and 3. As Martin Mansergh explained, the Irish had formed a view on their side that the negotiations would be deadlocked if they kept insisting on retaining the phraseology in the Irish Constitution describing the island of Ireland as the 'national territory'. This was a substantial change from the Irish Government's position during British–Irish discussions in 1994, when they had refused to delete the term 'national territory' from Article 2. This time, said Mansergh, the Irish realised that a more flexible response was absolutely vital to building up confidence between Ahern and Trimble. The UUP leader, acknowledged Mansergh, wanted an assurance that there would be serious negotiations that would lead to an agreement, not merely a public relations exercise.[52] This was partly true; Ahern's Fianna Fáil government was handicapped in this area by John Bruton's commitment, while Taoiseach, to end the Irish state's territorial claim in Article 2.

In discussions with the UUP, the Irish had also hoped to trade changes in Articles 2 and 3 for a North–South body with executive powers. The UUP refused.[53] Unconcerned with the Government of Ireland Act 1920, the UUP's primary aim in discussions on constitutional issues was to avoid any Irish focus on the Act of Union. Thus they felt no pressure to concede on cross-border bodies in return for changes to Articles 2 and 3.

It was after a meeting on 4 March that the UUP were first shown the proposed changes to Articles 2 and 3 in writing. These proved close to the final draft. The UUP, however, pushed for further movement. The Irish responded that they had their own domestic problems within Fianna Fáil concerning the proposed changes, and that it was very difficult to go much further. The Irish also pointed out that, from the Unionist point of view, the principle of a united Ireland by consent was now to be included. Indeed, they pointed out, they had moved considerably from their 1994 proposals to the current position in which they had dropped their territorial claim.

The UUP responded with criticism of the wording of Article 3 which, they feared, continued to contain a constitutional imperative to unity. However, the Irish Government explained that it wanted to include the legitimate aim of pursuing a united Ireland and that changes here would also allow their

Constitution to establish cross-border bodies. The Irish Government warned that it was close to losing wider Nationalist support on the issue.[54] The Irish were certain that, in the opinion of their legal advisors, the territorial claim to Northern Ireland and the constitutional imperative to Irish unity would be removed by their proposed changes. The Irish explained that as a result of the Irish Supreme Court's review of Articles 2 and 3 in the McGimpsey case it had become part of Irish constitutional law that

- the reintegration of the national territory is a constitutional imperative

- Article 2 of the Constitution consists of a declaration of the extent of the national territory as a claim of legal right

- the derogation in Article 3 underwrites the assertion in Article 3.

But the Irish Government's legal representatives pointed out that the above view 'could not survive' the explicit provisions of the new Articles 2 and 3 which contained

- a constitutional statement recognising two jurisdictions on the island of Ireland

- recognition that unity of the island of Ireland can only take place with the consent of the majority in both of the jurisdictions

- recognition that the wish for a united Ireland is 'a firm will'

- an assertion of a constitutional right of all persons born in the island of Ireland to be part of the Irish nation.

The Irish Government's legal representatives concluded, 'On this basis it is asserted that the replacement of the current text of Articles 2 and 3 by those now proposed would end the constitutional territorial claim to the "six counties" and the constitutional imperative to national unity.'[55] In essence then, the discussions on Constitutional Issues appeared to be close to resolution by the deadline of May 1998.

Rights and Safeguards

The question of Rights and Safeguards was crucial to the different negotiating positions of Unionists and Nationalists during the talks. All the Nationalist groupings believed the communal perception of substantial historical discrimination against Catholics in Northern Ireland. However, there were differences of emphasis between the SDLP and Sinn Féin. While the former acknowledged that there had been significant reforms in Northern Ireland, the latter held that such reforms were merely cosmetic in what was an inherently sectarian state which could only be remedied by ending partition. Sinn Féin believed that social and economic inequalities continued to permeate Northern Irish society because successive British Governments had propped up an unequal system. Injustice had been created by partition and only a single democratic island would present the best framework for addressing these problems.

Republicans complained that thirty years after the civil rights movement had been launched, inequality and injustice still prevailed and that the willingness of the British Government to address these matters remained questionable. The nationalist cultural tradition was continually undervalued and ignored, with the failure to provide for education in the Irish language the most obvious example. On the health and social fronts in matters such as ill health and indebtedness the north of Ireland was in the worst position in Europe. Sinn Féin concluded that it was time for the British Government to 'end the war economy in this part of Ireland'.[56] The answer for Sinn Féin was the 'equality agenda'. This meant that:

> The securing of equality, rights and justice needs to be visible and immediately tangible; 'equity' of treatment must be replaced by 'equality' of treatment; this should not even be a matter of negotiation and all provisions must be statutory, and must cover all aspects of life. For example, policing, human rights, the legal system and the administration of justice should come within the remit of North–South institutions; economic development, fair employment and an end to discrimination are other important areas, [and] cultural rights are central to any settlement.

> Equality needs to be accorded to the Irish language. Bilingualism needs to be proactively encouraged and statutory provision made, a human rights commission should be established on an all-Ireland basis to ensure that the principle of equality applies in all areas of government and social life. The establishment of a Bill of Rights and an all-Ireland constitutional court responsible to a North–South council is essential, combined with changes in the administration of justice.[57]

The British Government disputed many of Sinn Féin's complaints regarding its alleged inactivity in combating discrimination. It did, however, focus on those matters which were directly relevant to confidence building and to underpinning and reinforcing any settlement that might emerge. With this in mind, the British Government concentrated on five main areas – targeting social need, rural development, employment equality, cultural issues and rights and safeguards where they could point to progress.[58] However, the British also emphasised that they remained committed to strengthening rights and safeguards for the minority. At the core of British policy was to be a Human Rights Bill and the incorporation into domestic UK law of the European Convention on Human Rights. The British were also prepared to consider whether it would be necessary to supplement these measures with specific provisions tailored to suit circumstances in Northern Ireland. Areas to which additional measures would apply included policing, parades and employment equality. The British Government suggested that what was needed was a settlement based on a recognition by the people of Northern Ireland that they believed that the incorporation of human rights represented a vital addition to a lasting settlement.

The Irish Government supported the British position but added that there should be 'appropriate steps to ensure an equivalent level of protection in the Republic'. What was needed was an assurance that there would be a common standard of human rights throughout the island of Ireland. The SDLP agreed and saw value in the suggestion for an all-island rights Charter or Covenant. It observed that the idea had arisen from the previous round of talks in response to Ian Paisley's comment that a Northern Ireland Bill of Rights was based on the assumption of Northern Ireland remaining within the UK, and that any change in that status would leave Protestants unprotected. The SDLP believed it was possible that in the future Northern Ireland might opt, by consent, for reunification with the Republic; therefore it was important that rights were created which would apply equally for unionists in such an eventuality as well as for nationalists at the present time.

Rights were a political expression of identity which was why the SDLP did not believe in a purely internal settlement in Northern Ireland, just as it did not believe in a purely internal all-Ireland settlement should a majority vote for unification. This was just one aspect of the guarantees that an all-Ireland Charter could provide. If there was any change in Northern Ireland's position within the United Kingdom then surely Unionists would want to negotiate such a change using the principles contained in a Charter as a basis for protecting their rights in a united Ireland.[59]

The UUP, while not keen on an all-Ireland Charter, had also applied itself to the question of Rights and Safeguards by focusing on the question of minority rights elsewhere in the democratic world as a model for accommodating the cultural and national identity of nationalists within Northern Ireland. For example, in an internal party paper, Professor Antony Alcock pointed out that for twenty-five years after the Second World War national minorities had remained an object of suspicion by host states. Yet after 1970 everything had changed. The main reason was the process of European integration, led by states, on the basis that national boundaries were fixed. The only exception was the claim of the Irish Republic to Northern Ireland. This meant that, with the exception of Northern Ireland, minorities – at least in western Europe – gradually ceased to be considered threats to state integrity and security. This was coupled with the growing corpus of conventions setting standards of human, cultural and economic and social rights emanating from the Council of Europe and the EU which served to enhance the economic, social and cultural positions of minorities in their homelands.

Alcock argued that one significant manifestation of this liberalisation of attitudes to minorities was the granting of, or expansion of, regional autonomies with legislative and administrative powers. By the mid-1990s the spirit of regionalism was sweeping the European Community. The emergence of so many regions/provinces/cantons with legislative, executive and financial power to carry out decisions enabled these regions to proceed to the next stage in the process of European integration, namely, the development of cross-border co-operation. Alcock argued that the principle of the right of self-determination of peoples – not territories – was incorporated into the United Nations Charter in Articles 1 and 55. But what were 'peoples'? A right needed a definition; it needed a bearer. Neither was to be found in the Charter. There was however a general consensus that 'peoples' meant 'cultural communities', i.e. nations. But did this extend to groups? The answer had to be 'No'. Few areas were culturally homogeneous.

Alcock, in order to get round the hostility to the principle of self-determination based on its perception as a recipe for secession from a state, drew a distinction between *internal* and *external* self-determination. Since minorities could no longer easily claim the right to external self-determination, i.e. the right to change sovereignty and borders, they should be compensated by internal self-determination, namely, the right to decide all legislative and administrative measures necessary for the maintenance and development of their cultural characteristics, which could include economic and social as well as cultural measures; external self-determination should only be sought if the host state refused to grant legitimate requests.

From the above, Alcock argued, it should be clear that if the representatives of the nationalist community in Northern Ireland called for self-determination then one should enquire what they meant. Internal self-determination would be a legitimate subject for negotiation and should apply to both communities. If external self-determination was sought – secession from the United Kingdom – it should be rejected. But this line would only succeed if the bicultural – British and Irish – nature of Northern Ireland was stressed and defended and if the idea that Northern Ireland was 'filled only by Irish people', even if some did not want to live under all-Ireland institutions, was 'ruthlessly' rejected.[60]

However, one of the problems for the UUP was that Northern Nationalists did not regard themselves as a minority. The SDLP regarded both communities in Northern Ireland as equal; Sinn Féin saw unionists as an Irish national minority in Ireland. While the UUP saw the incorporation of rights conventions from elsewhere, into Northern Ireland, as a mechanism for safeguarding the rights of those they considered a national minority within the UK – Northern Irish Catholics – Nationalists disagreed. The key problem for the UUP was that the SDLP sought the incorporation of such conventions plus a North-South body with executive power as the means of safeguarding and expressing the Northern nationalist community's rights. But for the UUP this went beyond internal self-determination and was seen as a mechanism for Nationalists achieving external self-determination.

The UUP accepted that constitutional Nationalists and Unionists were agreed that the problem they were dealing with was that communal identity and allegiances did not correspond with the state. They pointed out that the European Frameworks Convention for the Protection of National Minorities contained a long list of rights, all of which needed protection in Northern Ireland, and should be the guiding principle for additional rights. But the UUP rejected the Frameworks Documents when they spoke of the rights of the two communities being balanced, for to accord equality to a national minority in the way proposed flew in the face of international conventions. As the UUP acknowledged, although Nationalists might not regard themselves as being part of a minority, the Framework Convention on the Protection of National Minorities stated that it was not group rights but individual rights which had to be considered and individuals were free to choose whether they regarded themselves as being in a minority or not. While individuals had that right it was up to others like the talks participants to put the mechanisms in place to honour this position. The UUP was not worried about groups or individuals. It was more concerned with the rights which individuals and groups had.[61] But this, on its own, appeared to be insufficient for Nationalists. In the end, all roads seemed to lead back to Strand Two.

Decommissioning, Policing and Criminal Justice

To the surprise of many of the talks participants General John de Chasterlain's Independent International Commission on Decommissioning, established by the British and Irish Governments in September 1997, took its mandate seriously. While no one realistically expected any decommissioning this side of an agreement, the Commission set about drawing up decommissioning schemes anyway. The Commission's consultations with both British and Irish security forces had produced detailed estimates of paramilitary arms. The Commission was satisfied that decommissioning was unlikely to be a one-time event but was more likely to involve a series of such events. Recognising a need for flexibility, the Commission came to the conclusion that any decommissioning scheme had to make provision for a number of key elements irrespective of the method or location of decommissioning chosen. These included: a set standard for verification; complete destruction of the arms, ammunition or explosives made available for decommissioning; compliance with the statutory prohibitions on forensic testing; and acceptance that the requirement for public safety could not be compromised.

Since the vast majority of illegal weapons were held by paramilitary groups that claimed to have tight control and discipline over them, the Commission did not expect decommissioning to be a casual or random event. When paramilitary groups took the decision to proceed with decommissioning, the Commission expected and believed they would communicate this decision through some trusted and carefully chosen person. As a result, the decommissioning scenario envisaged was not one that contemplated a random phone call by an unknown voice, stating that weapons could be picked up at a certain site. Instead, the decommissioning scenario was based on the expectation, confirmed beforehand, that the Commission would be dealing with an authorised representative of the paramilitary organisation concerned. Thus when the initial contact to discuss an individual act of decommissioning occurred, the Commission would wish to know it was dealing with such a person. It would be understood, however, that this person might not be able to commit to a certain course of action without referring back to the paramilitary group he or she represented.

Discussion at this stage would cover a predictable range of topics. The Commission would wish to know: the type of weapon, explosive or ammunition contemplated for the decommissioning event; the quantity (numbers or weight); the general condition of the items with the assessment at this stage simply being the paramilitary group's estimate of the safety or state of the item; the decommissioning modality anticipated; and whether any member or representative of the paramilitary group would accompany Commission members to the site or be present at the site. The contact-person would be given confirmation of the Commission's requirements for verification, destruction, control and safety during the event.[62]

The paramilitary related parties had a common strategy to deal with decommissioning. This was to ignore it. None of them, particularly Sinn Féin, appeared to attach much importance to the issue. Indeed, at times, it seemed that it was only the UUP which harped on about decommissioning. Instead, Sinn Féin outlined its own concerns about security related matters, as follows:

> The six counties is a highly militarised zone. A complete demilitarisation of the situation is required. Immediate transitional steps should include the following:
>
> –   The E[mergency] P[rovisions] A[ct] and P[revention of]T[erroism] A[ct] and all other repressive legislation must be repealed.
>
> –   A proper policing service must be created to replace the RUC which must be disbanded. It must have a minimum of forty per cent nationalists in its ranks.
>
> –   This should be achieved in an agreed timetable in the context of specific affirmative action measures [for nationalists].
>
> –   Pending the disbandment of the RUC British political and cultural symbols and the paramilitary trappings of this force must be removed. Interrogation centres must be closed.
>
> –   A screening process must be initiated to remove officers with a record of human rights abuse.
>
> –   The British Army must be withdrawn to barracks as a first step in overall demilitarisation.

–   The Royal Irish Regiment must be removed permanently from contact with the civilian population pending the early disbandment of its locally deployed units.

–   All political prisoners must be released.[63]

The British Government, which had primary responsibility for such matters, responded to Republican concerns. The British argued that they wanted to see a return to 'normal' policing arrangements in Northern Ireland. This also meant that the British Army would no longer need to fulfil an operational role in support of the police; protective security measures would be removed; and there would be no further need for temporary emergency legislation. However, the British cautioned that the speed at which this would be possible would depend on the level of violence and the extent of the threat of terrorist attack as well as public disorder at the time. To illustrate this, the British identified three scenarios to indicate the types of de-escalatory steps which could be taken in response to changes in the level or threat of violence.

Scenario 1. Main terrorist organisations dismantled and disarmed, a minimal residual terrorist threat, criminal activity ongoing and improving community relations leading to a lower potential for public disorder.

Security profile: A police service operating without military support (other than routine specialist support as provided elsewhere in the UK) and providing high quality service without counter-terrorism constraints.

Scenario 2. A spectrum of threat levels, ranging from a situation where terrorist groupings are beginning to dismantle their organisations and/or disarm, and are quiescent or only sporadically active; through a somewhat higher level of threat, where smaller groups continue to carry out attacks against a range of targets; to a situation where significant terrorist activity continues, albeit at a reduced level from Scenario 3. In addition, a similar spectrum of public disorder. (It should be noted that this scenario is particularly wide-ranging and that the security force profile could therefore vary considerably in response.)

Security profile: Continuing requirement for counter-terrorist policing, with military support as necessary, the level depending on the actual situation.

Scenario 3. A high level of terrorist activity, including bombings, shootings and so-called 'punishment' attacks, probably coupled with serious public disorder.

Security profile: Where appropriate, a high level of counter-terrorist policing, supported by the military.

Clearly, the British Government stated, in a situation where a high level of threat obtained – Scenario 3 – security force operations and presence would have to remain at a high level and the supporting security infrastructure and counter-terrorist legislative framework retained. But at lower levels of threat, as a normal law and order situation began to prevail, the security forces would continue to respond in 'imaginative and constructive' ways. The sorts of measures which it would be progressively possible to implement included:

-     ... a relaxation in security force posture (operating procedures, use of protective equipment etc) in line with the reducing threat; a reduction in military support to routine RUC patrols ... reductions in operations specifically designed to counter terrorist activity (... searches, helicopter operations, etc); and eventually an end to routine military support to the police.

-     Army force levels: ... battalions sequentially withdrawn from Northern Ireland, while remaining under the G[eneral] O[fficer] C[ommanding]'s command; force levels under the GOC's command reduced; and a progressive return to barracks by resident and Royal Irish units.

-     Security installations: security barriers and gates opened and remaining control zone orders lifted; a progressive defortification of police and army bases and public buildings; and the phasing out of counter-terrorist military bases and other installations.

-     Legislation: a steady reduction in the use of emergency powers as the security situation eases; suspension of individual EPA powers as the requirement for them ends ...; and a return to greater use of jury trials as incidence of scheduled [terrorist] offences fails.

The British Government's aim was to see a situation – Scenario 1 – where the police were able to serve the entire community unconstrained by the threat of terrorism; where the army had returned to its normal peacetime function and no longer had an operational role in support of the RUC; where counter-terrorist security installations had been removed; and where Northern Ireland-specific measures did not form part of any future United Kingdom counter-terrorist legislation. Progress towards this objective had, however, to be determined by the level of threat; and an irreducible minimum of security capabilities would need to be retained so long as paramilitary organisations and stocks of illegal weapons remained intact.[64]

Once again it seemed that key participants in the talks – here it was the British Government and Sinn Féin – were poles apart with time ebbing away and most attention diverted towards Strand Two. But the germ of a solution was suggested by the SDLP. They raised the possibility of an Independent Commission to review the role of the police. They advanced the idea on condition that it was a meaningful, independent, possibly international body to report back to a post-agreement administration.[65] The remit of the commission would cover: the structures and organisation of the police; the case for a unitary and regionalised or autonomous regionalised police service; the ethos and symbols appropriate for a new political agreement; the recruitment, policies and practices of the police service; arrangements for training; arrangements for increased accountability over the police service; and the scope for increased co-operation with the Garda Síochána. The SDLP also advanced the idea that an Independent Commission could be used to develop a new approach to criminal justice matters. Sinn Féin supported a commission but only on condition that it should oversee the disbanding of the RUC.[66]

Prisoners

For both Republicans and Loyalists the issue of prisoners remained crucial to any political settlement. In December 1997, Gerry Adams made it clear that Sinn Féin would refuse to sign up to any agreement unless 'political prisoners' were released. Adams warned 'There cannot be any settlement while there are prisoners in prison. We have been clear about this from day one. The release of prisoners has to be part of any settlement. ... We want to see the release of all prisoners.' He added that he would be 'very surprised' if the SDLP or the Irish Government would give any backing to a peace deal which did not include prisoner releases, claiming that Fianna Fáil knew that this was a 'central sinew' in the whole infrastructure of a peace settlement. Adams stated that a political arrangement would be unworkable if Republican and Loyalist prisoners were still locked up.[67]

Inside Castle Buildings, both the UDP and the PUP supported Sinn Féin's position. The UDP argued that any objective observer would agree that political prisoners, their families and friends were also victims of the conflict over the previous three decades. The acknowledgement of this meant that some talks participants had to move away from their position of denying the very existence of political prisoners. If there were no political prisoners, why was the issue being discussed in a political process? Similarly, were those people saying that Northern Ireland had, for the past 27 years, been subjected to an amazing and unprecedented upsurge in ordinary criminality? The UDP believed it was time to stop this pretence and deal with the issue.

The issue of political prisoners had to be resolved within the process and not as some form of peripheral matter. Loyalist prisoners had played a vital role in securing the Loyalist ceasefire three years previously. They had also helped to maintain it. Yet the British Government had abjectly failed to make any significant movement towards a process of release for political prisoners. A previous Secretary of State had spoken about acting on the prisoner issue with 'generosity and imagination' but, in effect, prisoners had been waiting in vain. In December 1995, 50 per cent remission for political prisoners had been introduced by the British Government, but what this actually meant was bringing political prisoners back into line with so called 'ordinary decent criminals'. That category of prisoner had, until December 1995, enjoyed a more generous rate of remission than political prisoners.

From the UDP's perspective, the British Government had failed to implement any measures designed to shorten the period of imprisonment for life sentence prisoners. The UDP contrasted the difference in attitude adopted by the British Government when dealing with Loyalist and Republican prisoners. Five months after the renewed PIRA ceasefire, the British Government had moved swiftly to bring Republican prisoners back from the British mainland. This, along with a host of other confidence-building measures, directed solely towards the republican and nationalist community, had given the impression of a less than even-handed approach. This gave the UDP a major problem in respect of even-handed confidence-building measures. Were Loyalist prisoners seen to be less important than others? The UDP hoped not.

The Irish Government emphasised the deep importance it attached to prisoner issues by supporting the position taken by the paramilitaries. It saw confidence building as an essential element in the promotion of trust and the underpinning of peace in Northern Ireland. Its experience in the talks had confirmed that confidence was a key ingredient to progress. Where progress had been made it had been where a degree of confidence had been imparted to all sides. As progress was made, confidence grew. The Irish Government had always believed that the Peace Process ultimately depended on creating and sustaining this virtuous cycle of confidence and progress. The Report of the International Body identified continued action by both Governments on prisoners as one of the measures that would bolster trust. The Irish Government fully shared this view. It regarded the maintenance of the Republican and Loyalist ceasefires as critically important confidence-building measures in themselves. The assurance of a peaceful atmosphere had helped provide the necessary foundation on which to develop further measures to increase reconciliation and trust. It was essential, therefore, to continue to focus in an imaginative and progressive way on all the questions relating to those who had been imprisoned in the context of the conflict, both Republican and Loyalist, while also giving full attention to the concerns of victims of violence.

Comments such as this infuriated the UUP, which objected to terms such as 'prisoners of war' being used in the formal record. There were no prisoners of war in Northern Ireland. The UUP even had some doubt about the term 'political' to describe prisoners; but whatever description was used the UUP objected to it being used in the formal record. The UUP referred to the release of 36 prisoners by the Irish Government during the first PIRA ceasefire, which had supposedly established confidence. The UUP asked the Irish Government how these releases increased confidence in the community when incidents such as Canary Wharf and the murder of RUC officers were subsequently perpetrated. The Irish Government responded by saying that the ceasefires had had a positive effect on confidence building. However, such confidence building had to be reinforced by specific measures as well. Taking into account the fact that the ceasefires had a sound basis, it seemed reasonable to underpin this situation by taking action on an issue which was close to both communities. There was no doubt that the durability of the ceasefires was a confidence-building measure but action should be taken to underpin this and the prison issue was of relevance to both communities.

The UUP, however, said it could not follow the logic of the Irish Government's position. It seemed contradictory for the Irish Government to be saying that the release of prisoners was a confidence-building measure when one did not know the durability of the PIRA ceasefire. The UUP argued that it ill beheld the Irish Government to manufacture confidence-building measures when there was a lack of confidence apparent between the Republic and the United Kingdom on the handling of terrorist matters.[68]

However, despite the protests of the UUP, it was clear that the party was becoming increasingly isolated on the prisoner issue. As the British Government noted, a number of the parties to the talks – the UDP, PUP, SDLP, Sinn Féin, and the Irish Government – had now made specific recommendations regarding the release of prisoners in their submissions to the Sub-Committee on Confidence Building Measures. Among the proposals put forward were the following:

–   There should be some form of early release for terrorist prisoners. Eligibility for early release should take account of the paramilitary affiliation of a prisoner, the attitude of his paramilitary group to the political process and if the group has maintained a ceasefire.

–   The life sentence review procedures should be changed for terrorist prisoners. There should be automatic release after a set period (perhaps 10 years) and the first review should be advanced. The procedure should also be more open.

–   Determinate sentence terrorist prisoners should receive sixty-six per cent remission.

–   More generous treatment might be given to prisoners who have been convicted of certain offences, or who are serving long sentences.[69]

A consensus for substantial movement on the prisoner issue was now clearly developing among the Nationalist and Loyalist representatives.

Expulsions

Prisoners and decommissioning were controversial issues. Many Republican and Loyalist prisoners were serving sentences for horrendous crimes against the person. Decommissioning was an issue which would not go away because the legitimate or illegitimate use of violence went to the heart of the Northern

Ireland conflict. The right to use armed struggle as a political weapon to end British rule in Ireland was championed by the Republican Movement. The right to use violence to retaliate against Republicans was claimed by Loyalists. Killings and bombings continued throughout the talks. The question was: who was behind them? If they were paramilitaries associated with some of the parties engaged in the talks then the whole process was devalued. On two occasions the Governments were forced to demonstrate to paramilitary related parties that the talks process could not sustain a twin-track approach of politics and violence.

In the early hours of Sunday 11 January 1998, Terry Enright, a Catholic doorman at a Belfast nightclub, was shot dead by Loyalist gunmen. The LVF claimed responsibility for the murder. In a statement, it said that the killing was in direct response to the murder of Billy Wright. It called on the Irish Government to drop Articles 2 and 3 of the Irish Constitution, adding, 'The Loyalist Volunteer Force is not against peace, but not peace at any price.'[70] On 18 January, the LVF murdered Fergal McCusker, in Maghera, County Londonderry. In a coded message, the LVF warned, 'This is not the end.'[71] The next day two more people lost their lives. The first to die was a leading Loyalist, Jim Guirney, 38, who was shot dead by the INLA. Later that evening Larry Brennan, a Catholic taxi driver, was shot dead outside his depot in south Belfast. Speculation spread that the LVF was not operating alone. On 21 January, another Catholic man, 55-year-old Benedict Hughes, from Suffolk Crescent in west Belfast, was shot dead. The next day, amid the deepening security crisis, the RUC Chief Constable confirmed the suspicion that the UFF were directly involved in the wave of sectarian killings.[72]

On 23 January 1998, the UFF issued a statement confirming its involvement in recent murders. The UFF recalled that it had adopted a policy of no first strike. However, since the Canary Wharf bomb, the UFF believed it had endured severe provocation from the Republican Movement, without response. The current phase of Republican aggression, initiated by the killing of Billy Wright, 'made a measured military response unavoidable. That response has concluded.'[73] With this admission it seemed inevitable that the UDP would be expelled from the talks, which had temporarily moved to Lancaster House in London for January.

When it seemed to some of the talks participants that Mo Mowlam was reluctant to expel the UDP, Sinn Féin, led by Gerry Adams and Martin McGuinness, were prominent in seeking an assurance that both Governments were going to 'face up to their responsibilities'. Sinn Féin warned that the British Government had no choice in this matter, as confirmed by intelligence provided by the RUC Chief Constable and the statement of the UFF itself, that the Mitchell Principles had been demonstrably dishonoured.[74] By now it was clear that there was no support from the major parties to the UDP's continued participation in the talks and, with the inevitability of being formally expelled, the UDP decided that they would leave the process first: they would not be humiliated. David Adams confirmed that, in the meantime, the UDP would be using 'all its influence ... to make sure that paramilitaries are convinced that the only way forward is through purely peaceful democratic methods'.[75] The UDP's expulsion was confirmed in a Plenary session of the talks. But an opening was left for the party's possible return: if, over a period of weeks, a complete, unequivocal and unqualified UFF ceasefire was demonstrated, and established through word and deed to have been fully and continuously observed, the Governments would consider the possibility of the UDP rejoining the negotiations.[76]

Now it was Sinn Féin's turn. On 9 February, a known drug dealer was shot dead outside a south Belfast restaurant. Brendan Campbell, aged 33, from west Belfast, was shot dead by Direct Action Against Drugs, a cover name for the PIRA. Only in January, DAAD had attempted to kill Campbell, shooting him twice in the chest as he sat drinking in the Meadows Tavern pub, in south Belfast. Campbell had been known to have taunted Republicans on a number of occasions. The next day, Robert Dougan, a prominent Loyalist with UDA connections, was shot dead as he sat in his car in a Belfast suburb. Soon afterwards, three suspected PIRA members were arrested in Twinbrook, Belfast, in a security operation. The INLA immediately denied any responsibility for the murder; the PIRA did not. Instead, two days later, the PIRA issued a brief statement which said, 'Contrary to speculation surrounding recent killings in Belfast, the IRA cessation of military operations remains intact.' The PIRA reiterated their preparedness to facilitate a climate which enhanced the search for a democratic settlement through real and inclusive negotiations.[77]

These two murders, given the suspicion of PIRA involvement in them, called into question Sinn Féin's continued participation in the talks. All eyes fell upon Ronnie Flanagan. On the morning of 13 February, the RUC Chief Constable informed the Secretary of State that he believed the PIRA was 'involved in the murders' of Robert Dougan and Brendan Campbell. Dr Mowlam immediately issued a statement in which she said she was now considering the right course of action. She added that the integrity of the talks process and the commitment to exclusively peaceful means were paramount and that all parties 'must be treated fairly and equally'.[78]

When the talks reconvened at Dublin Castle, on 16 February 1998, Mowlam recalled that, in their determination of September 1997, the two Governments had reiterated that they would expect the Republican Movement 'as a whole' to honour the commitment to the Mitchell Principles affirmed by Sinn Féin. The British Government then confirmed that it was the RUC Chief Constable's 'firm view' that both of the recent Belfast murders had been carried out by the Provisional IRA. These considerations clearly raised the questions of whether Sinn Féin was any longer entitled to participate in the negotiations.[79] Sinn Féin reacted angrily. It protested that, in effect, the British Government was both judge and jury. The British Government's approach seemed to be based on the assessment of the RUC Chief Constable, Ronnie Flanagan, as it had said that it shared his view. Therefore it was obvious that there was no other basis to the indictment apart from the assessment of a discredited and anti-nationalist police force.[80]

Back at Stormont, Mowlam held firm and confirmed that the Governments had decided to expel Sinn Féin from the talks. But, with little time left now until the deadline in May, both Governments were prepared to work with all the parties to produce a settlement over the coming six weeks. They wanted as many parties as possible – including Sinn Féin – to have the opportunity to contribute during this critical period. Consequently, subject to events on the ground and to convincing in word and deed that a complete, unqualified and unequivocal PIRA ceasefire was being fully and continuously observed, it was the expectation of both Governments that Sinn Féin would be able to return to the talks in March 1998. Both Governments would maintain contacts with Sinn Féin in the meantime.[81] Effectively, given that the talks only convened on certain days during the week, the expulsion amounted to six working days. Not surprisingly, the UUP was furious. David Trimble angrily complained that the talks process had reached a new low and that virtually all credibility was being squandered. He claimed that the Governments' decision confirmed the fears of many that it was the ability to resort to violence that defined one's status in the talks.[82]

The Governments were caught in a bind. The paramilitary associated parties had to be warned that violence was incompatible with the talks process. Yet, at the same time, the logic of the Peace Process was to draw paramilitaries in from the cold. So, the Governments settled for what amounted to a shot across the paramilitaries' bows. After their sin-binning, both the UDP and Sinn Féin duly returned to the talks for the finale.

PART IV

Agreement and Disagreement: The Belfast Agreement

The Mitchell Document

On 25 March, the Chairman of the talks, Senator George Mitchell, made a dramatic announcement. 9 April 1998 was the deadline by which an agreement would have to be concluded.[1] This focused Unionist and Nationalist minds at the talks. Up to this point much of the negotiations had been shadowboxing. Everybody knew that the final week of the talks would decide whether or not there would be an agreement. Only then would each of the participants' bottom lines be revealed. The deadline was also in the interests of the Governments. As Dr Mowlam admitted, 'I don't think anybody would want to hold a referendum [on an agreement] during the marching season.'[2] As the deadline approached, the scale of the task was dramatically underlined by Bertie Ahern as he left Dublin, on 1 April, for negotiations in London. Ahern said that 'large disagreements' remained, which could not be 'cloaked'. He added ominously: 'I don't know whether we can surmount this.' In a move which infuriated Unionists, the Taoiseach added, 'As far as I am concerned, the Framework Document is what has to stand. That is why we are still negotiating and working on it. I would like to be able to tell you we can surmount this. I don't know if I can.'[3]

Back in Belfast, George Mitchell was determined to get to the first landmark in his schedule: an initial draft of a comprehensive agreement by 3 April, based on the discussions and papers submitted by the talks participants. The Governments had yet to agree on their differences in Strand One and Strand Two; but on most of the other areas – changes in the Irish Constitution and British constitutional law; prisoners; policing; criminal justice and a new British-Irish Council, there was a common British-Irish position. By 3 April, however, there was no draft document for the political parties to consider. The main area of discussion between the British and Irish Governments centred on Strand Two and what was required to keep Sinn Féin on board without alienating the Unionists.

Eventually, Tony Blair and Bertie Ahern reached agreement and their officials brought the agreed document to Mitchell in Belfast on 5 April. The Governments' officials now requested, on behalf of the premiers, that Mitchell present a composite document to the parties – including the section relating to Strand Two agreed in London – with the remainder composed by the Chairman's team in Belfast, as the Chairman's document. A reluctant Mitchell agreed, although the final draft of Strand Two, containing a number of annexes, was not available for the parties until late on 6 April.[4]

The Unionist parties were aware that the document which would eventually emerge would be most unpleasant in Strand Two. But there were also divisions between the UUP and the smaller Loyalist parties on power-sharing. It is important to note how isolated the UUP were on this issue. The UDP, as noted previously, were committed to some form of co-determination; on 6 April, the UUP found that the PUP were too. David Trimble informed the UDP and PUP that a meeting with the SDLP 'did not go very well'. Reg Empey explained that the SDLP wanted collegiate leadership on key issues and a 20 per cent trigger mechanism as an added safeguard in the Assembly. The UUP feared that this mechanism would be used on every occasion and that consequently the Assembly would be paralysed. Trimble was also unhappy with incorporating sufficient consensus into the Assembly, and was worried that this would entrench sectarianism into the institution from the very beginning. Hugh Smyth of the PUP asked Trimble if he could live with safeguards in the Assembly, such as a weighted majority; the UUP leader replied that he was 'unsure'. This seemed to Smyth an indication that the UUP were 'talking about majority rule' to which the PUP was opposed. Trimble conceded that the UUP were seriously considering the Nationalists' proposals – the SDLP, he accepted, 'need something'.

As the discussion turned to Strand Two, Gary McMichael informed the UUP and PUP of how his meeting had gone with Bertie Ahern, in Dublin, earlier that morning. The UDP had made it clear to the Taoiseach that it had 'major problems' with implementation bodies. Ahern had replied that he needed the implementation bodies to 'sell' any agreement. The UDP told the Taoiseach that if they were in any agreement at the outset then 'we could not sell it.' McMichael was now anxious that the Unionist parties agree a common position on this. Trimble confirmed these ominous signs when he informed the Loyalist parties how, during a conversation with Tony Blair earlier that morning, the Prime Minister had confirmed the British Government's acceptance of Ahern's position on implementation bodies. Blair, said Trimble, 'has to give something to Ahern'. However, as Reg Empey explained, the 'problem with implementation bodies is that the Assembly does not own them. We have blocked the front door and do not want them to slip in the back door. We need some means of accountability to the Assembly.' Empey now suggested a possible solution – a work plan which would 'slip in advance matters that need to be discussed'.[5] But would this prove acceptable to the Irish and the SDLP?

When the misnamed 'Mitchell Document' was finally revealed to the parties, later that night, the talks almost collapsed. There was much that alienated the UUP in 'policy areas', though not necessarily the UDP and the PUP; in particular sections concerning a commission on policing and criminal justice, the lack of a clear connection between decommissioning and the proportional allocation of seats in a new Northern Ireland administration, and an early release scheme for prisoners. But most of the constitutional aspects appeared satisfactory to the UUP – the recognition of consent; the recognition of the territorial integrity of the United Kingdom of Great Britain and Northern Ireland; and options including the SDLP and UUP models, for consideration in Strand One. It was Strand Two which produced the crisis. Here there were no options – everything had been decided for Unionists. Significantly, it appeared that the Irish had retreated from their demand that the proposed North-South Ministerial Council should have executive power. However, there was a sting in the tail for Unionists – what Reg Empey had referred to when he warned of the 'backdoor' undermining of the Northern Ireland Assembly.

Together with an outline of the envisaged North-South Ministerial Council the Document contained a series of Annexes outlining the areas in which the Council would decide common North-South policies, specific areas where decisions would be taken on action for North-South implementation and a series of North-South implementation bodies. The Council's authority and functions were to be derived directly from London and Dublin. Effectively, the Northern Ireland Assembly was by-passed. It was not Belfast, but London and Dublin which determined the remit of the Council. This meant, from a Unionist perspective, that the people of Northern Ireland – by which they meant the majority unionist community – had no control over the degree and pace of North-South co-operation. For example, it had been decided by London and Dublin, not the Assembly in Belfast, that the Council was to use its best endeavours to reach agreement on the adoption of common policies in the areas listed in Annex A, making determined efforts to overcome any disagreements.[6] These areas were listed as follows:

Annex A
List of specified areas where the Council is to use best endeavours to reach agreement on the adoption of common policies ...

Agriculture
– research, training and advisory services
– development of the bloodstock and greyhound industries
– rural development

Education
- tourism training
- education for students with special needs
- education for mutual understanding
- teacher qualifications and exchanges
- higher and further education
- combating educational disadvantage

Health
- general hospital services and accident/emergency planning
- food safety

Industry; Inland Fisheries
- management development services to industry
- trading standards
- public purchasing
- supervision of credit unions
- occupational health and safety
- inland fisheries
- approaches to the [EU] Common Fisheries Policy
- fish health
- fisheries education, research and training
- geological survey
- energy projects
- road and rail issues
- environment
- physical planning and development strategy
- road safety[7]

In specified areas set out in Annex B, London and Dublin had decided where the Council was to take decisions on action for implementation separately in each jurisdiction.[8] This was as follows:

Annex B
List of specified areas in which the Council is to take decisions on action for implementation separately in each jurisdiction ... (Items in brackets are not agreed [by the Governments].)

Agriculture
- animal and plant health
- (approaches to Common Agricultural Policy)

– education and training programmes

Social Welfare/Community Activity
– entitlements of cross-border workers and fraud control
– support for voluntary community activity

The Environment
– environmental protection, waste management and pollution control
– mapping
– wildlife conservation

Culture and the Arts
– heritage protection and restoration
– cultural promotion abroad

Health
– disease registries, clinical trials and high-cost, high-technology areas
– post-graduate medical teaching and training
– health promotion strategies

Marine and Waterways
– aquaculture and marine matters and drainage
– promotion and support of joint activities and strategic planning of facilities

Science and Technology
– promotion of scientific and technological research and its application[9]

But it was in Annex C that the Mitchell Document contained the most far-reaching proposals. The Council was to take decisions on action at an all-island and cross-border level through implementation bodies to be established.[10] For the areas listed in Annex C, it was 'agreed that new implementation bodies are to be established'. The two Governments were to 'make all necessary legislative and other preparations to ensure the establishment of these bodies at the inception of the British/Irish Agreement or as soon as feasible thereafter, such that these bodies function effectively as rapidly as possible'.[11] Only *further* bodies, in addition to those specified in the Annexes, and other developments of these arrangements, would be by agreement in the Council and with the specific endorsement of the Northern Ireland Assembly and the Oireachtas.[12] The list of implementation bodies was as follows:

Annex C

– ... [Items through Inland Waterways Body are agreed; all items thereafter are not agreed]

– a Tourism Body, covering promotion, marketing, research and product development for the island as a whole

– an Environmental Protection Body, covering co-operation on environmental protection, pollution, water quality and waste management and related matters in cross-border areas, as well as the development of a strategic approach for the island as a whole

– an EU Programmes Implementation Body ...

– a Transport Planning Body covering the co-ordination and development of the major transport services in Ireland, consideration of strategic issues in relation to road and rail networks and ports

– an Inland Waterways Body covering the joint development and management of inland waterways

– an Irish Language Promotion Body, promoting the use of the Irish Language to include an element of advice and support for Irish-medium education, supplementing and supporting the efforts of the voluntary support and co-ordination agencies in this latter sphere

– a Trade Promotion and Indigenous Company Development Body, supporting the development of indigenous enterprise and companies in the industrial and services sectors, including industrial training and the promotion of exports and of innovation and scientific and technological research and development ...

– an Arts Body, with functions in regard to promotion of the arts discharged in the Republic by An Chomhairle Ealaíon (The Arts Council) and in Northern Ireland by the Arts Council of Northern Ireland.[13]

The talks were immediately thrown into crisis. None of the Unionist parties was prepared to accept the Strand Two proposals. The transfer of functions, by London and Dublin, to the North–South Council clearly made it the source of authority for North–South co-operation and therefore it would, in Unionist eyes, be acting as a third level of government in Ireland. The power of the Northern Ireland Assembly to agree and develop areas of North–South co-operation, subject to a Unionist veto in the North–South Council, was neutered. Unionists were being given a preordained range of implementation bodies and told precisely where North–South co-operation would be conducted. The UUP's Deputy Leader, John Taylor declared, 'I wouldn't touch this paper with a 40-foot barge pole.'[14] David Adams of the UDP called on the Irish Government to 'plug into planet reality, and understand the situation we're in'.[15]

Jeffrey Donaldson, of the UUP, made it clear that there could not be agreement based on the proposals as set out in the Mitchell Document, adding, 'We can deliver a deal but we can't sign up to a hybrid, embryonic all-Ireland settlement.' The MP rejected an SDLP claim that his party was engaging in walk-out stunts: 'This is for real. We have major difficulties with this document. Our view is not reflected in it. Unless we get movement we are not going to get agreement. There must be a more realistic and balanced approach by the two governments, especially Dublin.'[16] The key disputed area was the source of authority for the implementation bodies. Acknowledging that accountability was built into the Document, Gary McMichael explained: 'That's not the point. Why not let the North-South Council decide a programme of work? That's not allowed because we're not trusted. The Assembly doesn't have any role.'[17] David Trimble now faxed a letter to Tony Blair warning:

> This document is not something the UUP could recommend to the greater number of people in Northern Ireland for approval. Before contemplating alternative proposals, I wish to know from you and the Irish Government if you are prepared to consider radically different measures. ... It is now 25 years from the failed Sunningdale Agreement and it now appears that the Irish Government has learned nothing from the reasons for its failure.
>
> In looking at the document it is also clear that all relevant international norms have been ignored.
>
> In all of this we have negotiated in good faith; it is now apparent that others have not. I await your early assurance that the Irish Government is prepared to negotiate in good faith.[18]

Perhaps shocked by the scale of the Unionist reaction, the Prime Minister reassured Trimble that the British Government was prepared to renegotiate the Document. Had he not agreed to do so, the talks were dead – the UUP bottom line had been reached. Blair arrived in Northern Ireland later that evening and went immediately to Hillsborough Castle where, within minutes, he was joined by Trimble. There, Blair identified two basic principles crucial to agreement. First, that Northern Ireland should remain part of the United Kingdom for as long as the majority of its people wanted it to be so; and secondly, that in return for this there was to be a recognition of the nationalist identity and fair and equal treatment for Catholics and Protestants alike in Northern Ireland. 'If there was agreement on those basic principles,' concluded the Prime Minister, 'then the rest is words and detail.'[19] Blair was summarising the basis of a deal – constitutional reassurance for Unionists; equality for Nationalists in Northern Ireland. By implication this meant resisting Nationalist claims in Strand Two. The British, it now seemed, realised that there would be no agreement at all if Unionist concerns in Strand Two were not met.

But what would be the attitude of the Irish? When a tired Bertie Ahern – distracted and emotionally drained from making arrangements for the burial of his mother – arrived at Castle Buildings he told reporters, 'We are here to listen ... everybody is required to move a little bit. I think we are all prepared to do that. I just hope we can make progress.'[20] However, Sinn Féin were now applying pressure on the Irish Government. Gerry Adams remained confident: 'There is no room for slippage and no room for this document to be unpicked,' he said. 'We are mindful of the unionist perspective, but on the core issues of justice, equality and the right of the people of this island to live together in peace without division, no British government will face us down. This generation of Irish republicans will not be faced down.'[21]

The UUP, as suggested earlier, had an alternative proposal for Strand Two. On 5 April, Reg Empey had suggested to Trimble that it might be time to put forward the UUP's plan 'B' for implementation bodies. These were effectively Empey's ideas. There could be, he suggested, a legislative enabling clause in a new 1998 Northern Ireland Constitution Act which would establish a North–South Council, in addition to a new British-Irish Treaty; a work plan for the North–South Council, the agenda of which might involve studies being commissioned by officials to establish the suitability of co-operation; the North–South Council could offer to 'inherit' the matters already being operated through the Anglo-Irish Intergovernmental Conference where they were within the area to be devolved to the Assembly, which would mean reports on progress going to the Council; the Council could be a suitable forum for discussion for Northern Ireland and the Republic's border counties to try and retain EU Objective 1 status funding for depressed regions; EU Peace and Reconciliation funding could be a suitable subject for cross-border co-operation; and cross-border co-operation on farming issues could be discussed in the EU context.[22]

Surprisingly, Strand Two issues were agreed along the UUP model relatively quickly, with Empey's work plan replacing the implementation bodies, although the Northern Ireland Assembly would be bound to agree at least 6 matters for future co-operation and implementation. This was the compromise – Nationalists were guaranteed that the North–South Ministerial Council would not be merely an 'empty house' and that there would be at least 6 areas of co-operation; Unionists were reassured that any implementation bodies would be agreed and established by the Assembly. Authority would thus flow from the Northern Ireland Assembly and not the North–South Council. Perhaps the crucial factor in shifting the Irish Government from their established position was Tony Blair. Immediately after agreement was reached on Strand Two, David Trimble had asked the Prime Minister how he had been able to persuade the Irish to shift their stance. Blair told the UUP leader that he had informed Ahern that unless the

Irish agreed to the Unionist model of Strand Two, he would declare the talks finished and blame the Irish Government. The Irish position shifted.[23]

Another, though not necessarily contradictory, impression of what happened came from George Mitchell, who credited Ahern with having come to his decision to renegotiate Strand Two on 7 April, after contemplating the implications of a refusal to do so. This was in defiance of the advice of his aides who felt that Dublin had negotiated in good faith with London and urged that the efforts of the two Governments be devoted to persuading the political parties to accept that agreement.[24] Whichever factor had the most influence on Ahern, one thing was clear: the talks were dead if Strand Two stood as it did. Ahern had to choose between insisting on a North-South model which satisfied and advanced Nationalist aspirations; or conclude an agreement which Unionists found acceptable. Essentially, this went to the heart of the Peace Process. Was this to be an intra-Nationalist agreement which kept Sinn Féin happy or the chance for an historic Nationalist-Unionist settlement which might not occur again? Ahern ignored his aides and chose the latter. It is doubtful whether any of his Fianna Fáil predecessors would have had the vision to do this.

Securing agreement on Strand Two proved to be the key to opening the door to Strand One, and indeed everything else. The SDLP leader, John Hume, indicated that he expected movement from the UUP in exchange for concessions from Nationalists: 'We pointed out to the Taoiseach and the Prime Minister that in the document supplied by Senator Mitchell there were proposals for changes to Articles 2 and 3 ... there was a clear acceptance of the principle of consent in relation to the changes in Northern Ireland, there was an acceptance of an assembly, and of east-west, British-Irish institutions. All of these proposals would be in the interests of unionists. The question is, what are they willing to do in return for all of that? Given that all the parties from the nationalist tradition are totally committed to agreement, how could the unionists be out in public arguing that they are being subsumed into a united Ireland against their will?' As Seamus Mallon explained, all parties had accepted a certain system for the appointment of ministers, but Unionists had not agreed to parallel consent. Mallon said, 'The unfortunate situation is that we have not been able to reach an understanding or approach an agreement on the very central basis of what is required by nationalists in relation to Strand One, and that is the consent of both sections of the community to every decision that will be made in that assembly.' He also pointed out that parallel consent meant that Nationalist *and* Unionist consent would be necessary for all important decisions.[25]

But even before their success in Strand Two, there were already signs that the UUP might be shifting its stance on Strand One towards that of the SDLP. Essentially there was little they could do to avoid this. As Hume and Mallon had quite rightly pointed out, given the above constitutional gains, to which was now added Strand Two, the UUP had little choice but to concede power-sharing in return. If the SDLP were to lose out on their preferred

Strand Two model – which it should be noted had been the policy of Nationalists since Sunningdale – then they had to be compensated in Strand One. Strand Two, after all, had been where the Unionists had most to fear; power-sharing in Strand One did not constitute a threat to the Union. As early as 5 April, in relation to Strand One, Reg Empey had warned David Trimble that he was 'becoming concerned that we are slowly being sucked into [the] SDLP's model'. But Empey added, 'I have always pointed out the weakness of our own model in regard to co-ordination and decision taking. However, the point of Seamus [Mallon]'s parallel consensus idea has possibilities if harnessed in a different way. Perhaps going the "full Monty" on the collegiate first/deputy Secretaryship has advantages over a hybrid approach. People don't understand parallel consensus (do you?). But they do understand "partnership government". Having a Unionist veto over the Assembly as a whole, including a negotiating position with any outside bodies, is not the worst thing that could happen. S[inn] F[éin] fears a unionist veto more than anything else.'[26]

Again, there was relatively quick progress in resolving Strand One issues between the SDLP and the UUP to the former's satisfaction with regards to a power-sharing cabinet, parallel consent and other safeguards. This was particularly so when one of the staunchest Unionist opponents of these, Jeffrey Donaldson, was detoured from SDLP-UUP meetings to a meaningless meeting between the UUP and the Irish Attorney-General on Articles 2 and 3 – the negotiations on which had already been concluded.[27] Primarily, David Trimble had aimed at securing the constitutional position of Northern Ireland within the Union. With the end of the Irish territorial claim, the UUP had also shielded the Act of Union from any 'balanced constitutional change'. Although the Government of Ireland Act 1920, including Section 75, was to be repealed, the British Government confirmed that this had no constitutional impact on Northern Ireland's position within the United Kingdom or its boundaries. Indeed, after all the Irish and Republican demands for the removal of the imagined British constitutional claim to Northern Ireland contained in Section 75, the British confirmed to the UUP that they would in fact be *enacting a similar provision* in a Northern Ireland Constitution Act. The British Government also confirmed that the effect of repealing Section 75 of the 1920's Act on Parliament's authority to legislate for Northern Ireland:

> is categorically that there is none: Parliament's power is unaffected. To put the matter beyond doubt, however, we intend to introduce, as part of the provisions of the Bill consequential on a settlement that confers legislative powers on the Assembly, provisions analogous to clause 27 (7) of the Scotland Bill currently before Parliament: ... 'This section does not affect the power of the Parliament of the United Kingdom to make laws for Scotland.'[28]

In fact the final drama of the talks occurred not on constitutional issues, but on prisoners and the question of whether there would be decommissioning before paramilitary related parties could serve in the Northern Ireland cabinet. As the UUP talks team gathered, in the afternoon of 10 April, to consider the final draft of the Agreement, David Trimble faced a rebellion on the possibility of Sinn Féin serving in a Northern Ireland Executive without decommissioning. Antony Alcock and Dermot Nesbitt were in favour of accepting the Agreement; Jeffrey Donaldson, David Campbell and Peter Weir were arguing for its rejection. The dissenters believed that the key passage in paragraph 25 of the Strand One section of the Agreement – referring to members of the Executive being committed to using 'only democratic, non-violent means, and those who do not should be excluded or removed from office under these provisions' – was not sufficient to bar Sinn Féin from office if the PIRA did not decommission its weapons. After all Sinn Féin claimed it was separate from the PIRA and had signed up to the Mitchell Principles while the PIRA had rejected them. Trimble, however, argued, as he had consistently done since becoming aware of the deletion of any explicit linkage between decommissioning and the holding of office, that there was sufficient linkage in the Agreement. How else could Sinn Féin which, as the Prime Minister had stated, was inextricably linked to the PIRA, demonstrate its commitment to democratic and peaceful means except by decommissioning?

Arguing in favour of acceptance was Ken Maginnis, the UUP's security spokesman. He pointed out that the Agreement gave the unionist community control of its own destiny for the first time in twenty-five years. No longer would unionists be powerless in their own land, having to be dictated to by people like Mo Mowlam. Trimble then gave his judgement on the Agreement. The UUP, he said, had entered the talks to secure the constitutional future of the Union. They had achieved those objectives. All of the other distasteful aspects of the Agreement – prisoners, the commission on policing – were *policy* issues which any British Government could introduce at any time. Rejecting the Agreement, and its constitutional gains, would not alter the Government's policy on these matters. Trimble asked what would be the one thing, at this late stage, he had to indicate to the Prime Minister that the UUP needed reassuring on; the answer was decommissioning. At this point, as Trimble prepared to meet Tony Blair, John Taylor indicated his support for the Agreement.[29] Without his Deputy Leader's support, Trimble would have been unable to have supported the Agreement. As a disenchanted Donaldson and Weir left Castle Buildings, Trimble received a letter from the Prime Minister, stating,

> I understand your problem with paragraph 25 of Strand One is that it requires decisions on those who should be excluded or removed from office in the Northern Ireland Executive to be taken on a cross-community basis.

> This letter is to let you know that if, during the course of the first six months of the shadow Assembly or the Assembly itself, these provisions

have been shown to be ineffective, we will support changes to these provisions to enable them to be made properly effective in preventing such people from holding office.

Furthermore, I confirm that in our view the effect of the decommissioning section of the agreement ... is that the process of decommissioning should begin straight away.[30]

Armed with this letter and having secured his constitutional objectives, Trimble indicated the UUP's support for the Belfast Agreement. In the end it was John Taylor who could have broken Trimble and the Agreement. As the UUP Deputy Leader subsequently explained, many unionists were angered by the release of prisoners and expressed great concern about the commission on policing; but these, as well as a review on criminal justice and the promotion of the Irish language 'will happen whether there is a "yes" or "no" vote [in the referendum]. The way to judge the agreement is to assess its stance on the broad constitutional issues. ... When I read it [the Agreement] on Good Friday, I itemised 18 points I was unhappy about, but there were many other points which I favoured and on balance I was positive to the overall agreement.'[31]

But where did all this leave Sinn Féin? Martin McGuinness had already warned the Prime Minister against the 'temptation to go for the Unionists' position. There can be no agreement which will work without Sinn Féin, just as there can be no agreement that will work without the support of David Trimble and his party.'[32] Shortly after 7 am, on 9 April, Mitchel McLaughlin had emerged from Castle Buildings claiming that Sinn Féin had reversed Unionist attempts to water down Strand Two issues. McLaughlin, who refused to take questions from the world's media, read a prepared statement which noted that his party had 'difficulties' with the Mitchell Document. The core issues remained British constitutional change, the proposed nature and power of all-Ireland institutions, the need to remove the Unionist Veto in institutions from all three strands, as well as concerns relating to policing and prisoners. McLaughlin pointed out that Unionists had sought to 'take the substance out of this paper in a number of key areas. They had succeeded to some degree in Strand Two. This has now been reversed.'[33] As has been seen, such was not the case and the statement appeared to be aimed at reassuring watching republicans. In effect Strand One had been settled between the SDLP and the UUP; and Strand Two between the British and Irish Government and the UUP. The Irish-UUP agreement on Strand Two represented the final collapse of Sinn Féin's pan-Nationalist strategy to create a Frameworks plus North-South body.

Having lost out on the constitutional issues – like the Irish Government it appeared unaware of this – Sinn Féin did, however, have the consolation of the 'Equality Agenda' involving extensive rights legislation and safeguards, commissions on policing and criminal justice, a commitment to demilitarisation and, perhaps most importantly, the extraction of a two-year limit on prisoner releases. Essentially, Sinn Féin were settling for the promise of reforming Northern Ireland to make it more acceptable to the nationalist community, something Gerry Adams dismissively attacked John Hume and the SDLP for working towards during the 1980s.

So, despite the effective spin put out by Sinn Féin, the final Agreement was a disappointment in the key constitutional areas. Here they found that constitutional Nationalism had taken the decision to reach an agreement with moderate Unionism, not militant Republicanism. One key Sinn Féin member, Pat Doherty, claimed the SDLP had 'bottled out' of the talks. Mitchel McLaughlin subsequently admitted, 'We could have got a better deal if the SDLP had been as nationalistic as we are. We could have got a better deal if the Irish government had been as strong on these issues.' He described the Agreement as a 'mixed bag'. There were issues in the Agreement which were there because Sinn Féin had fought for them, and other issues which they would have liked to have seen more fully developed. He accepted that 'We could have got a better deal, I think, if we had been stronger politically.' Sinn Féin had 'fought to firewall the north-south bodies but we did not succeed'.

McLaughlin admitted that the 'Assembly does have a controlling input in terms of both the establishment of the bodies and their functions'. In all elements of the package there were negative and positive aspects, although 'The negative, from a republican perspective, is that it [the Agreement] does, to an extent, legitimise the British state in Ireland.' McLaughlin pointed out that Republicans could only accept this in the context of a transitional phase itself, that is, the underlying processes of change meant that the Agreement was a time-limited arrangement that allowed for a constitutional political transference of the current political reality of two states in Ireland to an all-Ireland one. However, McLaughlin accepted that Sinn Féin had not received any guarantee from either Government that the Agreement represented a transitional phase, and consoled himself that 'no kind of policy issues would be trundled out by either government to prevent moving towards an all-Ireland scenario'.

Given that the North-South arrangements did not appear to offer the route to an all-Ireland polity, McLaughlin focused on an alternative, longer term, Republican gameplan which was compatible with an unarmed strategy. McLaughlin talked of bridging the difference between the existing electoral percentage, in broad terms between Nationalism and Unionism, with two dynamics. The first was the 'demographic trend of it' which, if left to itself, might ultimately resolve the issue of a majority in favour of all-Ireland structures at some undetermined time in the future. The second issue that could separately bring about the same situation was that 'somewhere in the order of ten to fifteen per cent of the present unionist community could be convinced to opt for an all-Ireland option'. The third aspect, 'which is probably the most realistic, is a combination of the two – that is, continued evidence of an increase, in an electoral sense, in nationalism impacting on a more pragmatic opinion within unionism ... And then people buy into the project.'[34]

This, if adopted, might effectively mean a long-term attempt by Republicans to persuade unionists of the value of Irish unity rather than relying on the British Government to do this for them. It would constitute a seismic compromising of Republican ideology. If any proof were needed that key members of Sinn Féin's leadership were committed to an unarmed strategy then it was surely accepting the final Agreement. But, for many, this could only be confirmed if the question of arms could be resolved.

The Belfast Agreement

Constitutional Issues

The final Belfast Agreement of 10 April 1998, commonly called the 'Good Friday Agreement', represented an historic compromise between Unionism and Nationalism within Northern Ireland; between Unionism and Nationalism within the island of Ireland; and between the sovereign states and nations within the British Isles. Consent underpinned the Agreement. It would be the people of Northern Ireland who would decide the constitutional future of the province.

For the first time since 1937 the Irish Government formally recognised the territorial integrity of the British state when it accepted Northern Ireland as a part of the United Kingdom in an international agreement. It also recognised the right of unionists to be British and the legitimacy of this. The British Government once again affirmed its commitment to legislate for a united Ireland if the Irish people – subject to the consent of the people of Northern Ireland – agreed to this. It also acknowledged the right of nationalists in Northern Ireland to regard themselves as Irish and recognised the legitimacy of this. Both Governments endorsed these commitments in a new British-Irish Agreement that replaced the Anglo-Irish Agreement. They agreed that they would:

> (i) recognise the legitimacy of whatever choice is freely exercised by a majority of the people of Northern Ireland with regard to its status, whether they prefer to continue to support the Union with Great Britain or a sovereign united Ireland

> (ii) recognise that it is for the people of the island of Ireland alone, by agreement between the two parts respectively and without external impediment, to exercise their right of self-determination on the basis of consent, freely and concurrently given, North and South, to bring about a united Ireland, if that is their wish; accepting that this right must be achieved and exercised with and subject to the agreement and consent of a majority of the people of Northern Ireland

> (iii) acknowledge that while a substantial section of the people in

Northern Ireland share the legitimate wish of a majority of the people of the island of Ireland for a united Ireland, the present wish of a majority of the people of Northern Ireland, freely exercised and legitimate, is to maintain the Union and, accordingly, that Northern Ireland's status as part of the United Kingdom reflects and relies upon that wish; and that it would be wrong to make any change in the status of Northern Ireland save with the consent of a majority of its people

(iv) affirm that if, in the future, the people of the island of Ireland exercise their right of self-determination on the basis set out in sections (i) and (ii) above to bring about a united Ireland, it will be a binding obligation on both Governments to introduce and support in the respective Parliaments legislation to give effect to that wish

(v) affirm that whatever choice is freely exercised by a majority of the people of Northern Ireland, the power of the sovereign government with jurisdiction there shall be exercised with rigorous impartiality on behalf of all the people in the diversity of their identities and traditions and shall be founded on the principles of full respect for, and equality of, civil, political, social and cultural rights, of freedom from discrimination for all citizens, and of parity of esteem and of just and equal treatment for the identity, ethos, and aspirations of both communities

(vi) recognise the birthright of all the people of Northern Ireland to identify themselves and be accepted as Irish or British, or both, as they may so choose, and accordingly confirm that their right to hold both British and Irish citizenship is accepted by both Governments and would not be affected by any future change in the status of Northern Ireland.[35]

Annex 'A' to this section of the Agreement contained the draft clauses/schedules for incorporation in British constitutional legislation:

1 (1) It is hereby declared that Northern Ireland in its entirety remains part of the United Kingdom and shall not cease to be so without the consent of a majority of the people of Northern Ireland voting in a poll held for the purposes of this section in accordance with Schedule 1 [see below].

(2) But if the wish expressed by a majority in such a poll is that Northern Ireland should cease to be part of the United Kingdom and form part of a united Ireland, the Secretary of State shall lay before Parliament such proposals to give effect to that wish as may be agreed between Her Majesty's Government in the United Kingdom and the Government of Ireland.

2   The Government of Ireland Act 1920 is repealed; and this Act shall have effect notwithstanding any other previous enactment.[36]

Schedule 1 covered the conditions by which the Secretary of State might direct the holding of a poll if at any time it appeared likely to him or her that a majority of those voting would express a wish that Northern Ireland should cease to be part of the United Kingdom and form part of a united Ireland.[37] The new British constitutional legislation did not remove a British territorial claim to Northern Ireland – there was none to remove. The Agreement did, however, remove the Irish territorial claim to Northern Ireland. At the same time, the new wording for Article 2 reassured Northern nationalists that they retained the right to be a part of the Irish nation; the corollary of this was that Ulster unionists were not to be automatically included in the Irish nation. The new Article 3, while retaining the Nationalist desire to one day establish a united Ireland, enshrined the principle of consent – North and South. It also recognised the existence of Northern Ireland. Effectively, the Irish Constitution would reflect the distinction between nation and state in the island of Ireland:

Article 2

It is the entitlement and birthright of every person born in the island of Ireland, which includes its islands and seas, to be part of the Irish nation. That is also the entitlement of all persons qualified in accordance with law to be citizens of Ireland. Furthermore, the Irish nation cherishes its special affinity with people of Irish ancestry living abroad who share its cultural identity and heritage.

Article 3

1   It is the firm will of the Irish nation, in harmony and friendship, to unite all the people who share the territory of the island of Ireland, in all the diversity of their identities and traditions, recognising that a united Ireland shall be brought about only by peaceful means with the consent of a majority of the people, democratically expressed, in both jurisdictions in the island. Until then, the laws enacted by the Parliament established by this Constitution shall have the like area and extent of application as the laws enacted by the Parliament that existed immediately before the coming into operation of this Constitution.

2   Institutions with executive powers and functions that are shared between those jurisdictions may be established by their respective responsible authorities for stated purposes and may exercise powers and functions in respect of all or any part of the island.[38]

Strand One

Strand One of the Belfast Agreement referred to Democratic Institutions in Northern Ireland. For Unionists this meant the ending of Direct Rule in

Northern Ireland. But the price for this was the institutionalisation of the Nationalist concept of parity of esteem in the Northern Ireland Assembly. Powersharing between Unionists and Nationalists – although 'Others' were recognised as well – meant national equality at the heart of government. The government of Northern Ireland would be bi-communal. The Agreement provided for a 'democratically elected Assembly in Northern Ireland which is inclusive in its membership', capable of exercising executive and legislative authority, and subject to safeguards to protect the rights and interests of all sides of the community.[39] An 108-member Assembly would be elected by proportional representation from existing Westminster constituencies. The Assembly would exercise full legislative and executive authority in respect of those matters currently within the responsibility of the six Northern Ireland Government Departments, with the possibility of taking on responsibility for other matters. The Assembly – operating where appropriate on a cross-community basis – would be the prime source of authority in respect of all devolved responsibilities.[40] The Agreement combined the UUP's concept of proportionality with the SDLP's concept of executive power-sharing and a minority veto. There would be safeguards to ensure that all sections of the community could participate and work together successfully in the operation of the new institutions and that all sections of the community were protected, through the following:

- allocations of Committee Chairs, Ministers and Committee membership in proportion to party strengths

- the European Convention on Human Rights (ECHR) and any Bill of Rights for Northern Ireland supplementing it, which neither the Assembly nor public bodies can infringe, together with a Human Rights Commission

- arrangements to provide that key decisions and legislation are proofed to ensure that they do not infringe the ECHR and any Bill of Rights for Northern Ireland

- arrangements to ensure key decisions are taken on a cross-community basis

    – either parallel consent, i.e. a majority of those members present and voting, including a majority of the unionist or nationalist designations present and voting

    – or, a weighted majority (sixty per cent) of members present and voting, including at least forty per cent of each of the nationalist and unionist delegations present and voting.

Key decisions requiring cross-community support will be designated in advance, including the election of the Chair of the Assembly, the First Minister and Deputy First Minister, standing orders and budget allocations. In other cases such decisions could be triggered by a petition of concern brought by a significant minority of Assembly members (30/108).

- an Equality Commission to monitor a statutory obligation to promote equality of opportunity in specified areas and parity of esteem between the two main communities, and to investigate individual complaints against public bodies.[41]

All of this was designed to reassure Nationalists that there would never be a return to majority rule and that the nationalist community would never experience the discrimination it had suffered under the old Stormont system. Nationalist consent would be required at every level of the Assembly. It also meant, of course, that Unionists would have a veto as well.

With regard to the Operation of the Assembly, members of the Assembly would register a disignation of identity – Nationalist, Unionist or Other – for the purposes of measuring cross-community support in Assembly votes under the relevant provisions.[42] The Chair and Deputy Chair of the Assembly would be elected on a cross-community basis.[43] Power-sharing would be enshrined at Cabinet level. The First Minister and Deputy First Minister, neither of whom would be subserviant to one another, would be jointly elected into office by the Assembly voting on a cross-community basis; following their election, the posts of Ministers would be allocated to parties on the basis of the d'Hondt system by reference to the number of seats each party had in the Assembly.[44]

These Ministers would 'constitute an Executive Committee', effectively a power-sharing Cabinet, which would be convened, and presided over, by the First Minister and Deputy First Minister, whose duties would include, *inter alia*, dealing with and co-ordinating the work of the Executive Committee and the response of the Northern Ireland administration to external relationships. The Executive Committee would provide a forum for the discussion of, and agreement on, issues which cut across the responsibilities of two or more Ministers, for prioritising executive and legislative proposals and for recommending a common position where necessary, for example in external relationships.

As a condition of appointment, Ministers would affirm the terms of a Pledge of Office undertaking to discharge effectively and in good faith all the responsibilities attaching to their office. An individual might be removed from office following a decision of the Assembly taken on a cross-community basis, if he or she lost the confidence of the Assembly, voting on a cross-community basis, for failure to meet his or her responsibilities, including those set out in the Pledge of Office. Those who 'hold office should use only democratic, non-violent means, and those who do not should be excluded or removed from office under these provisions'. The interpretation of this section was to be controversial.[45]

In terms of Relations with Other Institutions, arrangements were to be made to represent the Assembly as a whole, at Summit level and in dealings with other institutions, and 'will be such as to ensure cross-community involvement' – both Unionists and Nationalists would have to be present at North-South or East-West meetings where they would have a veto. The Westminster Parliament 'whose power to make legislation for Northern Ireland would remain unaffected' meant that the British retained sovereignty over Northern Ireland.[46]

Strand Two, the North-South Ministerial Council
In Strand Two, the Belfast Agreement established an intergovernmental confederal relationship between Northern Ireland and the Republic of Ireland. Dail Éireann and the Northern Ireland Assembly would control the nature and pace of North-South relations. The North-South Ministerial Council would have no executive power itself. It would have a consultative role providing a forum where a Council of Ministers from Northern Ireland and the Republic would meet, in which Unionists – and Nationalists – would have a veto over decision taking. There was also to be cross-community representation at such meetings. Unionists had secured agreement that the source of authority in North-South relations would originate from the Northern Ireland Assembly. While the North-South Council would be initially established by legislation at Westminster and in Dublin, the Northern Ireland Assembly would decide in what areas implementation bodies would be subsequently established.

The fact that the Assembly would have to accept that there would be cross-border implementation bodies reassured Northern Nationalists and the Irish Government that the Council would have a credible function. The Council also gave Northern Nationalists a separate, institutional expression of their identity. With the Council and the Northern Ireland Assembly mutually dependent on each other for their existence, Unionists and Nationalists knew that wrecking one institution would bring the other down. And, comforting for Unionists, was the removal of any overseeing British-Irish mechanism which could, conceivably, impose joint authority in the event of the Council's collapse.

The Agreement itself stated that a North-South Ministerial Council was to bring together those with executive responsibilities in Northern Ireland and the Irish Government, to develop consultation, co-operation and action within the island of Ireland – including through implementation on an all-island and cross-border basis – on matters of mutual interest within the competence of the administrations, North and South.[47] The purpose of the Council was:

- to exchange information, discuss and consult with a view to co-operating on matters of mutual interest within the competence of both Administrations, North and South

- to use best endeavours to reach agreement on the adoption of common policies in areas where there is a mutual cross-border and all-island benefit, and which are within the competence of both Administrations, North and South, making determined efforts to overcome any disagreements

- to take decisions by agreement on policies for implementation separately in each jurisdiction, in relevant meaningful areas within the competence of both administrations, North and South

- to take decisions by agreement on policies and action at an all-island and cross-border level to be implemented by the bodies to be established ...[48]

Unionists were satisfied that Northern Ireland Ministers were to be accountable to the Northern Ireland Assembly alone and not to the North-South Council. The Agreement stated that each side was to be in a position to take decisions in the Council within the 'defined authority of those attending', through the arrangements in place for co-ordination of executive functions within each jurisdiction. Each side was to 'remain accountable to the Assembly and Oireachtas respectively, whose approval, through the arrangements in place on either side, would be required for decisions beyond the defined authority of those attending'.[49]

During a transitional period between elections to the Assembly and the transfer of power to it, representatives of a Northern Ireland transitional Administration and the Irish Government, operating in the North-South Council, 'will undertake a work programme, in consultation with the British Government, covering at least 12 subject areas, with a view to identifying and agreeing by 31 October 1998 areas where co-operation and implementation for mutual benefit will take place'.[50] As part of the work programme, the Council would identify and agree at least 6 matters for co-operation and implementation in each of the following categories:

- Matters where existing bodies will be the appropriate mechanisms for co-operation in each separate jurisdiction

- Matters where the co-operation will take place through agreed implementation bodies on a cross-border or all-island level.[51]

The implementation bodies were to have a clear operational remit. They would implement, on an all-island and cross-border basis, policies agreed in the Council.[52] Any further development of these arrangements were to be by agreement in the Council and with the specific endorsement of the Northern Ireland Assembly and the Oireachtas, subject to the extent of the competences and responsibility of the two administrations.[53] It was 'understood that the North-South Ministerial Council and the Northern Ireland Assembly are mutually inter-dependent, and that one cannot successfully function without the other'.[54] The Northern Ireland Assembly and the Oireachtas were also to consider developing a joint parliamentary forum,[55] and an independent consultative forum appointed by the two administrations, representative of civil society.[56] The Annex to Strand Two stated that:

Areas for North–South co-operation and implementation may include the following:

- Agriculture – animal and plant health
- Education – teacher qualifications and exchanges
- Transport – strategic transport planning
- Environment – environmental protection, pollution, water quality, and waste management
- Waterways – inland waterways
- Social Security/Social Welfare – entitlements of cross-border workers and fraud control
- Tourism – promotion, marketing, research, and product development
- Relevant EU programmes and their successors
- Inland fisheries
- Aquaculture and marine matters
- Health: accident and emergency services and other related cross-border issues
- Urban and rural development.[57]

Strand Three, the British–Irish Council

In Strand Three, a confederal East–West relationship symmetrical to the North–South relationship was created. A consultative British–Irish Council would be created which included two sovereign states, all devolved national and regional entities within the United Kingdom – whatever their degree of autonomy – and those dependencies of the Crown within the British Isles. This was a unique combination of political entities which could co-operate in any bi-lateral or multi-lateral combination within their degree of authority. For example, an East–West implementation body could be established between the Irish Government, the Scottish Parliament and the Welsh Assembly in any particular area of mutual interest. The essential difference between the British–Irish Council and the North–South Ministerial Council was one of priority – the main devolved institutions in Scotland and Wales were still in the process of establishment.

The Agreement stated that the British–Irish Council was to be established under a new British–Irish Agreement to 'promote the harmonious and mutually beneficial development of the totality of relationships among the peoples of these islands'.[58] Membership of the British–Irish Council would comprise representatives of the British and Irish Governments, devolved institutions in Northern Ireland, Scotland and Wales, when established, and, if appropriate, elsewhere in the United Kingdom, together with representatives of the Isle of Man and the Channel Islands.[59] The Council would meet twice a year at Summit level, with other meetings on sectoral issues comprising appropriate representatives of the relevant members to be convened as necessary.[60] Representatives of members would operate in accordance with whatever procedures for democratic authority and accountability were in force in their respective elected institutions. The British–Irish Council would exchange information, discuss, consult and use best endeavours to reach agreement and co-operate on matters of mutual interest within the competence of the relevant Administrations.

Suitable issues for early discussion in the Council could include: transport links; agricultural issues, environmental issues; cultural issues; health issues; education issues, and approaches to European Union issues. Suitable arrangements would be made for practical co-operation on agreed policies. It would be open to the Council to agree common policies or common actions. Individual members might opt not to participate in such common policies and common action.[61] The British–Irish Council would normally operate by consensus. In relation to decisions on common policies or common actions, including their means of implementation, it would operate by agreement of all members participating in such policies or actions. The members of the Council, on a basis to be agreed between them, would provide such financial support as it might require. A secretariat for the Council would be provided by the British and Irish Governments in co-ordination with officials of each of the other members.[62]

In addition to the structures provided for under the Agreement, it would be open to two or more members to develop bilateral or multilateral arrangements between them. Such arrangements could include, subject to the agreement of the members concerned, mechanisms to enable consultation, co-operation and joint decision-making on matters of mutual interest; and mechanisms to implement any joint decisions they might reach. These arrangements would not require the prior approval of the Council as a whole and would operate independently of it.[63] The elected institutions of the members would be encouraged to develop interparliamentary links, perhaps building on the existing British–Irish Interparliamentary Body.[64] The full membership of the Council would keep under review the workings of the Council including a formal published review at an appropriate time after the Agreement came into effect and would contribute as appropriate to any review of the overall political agreement arising from the multi-party negotiations.[65]

Strand Three, the British–Irish Intergovernmental Conference
Strand Three of the Belfast Agreement also democratised the Intergovernmental Conference. Neither the British nor the Irish Governments were prepared to terminate the consultative process which had, from their perspective, successfully managed British–Irish relations

since 1985. Northern Nationalists were, in addition, reluctant to see a dilution of what they considered the Irish Government's special interest in Northern Ireland. For Unionists, Ministers from the new Northern Ireland Assembly would have access to British-Irish discussions including those relating to non-devolved matters in the new Intergovernmental Conference. But the new Intergovernmental Conference would not have an input into devolved matters relating to the Northern Ireland Assembly; discussions here would be between the Northern Ireland Administration and the Irish Government in the North-South Ministerial Council.

The Belfast Agreement thus established a new British-Irish Agreement, dealing with the totality of relationships, creating a new standing British-Irish Intergovernmental Conference, which would subsume both the Anglo-Irish Intergovernmental Council and the Intergovernmental Conference established under the 1985 Anglo-Irish Agreement.[66] The Conference would bring together the British and Irish Governments to promote bilateral co-operation at all levels on all matters of mutual interest within the competence of both Governments. It would meet as required at Summit level. Otherwise, Governments would be represented by the appropriate Ministers. Advisers, including police and security advisers, would attend as appropriate. All decisions would be by agreement between both Governments. The Governments would make determined efforts to resolve disagreements between them; but there 'will be no derogation from sovereignty of either Government'.[67]

In 'recognition of the Irish Government's special interest in Northern Ireland and of the extent to which issues of mutual concern arise in relation to Northern Ireland', there would be regular and frequent meetings of the Conference concerned with non-devolved Northern Ireland matters, on which the Irish Government might put forward views and proposals. These meetings, to be co-chaired by the Irish Minister for Foreign Affairs and the Secretary of State for Northern Ireland, would also deal with all-island and cross-border co-operation on non-devolved issues.[68] Co-operation within the framework of the Conference would include facilitation of co-operation in security matters; would address, in particular, the areas of rights, justice, prisons and policing in Northern Ireland – unless and until responsibility was devolved to a Northern Ireland administration – and would intensify co-operation between the two Governments on the all-island or cross border aspects of these matters. Relevant executive members of the Northern Ireland Administration 'will be involved in meetings of the Conference', and in reviews to discuss non-devolved Northern Ireland matters.

The Conference would keep under review the workings of the new British-Irish Agreement and the machinery and institutions established under it. Representatives of the Northern Ireland Administration would be invited to express views to the Conference in this context. The Conference would contribute as appropriate to any review of the overall political agreement arising from the multi-party negotiations but 'will have no power to override the democratic arrangements set up by this Agreement'.[69]

Rights and Safeguards

The aim of the second part of the Agreement was to institutionalise a structure of rights with which Nationalists could be reassured that their national identity was recognised in Northern Ireland and with which moderate Unionists could identify as practiced elsewhere in the democratic world to safeguard the rights of national minorities. The Agreement highlighted Rights, Safeguards and Equality of Opportunity; the first part of this section dealt with Human Rights. The parties to the Agreement affirmed their commitment to the 'mutual respect, the civil rights and the religious liberties of everyone in the community'. Against the background of the recent history of communal conflict, the parties affirmed in particular:

- the right of free political thought

- the right to freedom and expression of religion

- the right to pursue democratically national and political aspirations

- the right to seek constitutional change by peaceful and legitimate means

- the right to freely choose one's place of residence

- the right to equal opportunity in all social and economic activity, regardless of class, creed, disability, gender or ethnicity

- the right to freedom from sectarian harassment

- the right of women to full and equal political participation.[70]

In regard to United Kingdom legislation the British Government would complete the incorporation into Northern Ireland law of the European Convention on Human Rights, with direct access to the courts, and remedies for breach of the Convention, including the power for the courts to overrule Assembly legislation on grounds of inconsistency.[71] Subject to the outcome of public consultation underway, the British Government intended, as a particular priority, the creation of a statutory obligation on public authorities in Northern Ireland to carry out all their functions with due regard to the need to promote equality of opportunity in relation to religion and political opinion; gender; race; disability; age; marital status; dependants; and sexual orientation. Public bodies would be required to draw up statutory schemes showing how they would implement this obligation. Such schemes would cover arrangements for policy appraisal, public consultation, public access to services, monitoring and timetables.[72]

A new Northern Ireland Human Rights Commission would be invited to consult and advise on the scope for defining, in Westminster legislation, rights supplementary to those in the ECHR to reflect the particular circumstances of Northern Ireland, and drawing as appropriate on international instruments and experience. These additional rights were to reflect the principles of mutual respect for the identity, ethos and parity of esteem of both communities. They would, taken together with the ECHR, constitute a Bill of Rights for Northern Ireland. Among the issues for consideration by the Commission would be:

- the formulation of a general obligation on government and public bodies fully to respect, on the basis of equality of treatment, the identity and ethos of both communities in Northern Ireland

- a clear formulation of the rights not to be discriminated against and to equality of opportunity in both the public and private sectors.[73]

Regarding new institutions in Northern Ireland, the Northern Ireland Human Rights Commission, established by Westminster legislation and independent of government, would review the adequacy and effectiveness of laws and practices, making recommendations to government as necessary; providing information on, and promoting awareness of, human rights; considering draft legislation referred to them by the new Assembly; and, in appropriate cases, bringing court proceedings or providing assistance to individuals doing so.[74]

The British Government also intended to create a new statutory Equality Commission to replace the Fair Employment Commission, the Equal Opportunities Commission (NI), the Commission for Racial Equality (NI) and the Disability Council. Such a unified Commission would advise on, and would investigate, complaints of default. It would be up to the Northern Ireland Assembly to consider bringing together its responsibilities for these matters into a 'dedicated' Department of Equality. These improvements would build on existing protections in Westminster legislation in respect of the judiciary, the system of justice and policing.[75]

Comparable steps by the Irish Government would see it strengthen the protection of human rights in its jurisdiction. The Irish Government, taking account of the work of an All-Party Oireachtas Committee on the Constitution and the Report of the Constitution Review Group, would bring forward measures to strengthen and underpin the constitutional protection of human rights. These proposals would draw on the ECHR and other international legal instruments and would ensure at least an equivalent level of protection of human rights as would pertain in Northern Ireland. In addition, the Irish Government would:

- establish a Human Rights Commission with a mandate and remit equivalent to that within Northern Ireland

- proceed with arrangements as quickly as possible to ratify the Council of Europe Framework Convention on National Minorities (already ratified by the UK)

- implement enhanced employment equality legislation

- introduce equal status legislation

- continue to take further active steps to demonstrate its respect for the different traditions in the island of Ireland.[76]

It was also envisaged that there would be a joint committee of representatives of the two Human Rights Commissions, North and South, as a forum for consideration of human rights issues in the island of Ireland. The joint committee would consider the possibility of establishing a charter, open to signature by all democratic political parties, reflecting and endorsing agreed measures for the protection of the fundamental rights of everyone living in the island of Ireland.[77]

In terms of economic, social and cultural issues, the British Government committed itself to pursue broad policies for sustained economic growth and stability in Northern Ireland, and to promote social inclusion, including in particular community development and the advancement of women in public life.[78] The British Government also committed itself to make rapid progress with a new regional development strategy for Northern Ireland; a new economic development strategy for Northern Ireland; and measures on employment equality.[79] The Agreement recognised the importance of respect, understanding and tolerance in relation to linguistic diversity, including in Northern Ireland, the Irish language, Ulster-Scots, and the languages of the various ethnic communities. Although Irish was not to become an official language in Northern Ireland, the British Government paid particular attention to it, as it was considering signing the Council of Europe Charter for Regional or Minority Languages. Where appropriate and where people so desired it the British Government would:

- take resolute action to promote the language

- facilitate the use of the language in speech and writing in public and private life, where there is appropriate demand

- seek to remove, where possible, restrictions which would discourage or work against the maintenance or development of the language

- make provision for liaising with the Irish language community, representing their views to public authorities and investigating complaints

- place a statutory duty on the Department of Education for Northern Ireland to encourage and facilitate Irish-medium education in line with current provision for integrated education

- explore urgently with the relevant British authorities, and in cooperation with the Irish broadcasting authorities, the scope for achieving more widespread availability of Teilifís na Gaelige [the Republic's Irish language television station] in Northern Ireland

• seek more effective ways to encourage and provide financial support for the Irish language film and television production in Northern Ireland

• encourage the parties to secure agreement that this commitment will be sustained by a new Assembly in a way which takes account of the desires and sensitivities of the community.[80]

The Agreement also acknowledged the sensitivity of the use of symbols and emblems for public purposes, and the need, in creating the new institutions, to ensure that such symbols and emblems were used in a manner which promoted mutual respect rather than division. Arrangements would be made to monitor this issue and consider what action might be required.[81]

Decommissioning; Security; Policing and Justice; Prisoners
The most ambiguous area of the Belfast Agreement concerned decommissioning. The Agreement recalled the Procedural Motion adopted in September 1997, 'that the resolution of the decommissioning issue is an indispensable part of the process of negotiation', as well as the provisions of Strand One, linking Executive membership to a commitment to peaceful and democratic means. Decommissioning, therefore, remained an 'indispensable part of this agreement'. Noting the progress made by the Independent International Commission on Decommissioning and the Governments in developing schemes which represented a workable basis for achieving the decommissioning of illegally-held arms in the possession of paramilitary groups, the Agreement stated:

> All participants reaffirm their commitment to the total disarmament of all paramilitary organisations. They also confirm their intention to continue to work constructively and in good faith with the Independent Commission on Decommissioning, and to use any influence they may have, to achieve the decommissioning of all paramilitary arms within two years following endorsement in referendums North and South of the agreement and in the context of the implementation of the overall settlement.

The Independent Commission would monitor, review and verify progress on the decommissioning of illegal arms, and would report to both Governments at regular intervals. Both Governments were to take all necessary steps to facilitate the decommissioning process.[82] But, did any of this place an obligation on paramilitaries, particularly the PIRA, to disarm? Sinn Féin, regarding itself as a separate entity, did not believe that it did. In this, it was supported by some members of the UUP talks team who believed that this section allowed what they termed 'Sinn Féin-IRA' to wriggle out of any commitment to decommissioning by claiming that they were separate organisations; others, such as David Trimble, regarded the PIRA and Sinn Féin as inextricably linked, a precedent set by the latter's entry into, and expulsion from, the negotiations on the basis of the PIRA ceasefire and the breaches thereof. Trimble saw PIRA decommissioning as the test of a commitment to peaceful and democratic means and entry into the Northern Ireland Executive.

To encourage paramilitaries, and particularly the Republican Movement, to conclude that there was no need for a return to armed struggle, the Agreement noted that the development of a 'peaceful environment on the basis of this Agreement can and should mean a normalisation of security arrangements and practices'.[83] In referring to what Republicans would term demilitarisation, the Agreement committed the British Government to make progress towards the objective of a return as soon as possible to 'normal' security arrangements in Northern Ireland, although this was, crucially, to be 'consistent with the level of threat'. Given this, the British Government would publish an overall strategy, dealing with:

- the reduction of the numbers and role of the Armed Forces deployed in Northern Ireland to levels compatible with a normal peaceful society

- the removal of security installations

- the removal of emergency powers in Northern Ireland

- other measures appropriate to and compatible with a normal peaceful society.[84]

The Secretary of State was to consult regularly on progress toward this with the Irish Government and the political parties, as appropriate. The British Government would consult on firearms regulation while the Irish Government would initiate a wide-ranging review of their own emergency legislation – the Offences Against the State Acts 1939-85 – with a view to both reforming and dispensing with those elements no longer required as circumstances permitted.[85]

Referring to policing, the Agreement stated that the talks participants recognised that it was a 'central issue in any society'. They equally recognised that Northern Ireland's history of deep divisions had made it highly emotive, with great hurt suffered and sacrifices made by many individuals, including those in the RUC and other public servants. The Agreement sought the opportunity for a new beginning to policing in Northern Ireland, with a police service capable of attracting and sustaining support from the community as a whole. It argued that there was now a unique opportunity to bring about a new political dispensation which would recognise the full and equal legitimacy and worth of the identities, senses of allegiance and ethos of all sections of the community in Northern Ireland. This could inform and underpin the development of a police service representative in terms of the make-up of the community as a whole and which, in the absence of threats which would require otherwise, should be routinely unarmed.[86]

To this end, an independent Commission would be established to make recommendations for future policing arrangements in Northern Ireland. The Commission would have expert and international representation among its membership and would be asked to consult widely and to report no later than the summer of 1999.[87] The Agreement also stated that the criminal justice system in Northern Ireland should be designed to:

- deliver a fair and impartial system of justice to the community

- be responsive to the community's concerns, and encourage community involvement where appropriate

- have the confidence of all parts of the community

- deliver justice efficiently and effectively.[88]

There would thus be a parallel wide-ranging review of criminal justice, to be carried out by the British Government.[89]

Finally, in one of the most controversial sections of the Agreement, the Governments compensated Sinn Féin for their constitutional disappointments by promising to put in place mechanisms to provide for an accelerated programme for the release of prisoners, including prisoners transferred from Great Britain, those who had been convicted of scheduled – terrorist – offences in Northern Ireland or, in the case of those sentenced outside Northern Ireland, similar offences, referred to as 'qualifying prisoners'. Any such arrangements would protect the rights of individual prisoners under national and international law. Prisoners affiliated to organisations which had not established or were not maintaining a complete and unequivocal ceasefire would not benefit from the arrangements. The situation in this regard would be kept under review.[90]

The key addition to this section, from the Mitchell Document, was a time frame for the releases. Both Governments would complete a review process within a fixed time frame and set prospective release dates for all qualifying prisoners. The review process would provide for the advance of the release dates for prisoners while allowing account to be taken of the seriousness of the offences for which the person was convicted and the need to protect the community. In addition, the intention would be that, should the circumstances allow it, 'any qualifying prisoners who remained in custody two years after the commencement of the scheme would be released at that point.'[91]

Hearts and Minds

Following the media euphoria and the relief of the talks participants at concluding an agreement, thoughts turned to the impending referenda, in Northern Ireland on the Belfast Agreement, and in the Republic on the proposed constitutional changes contained therein. A copy of the Agreement was posted to every home in Northern Ireland. Initially, the general opinion in most circles was that the Republican grassroots might have some difficulty in accepting the historic compromising of traditional goals. The actions of the Governments in trying to support the Sinn Féin leadership's attempts to sell the deal were to have profoundly negative effects in the unionist community. The real battle for hearts and minds turned out to be in the Protestant community, the majority of whom were simply appalled at the release of what they regarded as terrorists – many convicted of multiple murders – back into the community. This was made worse with the prospect of leading Sinn Féin members – who were considered by the unionist community to have been the 'godfathers' organising the killing of the previous three decades – entering Northern Ireland's government.

Coupled with considerable doubt existing over the decommissioning of paramilitary weapons was concern for the future of the RUC: at the end of the day, although there had been an increase in support for the activities of Loyalist paramilitaries, for many Protestants the violence of the Troubles had been simply a case of right against wrong, of law and order on the one hand and terrorism on the other. Unlike Sunningdale, the constitutional issues were not paramount; the emotional issues were, and these related to prisoners, terrorists entering government without decommissioning, and the future of the forces of law and order – many of whose members had lost their lives at the hands of those about to be set free.

But at first attention focused on the Republican Movement. Sinn Féin put off making a conclusive response to the Agreement for several weeks. However, positive reports soon confirmed that the PIRA had changed 'general army orders' to allow Sinn Féin representatives to take their seats in a Northern Ireland Assembly. Changes to these orders, which formed the PIRA's constitution and rulebook, could only be taken at general army conventions. The PIRA constitution stated that such a convention 'shall be the supreme army authority'. News of the decision came a week before Sinn Féin held its special Ard Fheis on the Agreement.[92] In the run up to the Ard Fheis, as a confidence-building measure, the Irish Government released nine PIRA prisoners.

At the Ard Fheis, Martin McGuinness told the delegates that the Good Friday Agreement had weakened the Union because of a clause limiting its life to the will of a majority in the Six Counties – ignoring that this had been British Government policy since 1973. He accepted that the Agreement did not go as far as most nationalists wished but it was the basis for advancement. The Republican analysis was at the heart of Irish politics as never before. Britain's role in the Union was now somewhat akin to one partner saying the relationship was over but that he or she was willing to wait 'until the children have grown up'. There was now 'no absolute commitment, no raft of parliamentary Acts to back up an absolute claim, but only an agreement to stay until the majority decides otherwise. This is a long way from being as British as Finchley.'

The downside involved the proposed inclusion of the consent clause in the Irish Constitution and the definition of the nation in terms of its people rather than its territory. However, on a more positive note, McGuinness drew the delegates' attention to the Irish constitutional amendments which established North–South bodies. Although the Union had been weakened, partition remained. But this too could be weakened by the dynamic operation of all-Ireland structures which were part of the Agreement and which Unionists had fought 'tooth and nail to prevent'. From the beginning, explained McGuinness, Sinn Féin knew that the talks parameters laid down by the two Governments meant that Irish unity would not come out of this phase of the negotiations. So the party set itself the task of 'weakening the British link while defending the rights of Irish men and women and it is in this context that we must honestly measure the gains and losses'.[93]

In the event, there was a huge majority in favour of Sinn Féin's successful candidates taking their seats in a Northern Ireland Assembly. The motion advocating the move, submitted by the party's Ard Chomhairle, involved a change to Sinn Féin's constitution and required a two-thirds majority; 331 of the 350 delegates voted to support it.[94] The delegates placed their trust in the Sinn Féin leadership, a leadership which had the pedigree of leading the Republican Movement in war and, now, in relative peace. Widespread briefings of PIRA members had taken place since the Agreement. These indicated that the Agreement was 'better than expected'; that the Northern Ireland Assembly was part of 'transitional' arrangements; and that there would be no further point in continued violence, because within '10 to 15 years' there would be significant 'demographic' change in the North's population to provide for a nationalist majority in favour of unity. This message, reinforced by the release of all prisoners within two years, meant that the PIRA was prepared to accept the Agreement. It was understood that Sinn Féin negotiators at the talks had rejected a longer period for prisoner releases. The offer of a two-year release deadline had been communicated to PIRA prisoners at the Maze and was immediately accepted.[95] The role of the prisoners in supporting the Peace Process and the emotional pull of getting their comrades home was a decisive factor in convincing members of the Republican Movement to support the Agreement.

From the UUP, John Taylor welcomed Sinn Féin's decision. He claimed that, after 77 years, Sinn Féin had finally faced up to reality. The party now recognised that Northern Ireland remained part of the United Kingdom and that its status could not be changed without the consent of the people of Northern Ireland. From the opposite corner of Unionism, the DUP's Deputy Leader, Peter Robinson, claimed that it should now be clear to all unionists that the Agreement was a 'vehicle to trundle us into a united Ireland'.[96] This revealed the fundamental schism at the heart of Unionist politics. David Trimble claimed that the people crying treachery over the Agreement had no alternative strategy except maintaining the *status quo*, which meant the continuation of the Anglo-Irish Agreement. They were the

'No' voices who 'deserted the battlefield'.

The UUP leader claimed that he had kept all the promises made at the start of the talks, such as the ending of the Republic's territorial claim and a recognition of the territorial integrity of the United Kingdom. It was important to distinguish between the parts of the Agreement which related to structures and those which related to policies. The structures, such as the Assembly and the British-Irish Council, were 'as good as they could be'. The Union was safe: 'Dublin cannot dictate to us.' Trimble argued that unionists were not bound to accept the policies the British Government was pursuing: 'They are not good. By policies I mean the so-called equality agenda, policing, prisoners, and so on.' The UUP would press the Government for more changes on these; but it 'must be obvious that we are in a better position to achieve change in those policies within the new structures than without them'.[97]

On the other hand, Ian Paisley claimed that the deal put together by Trimble and Adams – what he termed the 'Trimble-Adams' pact – was 'worse than the Anglo-Irish Agreement, more treacherous than the Framework Document and poses far greater dangers to the Union than the Sunningdale Agreement ever did. Under the deal, the Union is weakened. It is nothing short of deception and lies to portray this deal as strengthening the Union. Unionists know that any deal so enthusiastically endorsed by the Dublin Government and the SDLP is something which represents a dilution and diminution of the Union.'[98] On 5 May, Unionists opposed to the Agreement officially launched their campaign with the slogan 'It's Right to Say No.' Calling themselves the United Unionists, their campaign composed the DUP, the UKUP and dissident UUP MPs Willie Ross and Willie Thompson. The former UUP leader, Lord Molyneaux, also launched an attack on the Agreement from the House of Lords, warning that the PIRA's resistance to decommissioning threatened a 'nightmare situation' of elected politicians 'sitting at the table side by side with terrorists with guns on the table, under the table or outside the door'.[99]

Peter Robinson outlined the strategy of the United Unionists. He was increasingly confident that a majority of unionists would vote No in the referendum. Once this was achieved, the plan was to elect as many anti-Agreement Unionists as possible to the Assembly, where they could destroy the process from within. They would attempt to frustrate the establishment of cross-border bodies; would vote against Sinn Féin entering government; and would oppose the release of prisoners. Robinson thought that Nationalists had provided the anti-Agreement Unionists with the weapon to do this: 'John Hume has been too clever by half. By insisting on an Assembly with a nationalist veto, he has also provided an Assembly with a unionist veto. He may regret that.' Robinson predicted that the Agreement would inevitably collapse and that 'for the first time in generations the thrust of government policy will have to be: "How can we accommodate unionists?"'

Robinson   denied   that   anti-Agreement   Unionists   were   acting irresponsibly. It was the Yes campaign who was acting immorally. They supported the establishment of a 'rigged and undemocratic' Assembly not based on majoritarian principles. They had agreed to cross-border bodies, which allowed a 'hostile foreign state' a growing role in Northern Ireland's internal affairs. They were proposing to sit 'cheek-to-cheek with Adams and McGuinness in government' while the PIRA remained 'armed to the teeth'. They would allow the release of 'unrepentant' prisoners and the destruction of a police force, which had valiantly upheld law and order. The only way for Adams and McGuinness to be removed from office – because of the need for cross-community support – was if they were 'found with a smoking gun in their hand'. Furthermore, Robinson believed that the PIRA would resume its campaign. He found it 'unbelievable' that the UUP leaders who opposed the Sunningdale Agreement would support the Belfast Agreement: 'I stood shoulder to shoulder with David Trimble and John Taylor back then. They told us that agreement was bad for the Union because it put Gerry Fitt in government. Now they tell us this agreement strengthens the Union when it puts Gerry Adams in government.'

Robinson rejected the arguments of the 32-County Sovereignty Committee and Republican Sinn Féin that the Belfast Agreement copper-fastened partition: 'Those people simply want a united Ireland today. They are not prepared to wait even a few months like the Sinn Féin leadership.' The repeal of the Government of Ireland Act 1920 meant that Northern Ireland was no longer an integral part of the United Kingdom: 'The mooring ropes have been loosened and we have been set adrift and pushed towards a united Ireland.'[100]

By now it was becoming clear that the tide of opinion within the unionist community was moving against the Agreement. Some of this had been inflicted by the UUP itself. Soon after the conclusion of negotiations at Stormont, David Trimble had flown to a long-standing engagement in the United States; John Taylor returned to his political commitments in Europe; and Ken Maginnis – who had not been an official member of the talks team anyway – left for a holiday in Cyprus. Effectively, this meant that the UUP's big hitters were out of the country in the opening stages of the referendum campaign. Senior party organisers decided to concentrate on the Assembly rather than the referendum campaign. This proved to be a major blunder. In such an environment, the anti-Agreement Unionists had virtually a free run. Things went from bad to worse when the UUP found that it had lost nearly all its potential campaign staff. Younger members of the talks team – such as Peter King and Peter Weir – joined the No camp. The UUP found that it could not get party workers to put up posters or canvass in support of the Agreement.[101]

Only now did it become obvious to the British Government that the main area of slippage was in the unionist community. On 16 April, an *Irish Times* opinion poll had found that, even in the euphoria generated by the events of Good Friday, unionists were less enthusiastic than nationalists about the

Agreement. Then, with five weeks to go to polling day, there was 90 per cent support for the Agreement among Catholics. There was a more muted 62 per cent support in the Protestant community. Among supporters of the UUP, 70 per cent declared their intention of casting a Yes vote. But by the middle of May, a rather different picture was emerging. As expected, the Catholic vote had held up, with 87 per cent supporting the Agreement. But there had been a substantial decline in Protestant support for a Yes vote, to 36 per cent. The No vote among Protestants had risen from 22 per cent following Good Friday, to 40 per cent. The proportion of Protestant 'don't knows' had risen from 16 to 24 per cent.

Among UUP supporters, the Yes vote had fallen 18 points to 52 per cent; the No vote had risen slightly, from 16 per cent to 19 per cent; but the 'don't knows' had risen from 14 to 30 per cent. The DUP had also solidified opposition to the Agreement among its own supporters. Immediately after Good Friday, 30 per cent of DUP supporters had been prepared to support the Agreement. This had now collapsed to 3 per cent. The release of prisoners was the main reason for not supporting the Agreement. It was cited by 45 per cent of No voters, including 50 per cent of UUP supporters voting No, as the primary reason for voting against the Agreement. Next, at 18 per cent, was 'The beginning of a move towards a united Ireland'.[102]

Two events in particular revolted many unionist voters. At the Sinn Féin Ard Fheis, a number of PIRA prisoners, who had been transferred from England to Irish prisons, were allowed to attend in order to demonstrate their support for the Peace Process. This was the notorious Balcombe Street gang, which had served over twenty years in English prisons. The sight of the prisoners on the main platform and the rapturous reception from the audience had all the earmarks of a victory rally. Their temporary release had been sanctioned by both the Irish and British Governments. It had a devastating impact on unionist opinion. This was compounded when the UDP held a rally in Belfast in support of the Agreement. On this occasion many unionists were alienated by the sight of Loyalist prisoners, in particular the killer Michael Stone, at the gathering. These two instances, more than any other, symbolised the amoral nature of a deal which would release terrorists back into the community. A rather pathetic report on victims of the Troubles, under the chairmanship of Sir Kenneth Bloomfield and commissioned by the British Government, seemed to confirm that they were the forgotten casualties of the conflict.

The United Unionists now, rather cleverly, turned sufficient consensus on its heads. After decades insisting that the majority in Northern Ireland – effectively the unionist population – should decide the constitutional future of Northern Ireland, anti-Agreement Unionists, such as Ian Paisley, now claimed that a Yes vote would be invalid unless a majority of unionists and nationalists *separately* voted in favour of the Agreement. This view was widely accepted in government as well. Tony Blair now moved into overdrive to reassure the unionist community. He returned to Northern Ireland and claimed that the British Government would 'clean up' any dissident groups who tried to wreck the Agreement through violence. Furthermore, if the Agreement were carried by a Yes vote, then the British Government would have a mandate to bring this into effect. The Prime Minister insisted that there had to be PIRA decommissioning within the two-year timeframe laid down in the Agreement. It had been made clear to Republicans that 'unless they give up violence for good, and decommissioning is a part of it, then the provisions are there in the Agreement that ensure they are excluded or removed from office. We can't have a situation where people who have not given up the path of violence are taking office in the Northern Ireland Government.'

Blair also reassured unionists that the RUC was not to be disbanded. He wanted to create a police service that was representative of both communities. He rubbished claims by anti-Agreement Unionists that former paramilitaries would end up as part of local police units. He understood how people were offended by early prisoner releases. But he reassured unionists that prisoners would be released from jails on licence only if both the individuals and their organisations had given up violence.[103] In attempting to clarify whether the terms and spirit of the Agreement were being met and whether violence had genuinely been given up for good, Blair said a range of factors had to be taken into account:

> ... first and foremost, a clear and unequivocal commitment that there is an end to violence for good on the part of republicans and loyalists alike, and that the so-called war is finished, done with, gone; that, as the Agreement says, non-violence and exclusively peaceful and democratic means are the only means to be used; that again, as the Agreement expressly states, the ceasefires are indeed complete and unequivocal: an end to bombings, killings and beatings, claimed or unclaimed; and to targeting and procurement of weapons; progressive abandonment and dismantling of paramilitary structures actively directing and promoting violence; full co-operation with the Independent Commission on Decommissioning, to implement the provisions of the Agreement; and no other organisations being deliberately used as proxies for violence.[104]

Blair was also pitching his reassurances at one individual in particular. The key figure on the Unionist side was Jeffrey Donaldson. Unlike many anti-Agreement Unionists, he had supported the constitutional arrangements in the Agreement. But his conscience would not allow him to sanction what he believed were weaknesses and amoral elements in the Agreement. Intensive pressure was applied by Downing Street to persuade Donaldson to come out in favour of a Yes vote. It was believed that such an outcome would sway many wavering unionist voters. Finally, a week before the referendum, Donaldson confirmed that he would be voting No. While Donaldson and his supporters – which included former members of the UUP talks team, Peter King and Peter Weir – welcomed the positive sentiments expressed by the

Prime Minister, they maintained there were a number of ambiguities and omissions which caused them some concern. The position of the Prime Minister appeared to be that the terms of the Agreement remained unalterable, and that it therefore remained to be seen whether this permitted him to include the necessary, effective safeguards which needed to be inserted into any Westminster legislation.

In particular, Donaldson and his supporters stated that their concerns included: an inadequate reassurance on the future of the RUC; no clear requirement for paramilitaries to decommission before holding ministerial office; the absence of clear measures to exclude from office those who failed to honour the commitment to non-violence and exclusively peaceful means beyond the cross-community vote proposed in the Agreement; the absence of clearly defined linkages between the need for the commencement of actual and ongoing decommissioning and the release of prisoners; and the absence of any provisions to exclude from office in a 'shadow' Assembly those committed to the twin approach of the ballot-box and the gun.[105] This was followed by confirmation from Lord Molyneaux that he also would be voting No.[106] The Grand Orange Lodge of Ireland added further to the British Government's gloom when it declared that as an 'organisation committed to civil and religious liberty' it could not instruct anyone how to vote but it was 'unable to recommend the Agreement to the people of Ulster'.[107]

With the referendum vote ever closer, David Trimble rejected suggestions that he had not prepared unionists sufficiently for the terms of the Agreement. He noted the 'remarkable absence' of argument in the campaign over constitutional matters and the three strands, particularly the 'very elaborate' provisions for running the Assembly. Instead, the 'problem has been prisoners'. Trimble insisted that prisoners 'are not our problem'. It was a Government problem. He blamed the Irish Government and the NIO which had 'spectacularly screwed up' on this issue with the 'conniving at the Balcombe Street extravaganza in Dublin'.[108] Trimble explained that the difference between himself and Jeffrey Donaldson centred on the small but important point about the 'effectiveness of the mechanism that would be used to exclude unreconstructed terrorists'. As far as the UUP leader was concerned, the decommissioning issue had been dealt with and there was 'no point in worrying around the edges. It has been dealt with in a way which I am sure we can work.'[109] The key phrase here was 'unreconstructed terrorists'. Trimble was quick to point out that he had no fundamental objection to Sinn Féin in government – provided Republicans proved that they had abandoned violence for good, as demonstrated by PIRA decommissioning.

22 May 1998 was polling day for voters in the Republic and in Northern Ireland. Voters in the Republic were asked: 'Do you approve of the proposal to amend the Constitution contained in the undermentioned Bill? Nineteenth Amendment of the Constitution Bill 1998.' The Bill provided for constitutional change arising from the Belfast Agreement. As well as

including changes to Articles 2 and 3, it also proposed additions to Article 29 of the Irish Constitution to allow the Irish state to be bound by the terms of the Agreement. The constitutional changes would not come into effect until the necessary measures were taken in both the Republic and Northern Ireland to implement all the provisions of the Agreement. Voters in Northern Ireland were asked: 'Do you support the agreement reached in the multi-party talks on Northern Ireland and set out in Command Paper 3883?'

When the votes were counted, the referendum produced a resounding Yes vote on both sides of the border. Overall in the two referenda there was an 85.46 per cent Yes vote. In Northern Ireland, 71.12 per cent voted Yes with an 81.1 per cent turnout. In the Republic 94.39 per cent of voters agreed to alter Articles 2, 3 and 29 of the Irish Constitution. While Ian Paisley claimed that the majority of the unionist community voted No, and the UKUP leader, Robert McCartney, said that a lot of the 'soft Yes' voters would switch back to his party and the DUP in elections to the Northern Ireland Assembly, it seems clear that Tony Blair's promises swung enough Protestant voters to give a slim Yes majority in the unionist community.

With the referendum out of the way, attention switched to the Assembly elections. The key word to describe the mood of the campaign was apathy. It was as if Northern Ireland's media and electorate were suffering from collective exhaustion. The result, on 25 June, saw the considerable achievement for the SDLP of securing the highest number of first preference votes for any political party; it was the first time in Northern Ireland's history that a Nationalist party had ever done this. The final distribution of seats in the Assembly revealed the split in Unionism, with a number of the UUP's Assembly members being openly against the Agreement. The results were as follows:

Party	Seats
Ulster Unionist Party	28
Social Democratic & Labour Party	24
Democratic Unionist Party	20
Sinn Féin	18
Alliance Party	6
United Kingdom Unionist Party	5
Progressive Unionist Party	2
Northern Ireland Women's Coalition	2
Others	3

The new Assembly met in 'shadow' form for the first time on 1 July 1998, with Lord Alderdice of the Alliance Party as initial Presiding Officer. David Trimble was elected as First Minister designate; John Hume stood aside to let his colleague Seamus Mallon become Deputy First Minister designate.

The Northern Ireland Constitution Act 1998

The Northern Ireland Constitution Act 1998, passed in Westminster, gave legal standing to the provisions of the Belfast Agreement. Bertie Ahern had claimed the Agreement meant that 'The British Government are effectively out of the equation'; Martin McGuinness claimed, 'We fought for and got the repeal of the Government of Ireland Act which underpinned the union, and insisted that other relevant legislation, including the Act of Union and the NI Constitution Act of 1973 be repealed or rendered inoperable by any new Act'; and Gerry Adams added that the British claim to Northern Ireland had been reduced to the 'one hinge' of the will of a majority of the people in Northern Ireland.[110]

The Northern Ireland Constitution Act 1998 showed these interpretations to be incorrect on a number of counts. Firstly, Section 75 of the Government of Ireland Act 1920 was, in law, unnecessary; its context was provided by the system of devolution introduced by the 1920 Act – the Northern Ireland Parliament – and the termination of that entire system terminated Section 75; and the inclusion, in the Northern Ireland Act 1998 of Section 5(6) – stating that 'This section does not affect the power of the Parliament of the United Kingdom to make laws for Northern Ireland' – was the substantive equivalent of Section 75 and would operate in the context of the system of devolution to be introduced by the 1998 Act. The Act did not expressly repeal the Acts of Union.[111]

For example, Section 1 of the Northern Ireland Act 1998 did not in any way sever the Union. What Section 1 did was to incorporate the consent principle into mechanisms for the most fundamental of all changes to the Union – termination. Section 1(1) declared that Northern Ireland in its entirety remained a part of the United Kingdom and should not cease to be, without majority consent.[112] The repeal of Section 75 was, legally, of no significance. The Union now depended upon the consent of the people of Northern Ireland. Furthermore, Britain was not out of the equation because Westminster would have to approve the legislation for ending the Union.[113]

In terms of sovereignty, Clause 43 of the Northern Ireland Act 1998 was explicit: it provided that 'Her Majesty may by Order in Council prorogue or further prorogue the Assembly.'[114] Domestic law took precedence over international agreements and Westminster remained sovereign over Northern Ireland. The Northern Ireland Act 1998, not the Belfast Agreement, was the crucial constitutional document in matters relating to the concept of self-determination and supremacy in British law.

No Way Forward

The end of electioneering and the passing of constitutional legislation at Westminster brought no immediate prospect of devolved government to Northern Ireland. Centre stage were the UUP and Sinn Féin. The UUP had committed itself, in its election manifesto, to insist on prior PIRA decommissioning before it would enter a power-sharing executive with Sinn Féin. Sinn Féin insisted that it was not the PIRA and that the Agreement did not place any preconditions on the formation of an executive. At this stage, as during the talks, the UUP refused to directly engage with Sinn Féin. David Trimble's own position seemed to be under considerable threat as the Drumcree march was once again banned from returning down the Garvaghy Road. It seemed that the gathering mass of Orangemen around Drumcree, and the potential for a bloody clash with the security forces standing in their way, offered a parallel with the UWC strike of 1974. Certainly, many leading anti-Agreement Unionists, such as Ian Paisley, seemed to relish the coming clash. It was doubtful whether Trimble's leadership could survive such an encounter. Then the situation suddenly changed with the murder of three young Catholic boys in an arson attack. The motivation was widely regarded at the time as resulting from the feverish atmosphere surrounding Drumcree. The shock of such an atrocity meant that many Orangemen no longer had the stomach for carrying on the Drumcree protest, which quickly dissipated.

A second atrocity allowed political movement between the UUP and Sinn Féin. This was the Omagh bomb. The Real IRA, associated with the viewpoint taken by the anti-Agreement 32-County Sovereignty Committee, detonated a car bomb in the town of Omagh. Twenty-nine people, of both faiths, were killed. It was the single most deadly attack by any party to the conflict in Northern Ireland during the whole of the Troubles. In the shocked aftermath, both the British and Irish Governments passed even more repressive security legislation. Politically, it highlighted the necessity for decommissioning. It also allowed for a sequence of events which saw the UUP and Sinn Féin end their cold war stand-off. Gerry Adams, on 1 September, issued a statement that Sinn Féin believed: 'the violence we have seen, must be for all of us now a thing of the past, over, done with and gone.'[115] This said nothing new, but in the aftermath of Omagh it allowed the first meeting to take place between Trimble and Adams.

However, this, and subsequent meetings, still brought no resolution of the decommissioning issue. So attention focused on other areas. The aim, particularly of the UUP, was to resolve all the outstanding issues until only one remained – decommissioning. There was continuing disagreement over the identity of the initial North-South implementation bodies, and over the number and functions of the departments of government in Northern Ireland that the new ministers, when selected, would preside over. Following intensive negotiations involving the political parties, and at times the British and Irish Governments, including the Prime Minister and Taoiseach, the First Minister and Deputy First Minister-designate reached agreement on 18 December 1998.

The agreement involved six implementation bodies, dealing with Inland Waterways; Food Safety; Trade and Business Development; Special EU Programmes; Language (Irish and Ulster-Scots); and Aquaculture and Marine Matters. Eleven Northern Ireland Departments were agreed upon to replace the existing six. There would be an Office of the First Minister and Deputy First Minister; Departments of Agriculture and Rural Development; Environment; Regional Development; Social Development; Education; Higher and Further Education; Training and Employment; Enterprise, Trade and Investment; Culture, Arts and Leisure; Health, Social Service and Public Safety; and Finance and Personnel.

The First and Deputy First Minister designates reported their agreement to the Northern Ireland Assembly, which approved the report.[116] On 15 February 1999, Trimble and Mallon put forward a comprehensive determination of the number and functions of offices to be occupied by the new Northern Ireland Ministers, and other proposals concerning the North-South Ministerial Council, the British-Irish Council and the Civic Forum.[117] On 8 March, the British and Irish Governments signed treaties establishing the North-South Ministerial Council;[118] the British-Irish Council;[119] and the British-Irish Intergovernmental Conference.[120] None of these bodies would become operative until power had been devolved to the Northern Ireland Executive.

Elsewhere, the Secretary of State announced a Review of the Criminal Justice System in Northern Ireland. A Northern Ireland Human Rights Commission was established. A commission investigating the future shape and role of policing in Northern Ireland was also set up under the chairmanship of former NIO minister and the last Governor of Hong Kong, Chris Patten. The Northern Ireland (Sentences) Act saw the release of the first terrorist prisoners. Despite continuing punishment attacks, and evidence that paramilitary groups were still importing arms and committing occasional murders, such as that of a PIRA member Charles Bennett by his own organisation, the British Government resisted calls to halt the releases or to link them to progress on decommissioning. By September 1998, routine British Army patrols in Belfast had been ended. There remained, however, a significant British military presence in the border areas of Northern Ireland, particularly south Armagh, which continued to be a source of constant irritation to Republicans.

The problem of decommissioning remained, with the UUP continuing to insist on prior PIRA decommissioning before it would serve in an executive with Sinn Féin. This was not based on a simple rejection of ever serving with Republicans in an executive. In January 1999, John Taylor emphasised that the UUP did not want the exclusion of any grouping. He acknowledged that before the collapse of the Northern Ireland Parliament, in 1972, his party represented the establishment; but that had changed. The UUP did not seek to exclude any party out of spite; but it was imperative that the PIRA make a gesture on decommissioning. As long as the PIRA remained intact, Sinn Féin could not take ministerial positions in the Executive.[121] Symbolically, pressure on the Republican Movement was increased when the LVF, now on ceasefire, decommissioned a small amount of firearms. This act demonstrated that decommissioning could move beyond the realm of the theoretical.

In an effort to inject some momentum into the process, the British Government set early March for the completion of the legislative process leading to the transfer of powers to the institutions set up under the Agreement. A transfer of powers by Dublin to the new North-South bodies was also required. However, until the issues of decommissioning and the formation of an executive had been resolved, the formal transfer would not happen. David Trimble suggested that if Republicans did not decommission then 'we will have to find some way of going forward without them'.[122] But the door on this option seemed to be shut when Bertie Ahern ruled out the formation of an executive without Sinn Féin, although he accepted that an executive would not begin to function unless the PIRA handed over some weapons, 'because Mr Trimble has made it absolutely clear that he will not set up the executive until this issue is resolved'.[123]

In Washington, for St Patrick's Day celebrations, Gerry Adams indicated he was prepared to 'reach out' to the UUP over the question of arms. But he had to be sure of a 'meaningful response' from David Trimble. Adams wanted to make sure that 'Mr Trimble and I jump together'. He explained that during a bilateral meeting between the two, Trimble had made it 'very, very clear that he wants from the IRA what he described as an "event"' – an act of decommissioning – which was larger than the LVF's event, that he wanted it to encompass a range of armaments through weaponry from detonators, timing devices, to explosives, and that he wanted it done in a credible and viable way. Adams told Trimble, 'I just couldn't deliver that; that isn't possible.' Adams stressed that any resolution of the impasse had to be within the terms of the Belfast Agreement and asserted, 'I cannot deliver from the IRA what the British Government couldn't achieve in the last 30 years.'[124]

By the end of March, as talks resumed in Belfast, a PIRA statement gave no hint of contemplating disarmament. Much to the annoyance of Republicans, this prompted the Taoiseach to tell the Dáil that although decommissioning was not a precondition of the Belfast Agreement 'it is an obligation'.[125] It seemed that only Republicans felt that the Agreement did not commit them to decommissioning. Intense negotiations between the British and Irish Governments, on the one hand, and the pro-Agreement parties, on the other, now took place at Hillsborough Castle, in County Down. Tony Blair, in particular, was demonstrating his determination to find a resolution to the problem – at the same time British forces were committed to the air campaign in the Kosovo war.

From these discussions a working draft of a declaration was put forward, by the Prime Minister and the Taoiseach, as a basis for agreement. It was called the Hillsborough Declaration. It attempted to set in motion the procedures to establish devolution, and then, secure decommissioning. Devolution would come first. The Declaration set out how ministerial nominations to the Northern Ireland Executive would be made under the d'Hondt procedure when powers would be devolved from Westminster; at a date, not later than a month from when the d'Hondt procedure began, a collective 'Act of Reconciliation' would take place which would see arms put beyond use on a voluntary basis; within the same timescale the Decommissioning body would report on progress.

Moves on demilitarisation and normalisation – meaning a reduction in British troop numbers and the removal of security installations – would be made in recognition of the changed security situation. In addition there would be, at the same time, ceremonies of remembrance for all victims of violence, to which representatives of all parties and the two Governments, and all churches, would be invited. Around the time of the Act of Reconciliation, powers would be devolved and the British-Irish Agreement would enter into force. The North-South Ministerial Council, the North-South implementation bodies, the British-Irish Council and the British-Irish Intergovernmental Conference would be established. By one month later, the Decommissioning Commission would make a report on the progress of disarmament. It would be understood by all parties that the successful implementation of the Belfast Agreement would be achieved if these steps were taken within the proposed timescale; if they were not taken, the nominations to the Executive would fall.[126] Initially, David Trimble was pleased with the Declaration[127] – it committed the Republican Movement to actual decommissioning; this was something they had never even admitted was an obligation arising from signing up to the Belfast Agreement.

However, resistance grew from within the UUP. There were no guarantees, no timetables of decommissioning, and no failsafe to continue the Executive while excluding Sinn Féin from office. But, before a critical mass could build up within the UUP to reject the Declaration, Sinn Féin and the PIRA rejected it for them. They saw it as an attempt to rewrite the Agreement. Sinn Féin and the PIRA were two separate organisations and it was wrong to hold one responsible for the actions of the other.

So, the two Governments started again. This time, instead of applying pressure on Sinn Féin they turned their attention to the UUP. This was based upon an assumption that the PIRA had accepted that decommissioning must occur. If devolution came first, then the onus would be on the Republicans to reciprocate and decommission some arms soon after. For example, Tony Blair interpreted the impasse over decommissioning as resolving around the question of trust: 'without trust, there can be no political settlement.' Republicans, he believed, feared that Unionists were not serious about letting them into the democratic process. They thought that Unionists wanted to re-write the Agreement. Unionists, on the other hand, believed that the Republicans, or a significant section of them, were addicted to violence as a tactic. The Prime Minister warned Republicans that decommissioning 'can be got through, but it cannot be got round'. Whatever the history, once it had been raised in 1995, decommissioning took on a special significance. Decommissioning was not a prior pre-condition of forming the Executive: 'But it is plainly part of the process. All parties are obliged to help bring it about. No one will believe that a party with a close connection with a paramilitary group could not bring about decommissioning.'[128]

After more inconclusive talks in Downing Street, in mid–May, a frustrated Prime Minister declared that 30 June would be the 'absolute deadline' for devolution to occur. This coincided with the transfer of devolved powers to Scotland and Wales. As the deadline approached, discussions between the Governments and parties once more intensified. On 25 June, the pro-Agreement parties declared their commitment to three principles: an inclusive Executive exercising devolved powers; the decommissioning of all paramilitary arms by May 2000 as stated in the Belfast Agreement; and decommissioning to be carried out in a manner determined by the International Commission on Decommissioning. A week of intensive discussions, ending on 2 July, yielded no final agreement between the parties, but led to another joint initiative from the two Governments.

The basis of this was the conviction that Sinn Féin had shifted its position on decommissioning. As the 'absolute deadline' came and went, indicating that the Governments had no plan B, Pat Doherty predicted that 'If we get politics working, if we get a new political dispensation, if we get total demilitarisation, I think we can create a new political context to which the IRA will respond in the appropriate manner.'[129] What precisely this meant or how long it would take was unclear, since, initially at least, Sinn Féin refused to put their proposals down on paper for fear they could be misinterpreted.

The UUP wanted the guarantee of a specific and very short period that would elapse between the formation of an executive and the beginning of the decommissioning process. But Sinn Féin's strategy was merely to agree a form of words with the two Governments, which would then be submitted to General de Chastelain when completing his report. Tony Blair seized on this to claim there had been 'historic, seismic shifts' in the political landscape. He added that the British and Irish Governments were prepared to give 'absolute legislative failsafe guarantees' to underpin any deal.[130] Sinn Féin's form of words, when finally committed to paper, stated that 'we believe that all of us, as participants acting in good faith, could succeed in persuading those with arms to decommission them in accordance with the Agreement. We agree that this should be in the manner set down by the Independent Commission on Decommissioning within the terms of the Good Friday Agreement ...'[131] This was seen by the Governments as an advance from the previous Sinn Féin position that it would merely use its influence, as required by the Agreement, to secure PIRA decommissioning, to a more confident prediction that it could persuade the PIRA to decommission.

Blair and Bertie Ahern then produced their Way Forward document. It earmarked a Devolution Order to be laid before the British Parliament on 16 July, and to take effect on 18 July. Within the period specified by the de Chastelain Commission, the Commission would confirm a start to the process of decommissioning. The Commission would then specify that actual decommissioning was to start within a specified time. It would report progress in September and December 1999 and in May 2000. There was also to be a 'failsafe' clause. The Governments undertook that, in accordance with the review provisions of the Belfast Agreement, if commitments to devolution and decommissioning were not met they would automatically, and with immediate effect, suspend the operations of the institutions set up by the Agreement. In relation to decommissioning, this action would be taken on receipt of a report at any time that the commitments now being entered into or steps which were subsequently laid down by the Commission, were not fulfilled, in accordance with the Good Friday Agreement. The British Government would legislate to this effect.[132]

In anticipation that this proposal might translate into a commitment to decommission paramilitary arms, the Decommissioning Commission reported that it believed that in order to complete its mandate by 22 May 2000, the decommissioning process should begin 'as soon as possible'.[133] Bertie Ahern called all this a 'great day for Ireland' and a 'glorious opportunity'. While he would not set a date by which he believed actual decommissioning would occur he referred to the decommissioning body delivering its series of reports in September, December and the following May. But discussions on decommissioning would begin as soon as the PIRA nominated someone as a contact person with the decommissioning body. Gerry Adams was cautiously optimistic. He now believed that the consequence of the week's efforts was, 'we will now move ahead with the full implementation of the Good Friday Agreement.'[134]

But this time it was the Unionists who were to reject the joint British and Irish proposals. David Trimble expressed deep unease that the wording of Sinn Féin's document failed to contain a commitment that the PIRA would definitely disarm. What was lacking was certainty. Trimble complained that the paper was fundamentally flawed because it 'equates democracy with terrorism, and treats them as if they were the same'. Republicans, in their paper, had not signed up to disarmament. They used words such as 'can' and 'could' when instead they should be using words such as 'must' and 'will' disarm. The paper offered promises but no certainty. Trimble emphasised that the UUP was not opposed to partnership with Catholics, Nationalists and Republicans: 'We are ready to work with Sinn Féin if they commit themselves to peace and democracy – and they know it.'[135]

In the event, it took less than two days for Trimble to reject the package. The day after the break-up of the negotiations the UUP's party officers unanimously voted to reject the proposals. Both pro and anti-Agreement Unionists within the UUP were opposed to the terms. Trimble now accused

Sinn Féin of deceiving the British and Irish Governments about the PIRA's intentions to decommission. He had great difficulties with the proposals. Unionists had problems with the timing, commitment and the failsafe mechanisms to ensure promises were kept by all sides. The proposals needed more than a few 'cosmetic changes' to persuade Unionists to sign up to them.

Trimble contacted Blair to express his concerns. He asked the Prime Minister why democrats should be punished if terrorists failed to decommission. Proposing an end to the Executive if decommissioning failed to happen required Unionists to 'make a leap in the dark without an effective net'. That all the institutions were to be suspended just because a paramilitary organisation, which could be the PIRA or the UVF, failed to live up to its obligations meant that the 'democratic politicians suffer'. Trimble felt that this was not a reasonable or fair proposition for the two Governments to ask of the UUP. The UUP was now questioning Republicans' true intentions about decommissioning after an assurance from Blair, during the recent negotiations, that both Sinn Féin and the PIRA would issue a statement saying 'the war was over', failed to materialise: 'That leaves my colleagues with a very great concern. A lot of them think that this is a con job by Gerry Adams and that unfortunately Tony [Blair] has been deceived. I share those doubts myself.'[136]

Neither Government was yet ready to give up on its proposals. In an effort to soothe Unionist concerns, Bertie Ahern called on the PIRA to publicly declare its support for the new initiative. The Taoiseach noted how during all the years of violence it was claimed that Sinn Féin and the PIRA were one. But 'All of a sudden, when we come to this final position, it is "Sinn Féin, but they do not speak for the PIRA".' The two organisations were the 'opposite sides of the one coin' and it was up to Gerry Adams and Martin McGuinness, who had influence over the PIRA, to 'sell the message'.[137]

Tony Blair focused directly on the UUP. While he accepted that Republicans had never in their history agreed to decommission their weapons, he believed that the Way Forward 'can now deliver it'. Within days of devolution, the paramilitary organisations, including the PIRA, 'must notify intention to decommission. If they don't, there is a failsafe that unwinds devolution.' As far as the Prime Minister was concerned: 'Within weeks, they must actually decommission.' He pointed out that the terms of the Way Forward were tougher than those contained in the Hillsborough Declaration, which offered 'at best a token act' of decommissioning simultaneously with devolution. Unlike the new proposal it offered no subsequent process to ensure all decommissioning, and no statement of intent to decommission on a specific timetable. Instead, it demanded equivalent acts of decommissioning from everyone, including the British Government.

Turning to Sinn Féin's argument that they were only saying that they 'could' rather than 'will' persuade the PIRA to decommission, Blair emphasised that decommissioning in this agreement was not dependent on words but on actions. If, within days of devolution, decommissioning had not occurred the failsafe mechanism would kick in and devolution would be reversed. The process of decommissioning meant that the PIRA, not Sinn Féin, had to give a clear and unambiguous indication of their intention to decommission. The argument that the failsafe possibility suspended the whole of devolution, and not just Sinn Féin, from the Executive, was simply a misunderstanding of the default mechanism. Should decommissioning not happen in the way set out by the Decommissioning Commission, 'we just go back to where we are now. So we are no worse off than today ... Back to square one.'

But there would be a clear difference. It would be obvious that the defaulting party would be Sinn Féin, and it would be open to other parties to agree to move forward without Sinn Féin. The British Government could not make other parties do this on its own as it was outside the terms of the Good Friday Agreement. So the procedure was automatic suspension followed by a review of the Agreement that allowed the parties to move forward without the defaulting party should they want to do so.[138] As Blair understood it, Unionists wanted certainty that decommissioning would happen and a guarantee that, if it did not, they would not be left in an executive with those who refused to do so. Republicans, on the other hand, wanted certainty that Unionists were serious about participating in a genuinely inclusive government. This was what the Way Forward was designed to deliver.[139]

However, Blair's comments now opened a breach with the Irish Government. The Taoiseach emphasised his Government's opposition to any proposals to exclude Sinn Féin from the Executive. Amid mounting Nationalist concern, Bertie Ahern argued that both the Belfast Agreement and the Way Forward were based on 'inclusion and not on exclusion'. The Belfast Agreement was an exercise in 'inclusive, collective politics' and 'That is the only way forward.' Ahern now placed great emphasis on the PIRA statement he had called for earlier, to build confidence on the ground. All his negotiations had been with Sinn Féin, not the PIRA. He had now changed his view of the Sinn Féin–PIRA relationship. In the past he had believed that the PIRA and Sinn Féin were opposite sides of the same coin; but this was no longer the case. That was why the PIRA had to make its position clear.[140] Later, the Taoiseach went further, stating that 'they're two separate organisations.'

Ahern now appeared out of step with Blair who, when asked if Sinn Féin should remain in an executive if there was no PIRA decommissioning, replied: 'I believe the answer to that is no if they are holding a private army in reserve.' Sinn Féin spoke for the PIRA on disarmament, but although the organisations were not exactly the same: 'they are inextricably linked together.'[141] These remarks brought angry reactions from Republicans and Unionists. Pat Doherty repeated that 'Sinn Féin does not represent any other organisation. We are not the IRA, and we cannot and will not make commitments on its behalf.' John Taylor claimed that the Taoiseach's remarks had effectively given a 'kiss of death' to the talks process and had undermined the Way Forward. Taylor accused Ahern of attempting to create conditions for Sinn Féin to 'wash their hands' of a decision by the PIRA not to give up their arms, enabling them to continue in an executive without decommissioning.[142]

From this point on, events descended into farce. On 16 July the 110-strong UUP executive at the party's headquarters heard David Trimble confirm that he would not be participating in the d'Hondt procedure and in the appointment of ministers to the Executive. The following day, the First Minister designate announced that the UUP would be boycotting the sitting of the Northern Ireland Assembly. Trimble and the UUP considered it 'premature to form a shadow executive'. The process should not be 'crashed. It should be parked, which will lead to a review.' Inside the Assembly's chamber there was laughter when the Presiding Officer, Lord Alderdice, turned to the 28 empty UUP seats, called on the absent Trimble to begin his ministerial nominations and gave him five minutes to do so. John Hume then nominated Mark Durkan as the SDLP's first ministerial appointment. While Ian Paisley refused to nominate a DUP minister, Gerry Adams forwarded Bairbre de Brún as Sinn Féin's first ministerial appointment.

With Sinn Féin and the SDLP left to fill all of the 10 ministerial posts, Lord Alderdice announced that the ministerial appointments could not stand because they all came from the Nationalist side. An angry Seamus Mallon announced his resignation as Deputy First Minister designate and accused the UUP of using the political crisis to 'bleed more concessions out of the Governments – to bleed this very process dry'. The only pleased voice was Ian Paisley's; he described it as a 'good day for Northern Ireland. Democracy has triumphed and there are no IRA men in the government of Northern Ireland.'

Back at Westminster, in the House of Commons, Dr Mowlam made an emergency statement announcing a review of the workings of the Belfast Agreement. At Stormont, Lord Alderdice adjourned the Assembly explaining that the Secretary of State had suspended it from sitting until further notice.[143] The Prime Minister and Taoiseach considered the scope of a review, in London, on 20 July. There they were once more joined by Senator George Mitchell, who was invited to act as facilitator in the process. After preliminary discussions with the parties, it was decided that a cooling-off period was necessary, and the review was scheduled to resume in early September. The Prime Minister and Taoiseach made it clear that the review would be limited in focus to determining how to carry forward the three principles agreed on 25 June.

Breakthroughs and Breakdowns

To the surprise of many commentators, after a period of recriminations, the atmospherics between the UUP and Sinn Féin dramatically improved when the warring parties spent time together at the American embassy in London. It was felt that both sides were appreciating the problems each had with their own support base. By November, the basis of a deal seemed possible. Speaking at Sinn Féin's national women's conference, Gerry Adams accepted that Unionism was 'no longer a monolith. There are people there, leaders there, who want to set aside the old ways. We need to work with them to make this happen.'[144] Unlike when the Way Forward document was proposed, the UUP were now prepared to 'jump first' and enter into government with Sinn Féin. But, although no commitments were given by Sinn Féin regarding PIRA decommissioning, David Trimble reiterated on a number of occasions to the Sinn Féin leadership that, by taking this gamble, he could only hold for a few weeks in government without some decommissioning. From the UUP perspective everybody, including Sinn Féin, was well aware that the report of General de Chastelain, due at the end of January 2000, was effectively a deadline for PIRA decommissioning. Furthermore, the UUP received assurances from the new Secretary of State, Peter Mandelson, who had replaced Mo Mowlam, that if there were no PIRA decommissioning the British Government would suspend the new institutions.[145] Mandelson, who had a close relationship with the Prime Minister, was seen by the UUP as more understanding of Unionism than Mowlam.

A series of stage-managed statements heralded the formation of the Executive. First, the UUP reiterated its total commitment to the full implementation of the Belfast Agreement in all its aspects. The party stated its belief that the establishment of the new political institutions and the disarmament of all paramilitary organisations would herald a new beginning – a 'new, peaceful, and democratic society, free from the use or threat of force'. The UUP also emphasised that it was committed to the principles of 'inclusivity, equality and mutual respect', principles on which the institutions were to be based.[146] Sinn Féin, in a statement delivered by Gerry Adams, repeated that the conflict 'must be for all of us now a thing of the past, over, done with and gone'. Sinn Féin accepted that decommissioning was an 'essential part of the peace process' and that the issue of arms would be finally settled under the aegis of the de Chastelain Commission, as set out in the Agreement. All parties to the Agreement had an obligation to help bring about decommissioning. But, crucially, the Agreement 'makes clear that the context required for its resolution is the implementation of the overall settlement, including the operation of its institutions'. This was a collective responsibility. Sinn Féin also condemned punishment attacks.[147]

The PIRA followed this with a statement reiterating that the Good Friday Agreement was a 'significant' development and that its 'full implementation' would 'contribute' to the achievement of lasting peace. The PIRA acknowledged the leadership given by Sinn Féin throughout the peace process and was willing to enhance the process, following the establishment of the institutions, by appointing a representative to enter into discussions with General de Chastelain and the Decommissioning Commission.[148] However, they gave no commitment to deliver any 'product' nor recognised any obligation to accept any timetables set down by de Chastelain.

But the UUP was adamant that decommissioning had to occur, and soon. As Sir Reg Empey emphasised: 'If Unionism is to deliver an inclusive executive, Republicanism must deliver decommissioning. Both sides must demonstrate in word and deed their commitment to these issues respectively if the agreement is to work.'[149] With the sequencing complete, Senator Mitchell finally departed from Northern Ireland believing that a basis now existed for devolution to occur and for decommissioning to take place as soon as possible.[150] This was not the final obstacle, however, for David Trimble had to convince his party's main decision-making forum, the Ulster Unionist Council, to endorse his gamble. This they did by a relatively narrow margin. In order to have his policy endorsed Trimble had deposited a post-dated letter of resignation with a senior member of the party hierarchy, Sir Joshua Cunningham, and promised to recall the UUC in mid-February 2000 to assess the political situation. Essentially, Trimble had set his own personal deadline for decommissioning and offered the UUC the opportunity to rubber-stamp it. If he had not done this, it was unlikely that he would have had the necessary support from the party to enter an executive.

Thus, the stage was set for Northern Ireland's first power-sharing cabinet since 1974. The appointments were as follows:

Northern Ireland Executive

First Minister:	David Trimble (UUP)
Deputy First Minister:	Seamus Mallon (SDLP)
Minister for Enterprise Trade & Investment:	Sir Reg Empey (UUP)
Minister for Finance & Personnel:	Mark Durkan (SDLP)
Minister for Regional Development:	Peter Robinson (DUP)
Minister for Education:	Martin McGuinness (SF)
Minister for Higher & Further Education:	Seán Farren (SDLP)
Minister for Environment:	Sam Foster (UUP)
Minister for Social Development:	Nigel Dodds (DUP)
Minister for Culture, Arts & Leisure:	Michael McGimpsey (UUP)
Minister for Health, Social Services & Public Safety:	Bairbre de Brún (SF)
Minister for Agriculture & Rural Development:	Brid Rogers (SDLP)

Thereafter, with the establishment of an executive, the PIRA appointed a contact person to the Decommissioning body; the Irish Government formally changed Articles 2 and 3, dropping the territorial claim to Northern Ireland; the North-South Ministerial Council met in full session for the first time; the North-South implementation bodies were established; the British-Irish Council met in session for the first time; and the British-Irish Intergovernmental Conference met for the first time.

But then, in January 2000, with General de Chastelain's Commission due to report on the progress of decommissioning, the Peace Process was once again thrown into crisis. Republicans claimed that the UUP had imposed an artificial deadline. The PIRA would not dance to a British and Unionist decommissioning tune. When Peter Mandelson received de Chastelain's report there was a very real prospect that he would suspend the new institutions. Martin McGuinness, now the Northern Ireland Minister of Education, warned that suspension would be the 'greatest disaster to befall Ireland in the last 100 years'.[151] But Mandelson told the House of Commons that de Chastelain's report stated that there had not yet been any decommissioning of arms by a major paramilitary group and he declared that this was 'totally unacceptable'. Notably in the case of the PIRA it had to be clear that decommissioning was going to happen. The Commission still believed that decommissioning was going to happen, but needed further evidence to substantiate that conclusion. In particular it needed definite information about when decommissioning would actually start.

The Secretary of State warned that if it became clear that, because of a loss of confidence, the new institutions could not be sustained the Government was ready to put a hold on the operation of the institutions. If it came to this, the purpose of the exercise would be to preserve them from collapse and to create time and space in which to rebuild the confidence required to sustain them.[152] In particular it was imperative to prevent David Trimble's resignation as First Minister. Given the splits in the UUP Assembly team, it seemed highly unlikely that he would have enough Unionist votes to be re-elected to that post.

With Irish ministers and officials engaged in intense talks with key members of the Republican Movement, the British and Irish premiers urgently met in Cornwall. Both called for 'clarity' on the PIRA's position regarding decommissioning. But by mid-February, with the recall of the UUC impending, Peter Mandelson suspended the Northern Ireland Assembly and Executive and with it the operation of the other institutions. Despite Nationalist claims that this was illegal and contrary to the Belfast Agreement, it was perfectly compatible with the provisions of the Northern Ireland Constitution Act 1998. The British Government – and the demonstration of British sovereignty in Northern Ireland – was clearly not out of the equation.

Controversy erupted as claims and counter-claims were made of a breakthrough on decommissioning. Seamus Mallon accused Mandelson of a 'faulty decision' by making his priority the internal politics of the UUP.[153] Gerry Adams claimed that the Secretary of State had capitulated to Unionist pressure rather than testing whether a new PIRA position could overcome the decommissioning impasse. Early on the morning of the suspension, the Irish Government had been made aware of a 'major breakthrough' from the PIRA. This had been passed on to the British Government. The Decommissioning Commission, in a new report, stated that the 'commitment holds out the real prospect of an agreement which would enable it [the Commission] to fulfil the substance of its mandate'. Bertie Ahern confirmed, 'without breaking any confidence', the 'deep significance for the resolution of the decommissioning issue of the ... de Chastelain report'.[154]

But nobody seemed to know the details of the 'breakthrough'. Certainly not the UUP leader. David Trimble retorted that it was 'make your mind up time' for the Republican Movement. Did they want to be part of the political process and did they want to commit themselves to politics? If so, 'they know what they have to do.' The First Minister could see nothing from the second de Chastelain report that could be described as a plan to decommission by the PIRA. Progress on this issue had to be clear and unambiguous.[155] Trimble now promised that any further plans to re-enter government would have to have the prior consent of the 860-strong UUC. But the impasse on decommissioning was not the only concern for Trimble. The Patten Report on the future of policing in Northern Ireland shook UUP confidence in their leader.

The Report recommended radical reforms to the RUC. It concluded that there should be a comprehensive programme of action to focus policing in Northern Ireland on a human rights based approach. This would involve a new oath, no longer to the Queen, but expressing an explicit commitment to upholding human rights. A new Code of Ethics should replace the existing, largely procedural code, integrating the ECHR into police practice. All police officers should be trained in the fundamental principles and standards of human rights and the practical implications for policing. Community policing should be the core function of the police service and the core function of every police station. The approximate size of the police service, over the following ten years, should be 7,500 full-time officers. Early retirement or severance packages should be offered to regular officers over 50 years of age. This meant the phasing out of the RUC Reserve. Ultimately, the number of new Protestant and Catholic recruits should be on a 50:50 basis.

But most controversially of all, from the unionist community's point of view, although the report stated that the 'RUC is not to be disbanded' it concluded that the force's name should be change to the Police Service of Northern Ireland, and that its symbols should not reflect those of the British or Irish states.[156] For many nationalists the symbols and name of the RUC represented the cultural ethos of only one side of the community – the Britishness of unionists. For many unionists the proposed change to the title and symbols was an insult to the memory of the 302 officers who had lost their lives in the Troubles.

While Sinn Féin's demand for the disbandment of the force was not granted, the fact that many unionists saw it as yet another sop to nationalists was enough to encourage Republicans to adopt a low-key response to the report as unionist frustration with reform undermined David Trimble's position further. This was demonstrated by the challenge to his leadership from the Reverend Martin Symth, in March 2000, when Trimble's opponent gave the UUP leader a bloody nose, winning 43 per cent of the UUC vote. In the politics of Northern Ireland it remained the perceptions of the other side's gains and losses, rather than the reality – the zero sum game – which dictated the winners and the losers. The danger for both the Sinn Féin and UUP leaderships was that of running too far ahead of their supporters. The UUP may have succeeded in securing its constitutional aims but these were often intangible gains when contrasted with the very painful and visible policy decisions taken by government, such as prisoner releases and the reform of the RUC. Sinn Féin's rhetoric often gave the impression of a leadership dictating events rather than being at the mercy of the decisions of others. But the rhetoric of an undefeated army ill prepared the grassroots for many of the compromises to be made. And decommissioning was perhaps a compromise too far. If Sinn Féin accepted an agreement which saw it working a constitutional settlement that was worse, from a Nationalist view, than the Sunningdale Agreement, where did this place all the killing and sacrifice of the past generation? Decommissioning would be an admission that not only was the war over, but that it was wrong.

So, the possibility of resolving the impasse in the Peace Process now shifted to a redefinition, or at the very least an interim modification, of decommissioning, so as to make it palatable for Republicans. British and Irish legislation envisaged either the surrendering of arms to the Decommissioning Commission, or their destruction, possibly by the terrorist group concerned, albeit under the Commission's supervision. What the Governments were now exploring was how to implement the PIRA's statement to the Decommissioning Commission that they were willing to put their weapons beyond use. Following the UUP's decision to 'jump first' into devolved government with Sinn Féin, the refusal by Republicans to move on the arms issue became an unsustainable position. Attention began to focus on an old idea of securing weapons in PIRA arms dumps and connecting this with some form of demilitarisation on the British side. Were this to be the basis of a deal then it would clearly be a seismic shift on the part of the Republican Movement. They would still retain possession of their arms but never before had Republicans been willing to allow an outside agency to put any part of their arsenal beyond use. If nothing else, such a move demonstrated just how desperate senior Sinn Féin members had become to demonstrate that politics must work, and had to be seen to work; even if this was partitionist politics.

Early on the evening of 5 May, the British and Irish Governments signalled the breakthrough in a Joint Statement. The Governments now believed that the remaining steps necessary to secure full implementation of the Belfast Agreement could be achieved by June 2001. Subject to a positive response to this statement, the British Government would bring forward the necessary Order to enable the Northern Ireland Assembly and Executive to be restored. The Governments called for paramilitary groups to now state that they would put their arms 'completely and verifiably beyond use'. Such statements would constitute a clear reduction in threat. In response, the British Government would, subject to its assessment of the terrorist threat at the time, take 'further substantial normalisation measures by June 2001'. The Governments asked the Decommissioning Commission to consider whether any further proposals for decommissioning schemes would offer the Commission greater scope to proceed in more effective and satisfactory ways with the discharge of its basic mandate.[157] A Joint Letter set out in greater detail the contents of the Joint Statement. But, crucially, the British had inserted a section which stated that legislation to implement the Patten Report on Policing would be enacted by November 2000 'subject to Parliament'.[158] This gave the British Government latitude to make changes to the legislation through amendments proposed at Westminster. When the Police Bill was published, soon afterwards, although it gave the Secretary of State the power to change the name of the RUC it did not specify what that name would be.

The morning after the premiers' Joint Statement, Gerry Adams issued a statement in which Sinn Féin welcomed the Joint Statement and Joint Letter from the two Governments. He emphasised the Governments' commitments on human rights and equality, demilitarisation, the Irish language and the support for the families of all the victims of violence. He also pointed out that it was essential to have a new policing service to which nationalists and republicans could give their support and feel confident about joining. The Belfast Agreement had to be fully implemented; there could be no dilution or departure from it.[159]

This was followed, later in the day, by a statement from the PIRA. It reiterated that the British Government's claim to a part of Ireland, its denial of Irish national self-determination, the partition of Ireland and the maintenance of social and economic inequality in the Six Counties remained the root causes of conflict. But, significantly, the statement went on to say that the full implementation, on a progressive and irreversible basis of what had been agreed, would provide a political context, 'in an enduring political process, with the potential to remove the causes of conflict, and in which Irish republicans and unionists can, as equals, pursue our respective political objectives peacefully'. In that context, the PIRA leadership would initiate a process that 'will completely and verifiably put IRA arms beyond use. We will do it in such a way as to avoid risk to the public and misappropriation by others and ensure maximum public confidence.' The PIRA would resume contact with the Decommissioning Commission. The PIRA leadership also agreed to put in place a confidence-building measure to confirm that its weapons remained secure. The contents of a number of arms dumps would be inspected by agreed third parties who would report that they had done so to the Decommissioning Commission. The dumps would be re-inspected regularly to ensure that the weapons had remained silent.[160] The Prime Minister and Taoiseach welcomed the PIRA statement and announced that the weapons inspectors were to be Martti Ahtisaari, the former President of Finland, and Cyril Ramaphosa, the former Secretary-General of the African National Congress.[161]

In a statement to MPs, in the House of Commons, Peter Mandelson claimed that he had been vindicated in his decision to suspend the political institutions in Northern Ireland. He had done this because there would not only have been a total collapse of the institutions, but a total collapse of confidence within Unionism, from which the political process would not have been able to recover for a very long time. The aim of the British Government had been to achieve the clarity about the PIRA's intentions which was noticeably lacking in February; and, by doing so, to rebuild Unionist confidence and thereby to re-establish the institutions. The new PIRA statement was more of a clear-cut assurance of that organisation's intentions than had ever been heard before. An essential element of the inspection scheme was that the process should be continuous.[162]

Attention now refocused on the UUP. David Trimble had to go back to the UUC which had re-elected him leader by an uncomfortably narrow margin. The UUC had also decided that the UUP should not go back into a power-sharing executive if the RUC's name was to be discarded. Trimble's decision to respond cautiously to the PIRA offer sidefooted his anti-Agreement opponents within the UUP as he effectively stole their skeptic position. Trimble pronounced himself encouraged by the PIRA's statement; he went no further than to say that it 'appears to break new ground'.[163] However, Jeffrey Donaldson pointed out that there was nothing in the PIRA statement which indicated that it was going to disarm. The problem was that the PIRA still retained possession of its weapons and there was no guarantee that all of its weapons would be deposited in these bunkers or that the PIRA would not use them during the weeks between the proposed inspections.[164] With these concerns reflecting those of rank and file UUP members, John Taylor, in the Commons, asked the Secretary of State for a guarantee that all the PIRA's illegally held arms would be brought under control. Peter Mandelson replied that it was 'our requirement and our expectation' that all PIRA arms would be placed under control.[165]

The UUP leadership continued to play hardball in order to reassure its supporters. After meeting the inspectors, Trimble declared that there could be 'no minimalist approach' to decommissioning. If all that was being offered was the inspection of arms dumps then it could not be regarded as a satisfactory resolution of the issue. The dumps were 'not the permanent solution'. There were two different processes: putting arms beyond use, completely and finally, was to be done in consultation with the Decommissioning Commission; the inspection of arms dumps was an immediate confidence-building measure.[166]

Trimble received a letter of comfort from Mandelson to reassure UUP supporters that the party was not being sucked into an arrangement from which they could not retreat, or that many of the UUP's wider concerns were not being sacrificed in order to appease Republicans. Mandelson confirmed that the Northern Ireland Act 2000, which gave the Secretary of State the formal power to suspend Northern Ireland's political institutions, would not be repealed. If difficulties arose in the implementation of the Belfast

Agreement there would be an immediate formal review. Mandelson reiterated that the North-South Ministerial Council and the Northern Ireland Assembly were interdependent. If the Assembly collapsed the Council would not meet and the British Government envisaged the functions of the implementation bodies returning, within a reasonable period, to where they came from. The Secretary of State was to invite the new Policing Board to agree the design of the new service badge. If they were unable to agree, the Secretary of State would take a power in the Police Bill to decide the issue. Mandelson also confirmed that it was the intention of the Government to devolve policing and criminal justice issues to the Assembly 'sooner rather than later'.

Concerning Trimble's worries over the flying of flags from public buildings, Mandelson looked to the restored Executive to address the issue; but if the Executive could not reach a consensus the Secretary of State would take the power, by Order-in-Council, to provide a legal basis for the regulation of the flying of flags. Mandelson did not want this issue to become a 'running sore'. He noted that Trimble had made a strong case over the issue of the police name and the need to demonstrate clearly, as the Patten Report suggested, that the RUC was not being disbanded. The Secretary of State confirmed that the RUC 'is not being disbanded' and he believed that ways could be found of retaining an honourable and permanent place for the RUC name consistent with implementing the Patten proposals.[167] As a further sop to Trimble, Mandelson confirmed to the House of Commons that the Union Flag remained the flag of the United Kingdom of which Northern Ireland was a constituent part and while that was the wish of the majority of its people it would continue to fly over Northern Ireland.[168]

Armed with these reassurances, Trimble now went on the offensive against his opponents within the UUP. He announced that the UUP would quit any new executive if the PIRA failed to honour its pledges on disarmament. He acknowledged that there was concern within his party that 'if we move on this we are then locked into a situation'. However, Trimble argued that this simply was not the case: 'We retain complete freedom of action ourselves. From our point of view if there is any delay, if there is any foot dragging, then that is going to have serious political consequences.' In his assessment of the PIRA statement, Trimble went further than he had ever gone before when he argued that the Republican process of putting its arms beyond use was actual decommissioning. The suspension of the Executive had forced the PIRA to make an 'unprecedented offer'. In fact, 'There is no difference in practical terms if IRA weapons are made permanently inaccessible or unusable – this is decommissioning. The weapons are destroyed.' Turning to his own supporters he warned that if Unionists rejected the Belfast Agreement it would be replaced by 'green-tinged rule' and they would be in the 'wilderness for years'. He predicted that Sinn Féin could eventually become the largest Nationalist party in Northern Ireland and a substantially worse deal would await unionists.[169]

All of these apparent concessions to Trimble produced deep unease for Nationalists. When the Police Bill was eventually published, Bertie Ahern expressed concerns over the apparent diluting of its provisions when compared with the Patten Report. The main areas of concern were the provisions relating to the structures of accountability on the part of the proposed policing board and ombudsman, particularly their power to initiate inquiries, as was envisaged in the Patten Report. There were also concerns about the membership of the policing boards and the district partnerships. Ahern insisted that they should be representative of the broadest cross-section of the community. The Taoiseach was suggesting that a more limited interpretation of their roles was aimed at restricting Republican involvement. In respect of human rights, Ahern was also concerned about the content and scope of the oath. Since the Bill had been published, the Irish Government had received an 11-page list of concerns from the SDLP and a three-page list from Sinn Féin.[170]

An internal NIO document revealed the tensions between the British and the Irish. It noted that the view of the Irish Minister for Foreign Affairs, Brian Cowen, appeared to be that, beyond the constitutional acceptance that Northern Ireland remained part of the UK, there should be no further evidence of Britishness in the governance of Northern Ireland. The writer commented that this was 'an argument presented with all the subtlety and open-mindedness that one would expect from a member of Sinn Féin'. This apparently underlined the Secretary of State's view that 'Cowen has no feel or understanding of Unionist concerns and can usually be reliably counted on to tack to the green at every opportunity.'[171]

From the SDLP, Seamus Mallon criticised the UUP over the issue of the RUC's name and the flying of the Union Flag: 'For two years, we had a problem. The problem was decommissioning. One half-hour after the decommissioning issue was effectively resolved, then we had two more issues on the table.'[172] These were two more preconditions. Mallon felt that all of this undermined the crucial thrust of British-Irish intergovernmental arrangements from Sunningdale to the Belfast Agreement. In essence, the central problem was that the negotiating process often used by the two Governments over the past two years had fostered a 'shopping list syndrome'. During that time the UUP and Sinn Féin had beaten a path to Downing Street and Government Buildings in Dublin. Each time, more demands were made – and more met. Private undertakings and understandings replaced the politics of negotiation.

As an example of this, Mallon criticised the suspension of the political institutions as a unilateral decision to sustain the UUP. The decision to weaken and dilute the Patten recommendations was another overt attempt to save Unionism from itself, at the expense of the need to create a policing service that could command the support and involvement of all sections of the community. The Order-in-Council passed to give the Secretary of State the power to decide over the flying of flags was an obvious breach of the Belfast Agreement in yet another attempt to influence the outcome of the UUC's decision on whether to return to power-sharing. This drip-feed of concessions, for overtly party political reasons, had changed the perception of the British

Government as protector and guarantor of the Agreement. The Secretary of State had allowed himself to become a 'political crutch' for Ulster Unionism.[173]

Both the SDLP and Sinn Féin had been angered by the failure of the Police Bill to confirm that the name of the new force would be the Police Service of Northern Ireland and by Peter Mandelson's hints that, while this might be the force's working title, it might be possible to include 'RUC' in what he termed the 'title deeds' of the new service. Gerry Adams confirmed that Republicans were not prepared to support the new service on the basis of the legislation as drafted. However, with the UUC's decision in the balance, Trimble was in belligerent mood. He pointed out that he, and the UUP, had been encouraged not to humiliate the Republican Movement, and that it should not be emphasised that they had been defeated; but Trimble was annoyed that, at the same time, Nationalists were determined to inflict a defeat on the police: 'That is what the business about stripping them of their proud title, of the Royal title, of the Crown and of the flag; that's what it means.' This was a symbolic defeat, for some pique of Nationalism, that they wished to inflict on the police force and 'of course [unionist] people feel they're going to be humiliated, and what they're insisting with regard to this [UUC] resolution is "we will not be humiliated".' Trimble pronounced himself satisfied that the British Government had learned the lesson of the folly in the Patten Report, and that it was now anxious to ensure that the police and their families were not going to be humiliated. This would be reflected in future arrangements with regard to the name and the service's badge, although Trimble seemed to concede that the RUC name would not be part of the new working title.[174]

These concessions were enough to swing the vote for Trimble. In many respects Trimble's political weakness and the divisions within Unionism gave him a stronger hand in negotiations with the British Government than the electorally sound SDLP and Sinn Féin. The UUC meeting itself lasted over three hours. The final vote was close but Trimble secured a majority; 459, or 53 per cent, supported Trimble, while 403, or 47 per cent, rejected a return to power-sharing. The Northern Ireland power-sharing Executive then had devolved power returned to it on 27 May.

As the Police Bill continued on its way through Parliament, the British Government could now offer concessions to Nationalists following the restoration of devolved government. Some sixty amendments, many addressing Nationalist concerns, were still not enough to appease them. In particular, controversy surrounded the proposed name of the police. Peter Mandelson confirmed that the working title of the force would be the Police Service of Northern Ireland. But, to the fury of the SDLP and Sinn Féin, the Government was also prepared to accept two UUP amendments tabled by Ken Maginnis: '(1) The body of constables known as the Royal Ulster Constabulary shall continue in being as the Police Service of Northern Ireland (incorporating the Royal Ulster Constabulary)'; and '(2) the body of constables referred to in (1) above shall be styled for operational purposes the "Police Service of Northern Ireland".' The aim, as Maginnis explained, was to incorporate the RUC in the title deeds of the Bill which would retain 'RUC' as part of the formal title of the service and, more importantly, confirm that the force had not been disbanded.[175]

But, more significantly, on 26 June 2000, the PIRA announced that it had re-established contact with the Independent International Commission on Decommissioning and put in place a 'confidence-building measure'. A number of arms dumps had been examined by weapons inspectors.[176] Martti Ahtisaari and Cyril Ramaphosa announced that they had carried out their first inspection of dumps containing a substantial amount of military material, including explosives and related equipment, as well as weapons and other materials. They observed that the weapons and explosives were 'safely and adequately stored' and had 'ensured that the weapons and explosives cannot be used without our detection ... We plan to re-inspect the arms dumps on a regular basis to ensure that the weapons have remained secure.'[177]

The news disgusted Ruairí Ó Brádaigh of Republican Sinn Féin. It appeared that his prediction, in 1988, that Gerry Adams's talks with John Hume would lead to a fatal compromise recognising constitutionalism and partition had finally come true. The PIRA had committed an 'overt act of treachery' and had surrendered. No military force claiming to be an army could give its arsenal into the safe keeping of another party, in this case one which reported back to that army's enemy, without going into liquidation. The PIRA was no longer an army. It had surrendered, not just politically on its objectives, but it had also in effect disbanded without those objectives being realised. Worse still, its leaders had contravened their own rules, rated by General Order No 11 as 'treachery punishable by death'. The example of the Irish struggle for national independence, so long an inspiration to people fighting for liberation against colonialism and imperialism the world over, would now, insofar as the Provos were concerned, be cited as a classic case of betrayal, counter-revolution and collaboration. Ó Brádaigh, however, noted that there remained one section of the Irish people which continued to resist English rule in Ireland.[178] As the chairman of the 32-County Sovereignty Movement, Francie Mackey, told the organisation's annual general meeting: 'We haven't gone away, you know.'[179]

Conclusion

The remark attributed to Seamus Mallon, that the Multi-Party Talks process would be 'Sunningdale for slow learners', was an apt comment on both Unionists *and* Nationalists. Retrospectively, it seems highly unlikely that the Belfast Agreement could have been secured at an earlier stage of the Troubles. Primarily, this was because neither Unionists nor Nationalists either realised or wanted to make the necessary compromises to reach an agreement. For example, by 1998, there was still one central fact with which anti-Agreement Unionists had yet to come to terms: majority rule in Northern Ireland died in 1972. Furthermore, the political landscape of British-Irish relations changed forever in 1985. This was partly the failure of the Unionist political élite to develop a system of government which could have integrated Northern Nationalists into the Northern Ireland statelet. However, while this begs the question as to whether or not Northern Nationalists would have accepted such a system, it is clear that majority rule never held out any hope of this.

Unionists such as David Trimble finally came to accept consociationalism as the only hope, in the long term, of convincing Northern Catholics that they could compromise on their political sense of Irishness without abandoning their cultural sense of Irishness. But for anti-Agreement Unionists, such as Ian Paisley's DUP, there is no prospect of a return to majority rule. Politically, Paisley has outlived all other rivals for the relative, if not absolute, leadership of Ulster Unionism. However, this has been by remaining committed to the traditional Unionist policies of a previous generation. In the narrow field of party politics this has been a tactical success; but, strategically, the failure to move from a demand for the return of simple majority rule has allowed the idea of a Protestant Northern Ireland for a Protestant people to be eroded forever.

In 1985, the nature of Northern Ireland's relationship with the Irish Republic changed forever. From the moment the Anglo-Irish Agreement became a fact of Northern Ireland's political landscape, Unionists had to deal directly with the Irish Government and its concerns. Without the Anglo-Irish Agreement and, later, the Frameworks Documents, it is unlikely that any Unionists would have been moved to negotiate the Belfast Agreement. The fear that a failure to conclude a deal would allow greater slippage towards a united Ireland was crucial. This entire strategy depended on the belief that, after decades of violence and the need for Unionist consent to any agreement being essential, Nationalists were prepared to conclude an historic agreement with Unionism. The gamble paid off because of the British decision to back the UUP in its constitutional demands and the willingness of the Irish to compromise in this area. The price for this was the UUP swallowing the equality agenda and accepting that consent was a two-way process: Northern Ireland would be governed by both the Unionist and Nationalist representatives of Northern Ireland or not by either of them.

But constitutional Nationalism did not get off lightly either. Up to the Belfast Agreement, all the solutions suggested by the major representatives of Irish Nationalism – a unitary Irish state; a federal Ireland; joint British-Irish authority over Northern Ireland; or a North-South body with executive powers – were Nationalist solutions which only heightened or confirmed Unionist fears. John Hume's argument that national sovereignty was an outdated concept and that it might be pooled in an Irish context could have a realistic chance of success only if there was a consensus about the constitutional environment. This could not occur while one state claimed the territory of another. In the end, the Belfast Agreement created a new confederal relationship between the two sovereign states of the British Isles and a new confederal relationship between one of those states and a region of the United Kingdom – the Republic and Northern Ireland. This envisaged North-South relations in the control of the respective lines of authority – the Irish Parliament and the Northern Ireland Assembly. It was to be an inter-governmental rather than a neo-functionalist process. Unionists, ultimately, would have a brake on the development of North-South relations.

But this was not necessarily a negative development for Irish Nationalism. The North-South Ministerial Council could still be the vehicle which allowed trust to develop between North and South. It was the inherent dynamic and executive power of the Council of Ireland and the Frameworks Documents which contributed to the Unionist sense of siege. The Belfast Agreement was explicitly confederal. This did not shut the door on the evolution of a federal Ireland. It was for Nationalists to persuade Unionists that this was in their long-term interests. But Unionists would decide if they were to be persuaded. In the meantime all Nationalists could console themselves that they had taken a step towards the nebulous goal of a united Ireland.

Which brings us to the Republican Movement. Constitutionally, Sunningdale was a much better deal from the Republican point of view. At that stage Republicanism was locked into a mindset which believed that the British Army could be driven into the Irish Sea. But the greatest legacy of the PIRA's military campaign has been to alienate Ulster unionists from their sense of Irishness and increase their reliance on their sense of Britishness. For the Republican Movement the war has been against the British presence in Ireland. But the Unionists *are* the British presence in Ireland. The Northern Ireland conflict is not, primarily, a conflict between the British Government and the Irish people. It is an ethnic conflict between two national communities. Slowly, over the course of the Troubles, the reality of this has been faced by the adherents of constitutional Nationalism throughout the island of Ireland. If a similar process were to evolve within the Republican Movement, then a disturbing realisation will have to be faced by Republicans – just who was the war really against?

Quite rightly, Sinn Féin pointed out that the PIRA had not surrendered and was never beaten by the British military. But, in the long run, it did not have to be. After abandoning their own delusions that terrrorism could be defeated by military means, the British relied on containment. The PIRA war against British imperialism in Ireland was an illusion. The British could not leave Northern Ireland because a million of their citizens could not be expelled from the United Kingdom against their will. Northern Ireland was not some far-away colonial relic. It was an integral part of the United Kingdom itself. Whatever Britain's historic role in contributing to the causes of the conflict, in the late twentieth century the consent of the majority will in Northern Ireland governed the British determination to stay. Together with the Irish Government, the British sought to manoeuvre Republicans away from violence without alienating the unionist population to the point of insurrection. Even if decommissioning proved to be an insurmountable obstacle, the end of systematic paramilitary violence by the main terrorist groups would constitute success for the British.

The Republican Movement sought to create a pan-Nationalist alliance to force the British to become persuaders for a united Ireland and by-pass unionist consent by establishing all-Ireland structures to create the dynamic towards this. Instead Republicans ended up agreeing to a deal which recognised partition; established consent as its guiding principle; saw the Irish Constitution distinguish between nation and state; reinstated what they claimed was a British territorial claim in the Northern Ireland Constitution Act 1998; agreed to become what were effectively Ministers of the Crown in a Northern Ireland executive; and participated in a British-Irish Council.

This, perhaps more than anything, suggests that senior members of the Republican leadership realised that continuing violence would not achieve their long-term goals. Ending violence meant political respectability and entering the political process with the prospect of government North and, possibly, South in a coalition. In return they got their prisoners out; saw the establishment of the equality agenda; and the reform, but not the disbanding, of the RUC. At the height of the war against British rule in Northern Ireland an acceptance of the equality agenda and the reform of Northern Ireland were the very things Sinn Féin reserved the most spite for in their criticisms of the SDLP.

This was why decommissioning was a compromise too far. There was no evidence that the Republican Movement ever believed that it was obliged to decommission. For to do so, after all the other compromises, would be to call into question the entire legitimacy of their war. However it might be presented, decommissioning would mean defeat, because it would be an admission, after all the other compromises, that the PIRA could never have beaten the British.

Since partition the British have not been opposed to a united Ireland if the consent of Northern Ireland to this was secured by Nationalists. For the greater part of the current Troubles, the primary aim of the British was to secure the end of violence in Northern Ireland. It was true that the PIRA were not defeated militarily; but the British only need a draw to win.

Notes

Introduction (pp 1-18)

1. Bridgid Hadfield *The Constitution of Northern Ireland* (Belfast 1989) p. 5
2. Thomas Hennessey *Dividing Ireland: World War One and Partition* (London 1998) pp 218-19
3. Hadfield op. cit. p. 243
4. Ibid p. 246
5. Ibid pp 100-101
6. Ibid pp 104-10
7. *The Future of Northern Ireland. A Paper for Discussion* (Belfast 1972) pp 32-3
8. *Unionist Review* June 1973
9. Garret FitzGerald *All in a Life: An Autobiography* (Dublin 1991) p. 213
10. *SDLP News* Vol. 1 No. 1 5 October 1972
11. FitzGerald op. cit. p. 213
12. Ibid p. 201
13. Ibid p. 208
14. Ibid p. 213
15. Ibid p. 217
16. Ibid p. 221
17. Hafield op. cit. pp 113-14
18. Brian Faulkner *Memoirs of a Statesman* (London 1978) pp 236-7
19. FitzGerald op. cit. p. 226
20. Northern Ireland Constitutional Convention Debates UUUC Policy Position 26 August 1975 pp 587-8
21. Ibid 22 September 1975 pp 537-40

Part I (pp 19-66)

1. *Irish Times* 9 November 1978
2. Ibid 16 February 1978
3. *Foreign Affairs* March 1980
4. *Irish Times* 18 July 1980

5.   Hadfield op. cit. pp 179-80
6.   Ibid pp 152-4
7.   *Irish Times* 2 October 1982
8.   Ibid 5 May 1982
9.   Ibid 2 October 1982
10. Padráig O'Malley *The Uncivil Wars. Ireland Today* (Belfast 1983) pp 101-3
11. *New Ireland Forum Report* (Dublin 1984) p. 26
12. Ibid pp 19-21
13. Ibid p. 17
14. Ibid p. 23
15. Ibid pp 31-8
16. *Fortnight* 4 February 1985
17. Anthony Kenny 'Joint Authority' pp 221-7 in John McGarry and Brendan O'Leary (eds) *The Future of Northern Ireland* (Oxford 1990)
18. FitzGerald op. cit. pp 497-8
19. Margaret Thatcher *The Downing Street Years* (New York 1993) pp 386-7
20. Ibid pp 384-5
21. Ibid pp 400-401
22. Hadfield op. cit. pp 192-8
23. Brendan O'Brien *The Long War: The IRA and Sinn Féin 1985 to Today* (Dublin 1993), p. 289
24. *An Phoblacht* July 1972
25. Seán Mac Stiofáin *Revolutionary in Ireland* (Farnborough 1974) pp 281-2
26. Paul Bew and Gordon Gillespie *Northern Ireland: A Chronology of the Troubles 1993-1996* (Dublin 1993) pp 98-9
27. *An Phoblacht*, 15 March 1977
28. Ibid 4 January 1978
29. Bew and Gillespie op. cit. pp 164-5
30. *An Phoblacht/Republican News* 17 November 1983
31. Ibid 8 November 1984
32. Ibid 29 August 1985
33. Ibid 17 November 1983
34. Ibid 1 March 1984
35. Ibid 21 June 1984
36. Ibid 5 January 1984
37. Ibid 18 October 1984
38. Ibid 22 November 1984
39. Ibid 19 April 1984
40. Ibid 26 April 1984
41. Ibid 21 June 1984
42. Ibid 8 November 1984

43. Ibid 22 November 1984
44. Ibid
45. Ibid 26 September 1985
46. Ibid 7 November 1985
47. Ibid 12 December 1985
48. Ibid 7 November 1985
49. *Sunday Tribune* 14 September 1986
50. *Irish Times* 2 November 1986
51. *Observer* 19 June 1988
52. *Hot Press* 17 December 1987
53. *Irish Times* 12 January 1988
54. *Irish News* 14 May 1988
55. *Irish Times* 18 May 1988
56. Ibid 22 June 1988
57. Ibid 13 June 1988
58. Ibid 7 September 1988
59. Ibid 12 September 1988
60. Ibid 26 September 1988
61. Ibid 13 September 1988
62. Ibid 19 September 1988
63. Pádraig O'Malley *Northern Ireland: Questions of Nuance* (Belfast 1990) p. 18
64. Ibid p. 22
65. Brian Rowan *Behind the Lines: The Story of the IRA and Loyalist Ceasefires* (Belfast 1995) p. 16
66. *Sunday Tribune* 17 January 1988
67. Northern Ireland Assembly Official Report, Vol. 237, p. 44 (1986)
68. Hadfield op. cit. pp 192–8
69. *Irish Times* 21 January 1986
70. *Studies* September 1986
71. *Irish News* 14 November 1986
72. *Irish Times* 13 January 1989
73. *Common Sense* (Belfast 1987)
74. *Fortnight* April 1987
75. Brooke-Mayhew Talks Papers: Draft Proposals for a British–Irish Agreement
76. David Trimble 'Initiatives for Consensus. A Unionist Perspective' pp 78–89 in Charles Townshend (ed) *Consensus in Ireland. Approaches and Recessions* (Oxford 1988)
77. Brooke-Mayhew Talks Papers: Statement by the Secretary of State for Northern Ireland, Peter Brooke MP 26 March 1991
78. Ibid Annex A Agreeing the Nature of the Problem (SDLP Paper) 5 May 1992
79. Ibid Agreeing New Political Structures. Submission by the SDLP to the

Inter-Party Talks 11 May 1992

80. Ibid Ref:SC/4 Report of a Meeting of the Structures Sub-Committee held at Parliament Buildings on 12 May 1992

81. Ibid Ref:SC/5 Summary Record of a Meeting of the Structures Sub-Committee at Parliament Buildings on the Afternoon of 12 May 1992

82. Ibid Ref:SC/10 Summary Record of a Meeting of the Structures Sub-Committee at Parliament Buildings on the Morning of 15 May 1992

83. Ibid A Submission by the Ulster Unionist Party. Arrangements for the Internal Government and Administration of Northern Ireland. 11 May 1992; A Sure Advance. A Paper Submitted by the Democratic Unionist Party 11 May 1992

84. Ibid Ref:SC/9 Summary Record of a Meeting of the Structures Sub-Committee at Parliament Buildings on the Afternoon of 13 May 1992

85. Ibid Revised Ref:SC/6 Record of a Meeting of the Structures Sub-Committee at Parliament Buildings on the Morning of 13 May 1992

86. Ibid Revised Ref:SC/7 Record of a Meeting of the Structures Sub-Committee at Parliament Buildings on the Morning of 13 May 1992

87. Ibid Ref:PT/17 Summary Record of a Plenary Meeting held at Parliament Buildings on the Afternoon of 20 May 1992

88. Ibid Annex A: New Political Institutions in Northern Ireland 10 June 1992

89. Ibid Ref: PT/24 Summary Record of a Plenary Meeting held in Parliament Buildings on the Evening of 12 June 1992

90. Ibid 'Constitutional Issues' Paper Submitted by the Irish Government Delegation 28 August 1992

91. Ibid Submission by the Irish Government Delegation: Possible Institutional Structures

92. Ibid Irish-British and Inter-Party Talks Strand II Submission by the SDLP September 1992

93. Ibid 7 July Annexe 1 Strand 2 Opening Statement by Rev. Dr Ian Paisley MP MEP on behalf of the Ulster Democratic Unionist Party

94. Ibid Strand 2 Response Paper UDUP

95. Ibid A paper submitted by the Ulster Unionist Party, October 1992: An Inter-Irish Relations Committee

96. Ibid UUP Strand 3 proposal 1992

Part II (pp 67-114)

1. Gerry Adams *Free Ireland: Towards a Lasting Peace* (Dublin 1995) p. 209

2. O'Malley op. cit. (1990) p. 58

3. *Irish Times* 10 November 1990

4. O'Malley op. cit. (1990) p. 82

5. Eamon Mallie and David McKittrick *The Fight for Peace: The Secret Story Behind the Irish Peace Process* (London 1996) pp 246-8

6. *Irish Times* 17 February 1992
7. Messages Between the IRA and the Government: Secretary of State for Northern Ireland to The Rt Hon. John Smith MP QC December 1993
8. Ibid 29 November 1993
9. Ibid British Message sent 26 February 1993
10. Ibid Message from the leadership of the Provisional Movement, 5 March [1993]
11. Ibid British message sent 11 March 1993
12. Adams op. cit. (1995) p. 209
13. *Irish News* 27 July 1992
14. Messages Between the IRA and the Government: British 9-paragraph note, sent on 19 March 1993
15. Ibid Message from the leadership of the Republican Movement, 22 March 1993
16. John Major *The Autobiography* (London 1999) pp 446-7
17. Setting the Record Straight: Sinn Féin's 'April' document: Sinn Féin's basis for entering dialogue
18. Mallie and McKittrick op. cit. pp 118-19
19. Ibid pp 371-2
20. Major op. cit. pp 447-8
21. Mallie and McKittrick op. cit. pp 375-6
22. Ibid pp 176-7
23. Major op. cit. pp 441-2
24. Ibid pp 449-50
25. Setting the Record Straight: April 24 1993 – First Joint Statement from Gerry Adams and John Hume
26. Adams op. cit. p. 215
27. *Starry Plough* Vol. 1, Issue 2, November 1991
28. *Fingerpost Monthly* May 1991, Vol. 8, No.1
29. Major op. cit. p. 450
30. Joint Declaration by An Taoiseach, Mr Albert Reynolds TD and the British Prime Minister, the Rt Hon. John Major MP, 15 December 1993 (Dublin 1993)
31. *Irish Times* 16 December 1993
32. Ibid
33. Adams op. cit. p. 227
34. Gerry Adams *An Irish Voice: The Quest for Peace* pp 37-9 (Kerry 1997)
35. Ibid pp 87-9
36. Paul Bew and Gordon Gillespie *The Northern Ireland Peace Process 1993-1996* (London 1996) p. 63
37. Mallie and McKittrick op. cit. pp 381-3

38. Ibid p. 90
39. Ibid p. 123
40. *Irish Times* 26 July 1993
41. *Independent* 28 July 1993
42. *Irish Times* 7 October 1993
43. Ibid 4 November 1993
44. Ibid 24 November 1993
45. Ibid 18 October 1993
46. Ibid 29 October 1991
47. Ibid 16 December 1993
48. Rowan op. cit. p. 126
49. Ibid pp 71-2
50. Steve Bruce 'Loyalists in Northern Ireland: Further Thoughts on "Pro-State Terror"' in *Terrorism and Political Violence*, Vol. 5, No. 4, Winter 1993 pp 262-3
51. *News-Letter* 8 October 1994
52. *Sunday Tribune* 16 October 1994
53. *Belfast Telegraph* 12 October 1994
54. *Irish Times* 17 October 1994
55. Ibid 16 January 1995
56. Ibid 23 January 1995
57. Ibid 17 February 1995
58. Ibid 18 February 1995
59. Frameworks for the Future Cmmd.2964 (London 1995)
60. Ulster Unionist Party: *We Reject the Governments' 'Frameworks' Proposals as the Basis for Negotiations*; Ulster Unionist Party: *Response to 'Frameworks for the Future'* nd
61. *Forum for Peace and Reconciliation / Foram um Shíocháin Agus Athmhuintaras Report of Proceedings* Vol. 16 Friday 5 May 1995
62. *Remarks by the Taoiseach, Mr John Bruton, TD, to the Forum Debate on North-South Structures in the light of the Joint Framework Document and other documents.* Friday 19 May 1995
63. *Sinn Féin Submission to Forum for Peace and Reconciliation, Dublin Castle, 19 May 1995. On the Need for All-Ireland Institutions*
64. *Forum for Peace and Reconciliation / Foram um Shíocháin Agus Athmhuintaras Report of Proceedings* Vol. 16, Friday 19 May 1995
65. Major op. cit. pp 470-77
66. Ibid pp 479-81
67. Ibid p. 134
68. *Report of the International Body* 22 January 1996
69. Ibid

70. Multi-Party Talks Papers *All-Party Negotiations Background Documents* October 1997 pp 43-4
71. Ibid pp 25-6
72. Ibid pp 1-9
73. Confidential information
74. Paul Bew, Henry Patterson and Paul Teague *Northern Ireland: Between War and Peace. The Political Future of Northern Ireland* (London 1997) pp 217-22
75. Ibid pp 225-9
76. Confidential information
77. *An Phoblacht/Republican News* 11 September 1997
78. *News-Letter* 15 September 1997
79. Ibid
80. Multi-Party Talks Papers: Proposed Procedural Motion 24 September 1997
81. Ibid Joint Statement 15 September 1997
82. *News-Letter* 8 August 1997
83. Ibid
84. Ibid
85. BBC Radio Ulster, Inside Politics 20 September 1997
86. *Irish Times* 17 September 1997
87. Ibid 8 January 1998
88. *News-Letter* 6 April 1998
89. *Irish Times* 14 October 1997
90. Multi-Party Talks Papers Notice of Indictment against Sinn Féin/IRA made by the Ulster Unionist Party to the Plenary session of the Stormont Talks; 23 September 1997
91. Ibid Conclusions of the Governments on representations made by the UUP against Sinn Féin; 24 September 1997
92. *News-Letter* 18 November 1997
93. *Irish Times* 1 December 1997
94. Ibid

Part III (pp 115-158)

1. Multi-Party Talks Papers: Ulster Unionist Party Memo on Heads of Agreement 3 January 1998
2. Ibid Irish Government. Heads of Agreement: Possible Propositions 8 January 1998
3. Ibid Propositions on Heads of Agreement 12 January 1998
4. Ibid UUP Debrief on Meeting with the Irish Government morning 31 March 1998
5. Ibid Freedom, Justice, Democracy, Equality: Nature, Form and Extent of New Arrangements. A Sinn Féin submission to Strands One and Two of

the Peace Talks 27 October 1997

6. *Irish Times* 22 January 1998
7. Ibid 19 January 1998
8. *Irish News* 2 February 1998
9. Ibid 4 February 1998
10. Ibid 7 February 1998
11. *Irish Times* 7 February 1998
12. *Irish News* 10 February 1998
13. Multi-Party Talks Papers: The United Kingdom Government's Proposals for Decentralised Government in Great Britain (16 January 1998)
14. Ibid Strand One Synthesis Paper (2 March 1998)
15. Ibid Strand One, Twelfth Meeting, 4 March 1998
16. Ibid Strand One, Fourteenth Meeting, 23 March 1998
17. *Irish Times* 24 February 1998
18. Ibid
19. Multi-Party Talks Papers: Strand One, Twelfth Meeting, 4 March 1998
20. Ibid British Government Democratic Institutions in Northern Ireland 29 March 1998
21. Ibid UUP Memo to John Holmes from David Trimble 1 April 1998
22. *Irish Times* 2 April 1998
23. Multi-Party Talks Papers: UUP Minute: Talks Meeting on 31 March 1998 with SDLP
24. Ibid Note of UUP Points Agreed with SDLP 1 April 1998
25. Ibid Ulster Unionist Party Memo on Heads of Agreement 3 Janaury 1998
26. *News-Letter* 17 January 1998
27. *Ireland on Sunday* 18 January 1998
28. Multi-Party Talks Papers: 27 January 1998 Strand Two Structures, Lancaster House, London
29. Ibid UUP Minutes: Talks in London on Tuesday 27 January 1998. Ulster Unionist Party and Prime Minister
30. Confidential information
31. Ibid
32. Multi-Party Talks Papers: Summary Record of Strand Two Meeting, Tuesday 3 March 1998, at 10.40
33. Ibid Summary Record of Strand Two Meeting, Tuesday 24 February 1998, at 10.43
34. Ibid Summary Record of Strand Two Meeting, Tuesday 10 March 1998, at 10.41
35. Ibid Summary Record of Strand Two Meeting, Tuesday 24 February 1998, at 10.43
36. Ibid Summary Record of Strand Two Meeting, Tuesday 3 March 1998, at 10.40

37. Ibid Summary Record of Strand Two Meeting, Tuesday 24 February 1998, at 10.43

38. Ibid Summary Record of Strand Two Meeting, Tuesday 3 March 1998, at 14.30

39. Ibid A Sinn Féin Discussion Document Submitted for all 3 Strands 24 March 1998

40. Ibid UUP Debrief on Meeting with the Irish Government morning 31 March 1998

41. Ibid Irish Government The Legal Basis of Proposed North-South Institutions 1 April 1998

42. Ibid UUP Memo to John Holmes from David Trimble 1 April 1998

43. Ibid SDLP Strands 1 and 2: Constitutional Issues 20 October 1997

44. Ibid A Sinn Féin Discussion Document Submitted for all 3 Strands 24 March 1998

45. Ibid Strand Two – Constitutional Issues. Paper by the Irish Government 17 October 1997

46. Ibid UUP Minute: Meeting held on Wednesday 4 March 1998 with Irish Government

47. Hadfield op. cit. pp 34-5

48. *Sunday Independent* 8 March 1998

49. Multi-Party Talks Papers: Ulster Unionist Party Memo on Heads of Agreement 3 January 1998

50. Ibid Memo David Trimble to John Holmes 1 April 1998

51. *Irish News* 30 March 1998

52. *Parliamentary Brief* Vol. 5, No. 6 May/June 1998

53. Multi-Party Talks Papers: UUP Minute: Meeting held on Wednesday 4 March 1998 with Irish Government

54. Ibid UUP Debrief on Meeting with the Irish Government morning 31 March 1998

55. Ibid Irish Government Memorandum on Articles 2 and 3. 1 April 1998

56. Ibid Summary Record of Liaison Sub-Committee Meeting on Confidence Building Measures on Monday 15 December 1997 (15.00)

57. Ibid A Sinn Féin Discussion Document Submitted for all 3 Strands 24 March 1998

58. Ibid Liaison Sub-Committee on Confidence Building Measures: Meeting on 13 January 1998. Economic and Social Development: Further Paper by the British Government

59. Ibid Summary Record of Inaugural Cross-Strand Meeting Monday 2 March 1998 (14.15)

60. Ibid Professor Antony Alcock Divided Communities in Europe. A Briefing Paper for the Ulster Unionist Party

61. Ibid Summary Record of Inaugural Cross-Strand Meeting Monday

2 March 1998 (14.15)

62. Ibid Independent International Commission on Decommissioning Initial Report. November 1997
63. Ibid A Sinn Féin Discussion Document Submitted for all 3 Strands 24 March 1998
64. Ibid Liaison Sub-Committee on Confidence Building Measures; Security Issues – Paper by HMG 23 March 1998
65. Ibid Strand One, Thirteenth Meeting, 9 March 1998
66. Ibid Strand One, Fifteenth Meeting, 25 March 1998
67. *Irish News* 1 December 1997
68. Multi-Party Talks Papers: Summary Record of Liaison Sub-Committee Meeting on Confidence Building Measures on Tuesday 2 December 1997 (15.00)
69. Ibid Liaison Sub-Committee on Confidence Building Measures: Meeting on 4 February 1998. Paper by the British Government
70. *News-Letter* 12 January 1998
71. *Irish Times* 19 January 1998
72. *News-Letter* 23 January 1998
73. Multi-Party Talks Papers: Conclusions of the Governments on the position of the Ulster Democratic Party in the talks. 26 January 1998 Annex A
74. Ibid Summary of Plenary (1st) Monday 27 January 1998, Lancaster House, London
75. *Irish News* 27 January 1998
76. Multi-Party Talks Papers Summary Record of Plenary Session, Monday 27 January 1998 Lancaster House, London
77. *Irish News* 13 February 1998
78. *Daily Telegraph* 14 February 1998
79. Multi-Party Talks Papers Summary Record of Strand Two Meeting, Monday 16 February 1998, at 11.12, Dublin Castle
80. Ibid Summary Record of Plenary Session, Tuesday 17 February 1998, at 17.51, Dublin Castle
81. Ibid Determination in Respect of Sinn Féin 20 February 1998
82. *News-Letter* 21 February 1998

Part IV (pp 159–216)

1. *Irish News* 26 March 1998
2. *Irish Times* 2 March 1998
3. Ibid 2 April 1998
4. George J. Mitchell *Making Peace* (London 1999) pp 148–65
5. Multi-Party Talks Papers: UUP Meeting with PUP and UDP 6 April 1998
6. Ibid The Independent Chairmen. Draft Paper for Discussion. Strand Two, Paragraph 5 (ii)

7. Ibid Annex A
8. Ibid Paragraph 5 (iii)
9. Ibid Annex B
10. Ibid Paragraph 5 (iv)
11. Ibid Paragraph 7
12. Ibid Paragraph 8
13. Ibid Annex C
14. *News-Letter* 8 April 1998
15. *Financial Times* 8 April 1998
16. *News-Letter* 8 April 1998
17. *Irish Times* 8 April 1998
18. Multi-Party Talks Papers: Trimble to Blair 7 April 1998
19. *Belfast Telegraph* 8 April 1998
20. *News-Letter* 9 April 1998
21. *Irish News* 9 April 1998
22. Multi-Party Talks Papers: Memo Empey to Trimble 5 April 1998
23. Note of a Conversation with David Trimble 8 April 1998
24. Mitchell op. cit. pp 170-71
25. *Irish Times* 9 April 1998
26. Multi-Party Talks Papers: UUP Memo Empey to Trimble 5 April 1998
27. Confidential information
28. Multi-Party Talks Papers: Paul Murphy MP to the Rt Hon. David Trimble MP 9 April 1998
29. Ibid UUP Talks Team Meeting 10 April 1998
30. Ibid The Prime Minister to the Rt Hon. David Trimble MP 10 April 1998
31. *Parliamentary Brief* Vol. 5, No. 6, May/June 1998 p. 24
32. *News-Letter* 10 April 1998
33. *Belfast Telegraph* 10 April 1998
34. *Parliamentary Brief* Vol. 5, No. 6 May/June 1998 pp 18-20
35. The Belfast Agreement: Constitutional Issues Paragraph 1
36. Ibid Annex A
37. Ibid Schedule 1
38. Ibid Annex B
39. Ibid Strand 1 Paragraph 1
40. Ibid Paragraph 2
41. Ibid Paragraph 5
42. Ibid Paragraph 6
43. Ibid Paragraph 7
44. Ibid Paragraphs 15-18
45. Ibid Paragraph 25

46. Ibid Paragraphs 30–33
47. Ibid Strand 2 Paragraph 1
48. Ibid Paragraph 5
49. Ibid Paragraph 6
50. Ibid Paragraph 8
51. Ibid Paragraph 9
52. Ibid Paragraph 11
53. Ibid Paragraph 12
54. Ibid Paragraph 13
55. Ibid Paragraph 18
56. Ibid Paragraph 19
57. Ibid Annex
58. Ibid Strand Three British-Irish Council Paragraph 1
59. Ibid Paragraph 2
60. Ibid Paragraph 3
61. Ibid Paragraphs 3–6
62. Ibid Paragraphs 7–9
63. Ibid Paragraph 10
64. Ibid Paragraph 11
65. Ibid Paragraph 12
66. Ibid British-Irish Intergovernmental Conference Paragraph 1
67. Ibid Paragraphs 2–4
68. Ibid Paragraph 5
69. Ibid Paragraphs 6–9
70. Ibid Rights, Safeguards and Equality of Opportunity Paragraph 1
71. Ibid Paragraph 2
72. Ibid Paragraph 3
73. Ibid Paragraph 4
74. Ibid Paragraph 5
75. Ibid Paragraphs 6–8
76. Ibid Paragraph 9
77. Ibid Paragraph 10
78. Ibid Rights, Safeguards and Equality of Opportunity Paragraph 1
79. Ibid Paragraph 2
80. Ibid Paragraph 4
81. Ibid Paragraph 5
82. Ibid Decommissioning Paragraphs 1–6
83. Ibid Security Paragraph 1
84. Paragraph 2
85. Paragraphs 3–5
86. Ibid Policing and Justice Paragraph 1

87. Ibid Paragraph 3
88. Ibid Paragraph 4
89. Ibid Paragraph 5
90. Ibid Prisoners Paragraphs 1-2
91. Ibid Paragraphs 3-5
92. Ibid 7 May 1998
93. *Irish Times* 20 April 1998
94. Ibid 11 May 1998
95. Ibid 25 April 1998
96. Ibid 11 May 1998
97. Ibid 18 April 1998
98. Ibid 16 April 1998
99. Ibid 7 May 1998
100. Ibid 19 May 1998
101. Confidential information
102. *Irish Times* 15 May 1998
103. Ibid 12 May 1998
104. Ibid 15 May 1998
105. Ibid 16 May 1998
106. Ibid 18 May 1998
107. Ibid 14 May 1998
108. Ibid 20 May 1998
109. Ibid
110. Brigid Hadfield 'The Belfast Agreement, Sovereignty and the State of the Union', *Public Law*, Winter 1998 pp 599-600
111. Ibid pp 604-5
112. Ibid p. 610
113. Ibid pp 615-16
114. Clause 43 Northern Ireland Constitution Act 1998
115. *Irish Times* 2 September 1999
116. Proceedings of the Northern Ireland Assembly 18 January 1999
117. Report from the First Minister-designate and Deputy First Minister-designate 15 February 1999; Proceedings of the Northern Ireland Assembly 15 February 1999
118. Agreement between the Government of Ireland and the Government of the United Kingdom of Great Britain and Northern Ireland establishing a North-South Ministerial Council 8 March 1999
119. Agreement between the Government of Ireland and the Government of the United Kingdom of Great Britain and Northern Ireland establishing a British-Irish Council 8 March 1999

120. Agreement between the Government of Ireland and the Government of the United Kingdom of Great Britain and Northern Ireland establishing a British-Irish Intergovernmental Conference 8 March 1999
121. *Irish Times* 19 January 1999
122. Ibid 6 February 1999
123. Ibid 16 February 1999
124. Ibid 19 February 1999
125. Ibid 1 April 1999
126. Remarks by the Prime Minister, the Rt Hon. Tony Blair MP on Behalf of the UK and Irish Governments at a Press Conference with the Taoiseach, Bertie Ahern TD, Hillsborough Castle, County Down 1 April 1999
127. Confidential information
128. Speech by the Prime Minister, the Rt Hon. Tony Blair MP at Stranmillis University College, Befast on Tuesday 15 June 1999
129. *Irish Times* 1 July 1999
130. Ibid 2 July 1999
131. Ibid 3 July 1999
132. The Way Forward. A Joint Statement by the British and Irish Governments 2 July 1999
133. Report of the Independent Commission on Decommissioning 2 July 1999
134. *Irish Times* 3 July 1999
135. Ibid
136. Ibid 5 July 1999
137. Ibid
138. *Sunday Times* 4 July 1999
139. *Irish Times* 6 July 1999
140. Ibid 9 July 1999
141. Ibid
142. Ibid
143. Ibid 16 July 1999
144. Ibid 15 November 1999
145. Confidential information
146. UUP Statement 15 November 1999
147. Sinn Féin Statement 15 November 1999
148. PIRA Statement 17 November 1999
149. *Irish Times* 16 November 1999
150. Ibid 18 November 1999
151. Ibid 4 February 2000
152. Ibid
153. Ibid 14 February 2000
154. Ibid

155. Ibid
156. The Future of Policing in Northern Ireland. Summary of Conclusions
157. Joint Statement 5 May 2000
158. Joint Letter 5 May 2000
159. Statement by Sinn Féin 6 May 2000
160. IRA Statement 6 May 2000
161. Joint Statement by the Prime Minister and the Taoiseach 6 May 2000
162. *Irish Times* 9 May 2000
163. Ibid 8 May 2000
164. Ibid
165. Ibid 9 May 2000
166. Ibid 16 May 2000
167. Ibid 17 May 2000
168. Ibid
169. Ibid 18 May 2000
170. Ibid
171. Ibid 5 May 2000
172. Ibid 17 May 2000
173. Ibid 18 May 2000
174. Ibid 22 May 200
175. Ibid 4 July 200
176. PIRA Statement 26 June 2000
177. Statement by Martti Ahtisaari and Cyril Ramaphosa 26 June 2000
178. *Irish Times* 26 June 2000
179. Ibid

Bibliography

(1) Official Government and Political Party Papers
Brooke–Mayhew Talks Papers (1991–1992)
Plenary Minutes
Strand One Minutes
Strand Two Minutes
Strand Three Minutes
British Government Papers
Democratic Unionist Party Papers
Irish Government Papers
Social and Democratic Labour Party Papers
Ulster Unionist Party Papers

British Government – Republican Movement Contacts (1990–1993)
Messages Between the IRA and the Government (British Government 1995)
Setting the Record Straight (Sinn Féin 1995)

Multi-Party Talks Papers (1996–1998)
Cross-Strand Minutes
Draft Paper for Discussion (Mitchell Document)
Independent International Commission on Decommissioning
Plenary Minutes and Papers
Strand One Minutes and Papers
Strand Two Minutes and Papers
Strand Three Minutes and Papers
Sub-Committee on Confidence-Building Measures
British Government Papers
Irish Government Papers
Progressive Unionist Party Papers
Social and Democratic Labour Party Papers

Sinn Féin Papers
Ulster Democratic Party Papers
Ulster Unionist Party Papers

(2) Printed Records: Debates and Constitutional Documents
Anglo–Irish Agreement (1985)
Belfast Agreement (1998)
Forum for Peace and Reconciliation/Foram um Shíocháin Agus
Athmhuintaras Report of Proceedings (1995)
Frameworks for the Future (1995)
Future of Northern Ireland. A Paper for Discussion (1972)
Government of Ireland Act 1920
Joint Declaration by An Taoiseach, Mr Albert Reynolds TD and the British
Prime Minister, the Rt Hon. John Major MP, 15 December 1993 (1993)
New Ireland Forum Public Submissions (1983–1984)
New Ireland Forum Report (1984)
Northern Ireland Assembly Debates/Proceedings (1998–2000)
Northern Ireland Constitution Act 1973
Northern Ireland Constitution Act 1998
Report of the International Body on Decommissioning (1996)

(3) Newspapers and Journals
An Phoblacht
Belfast Telegraph
Daily Telegraph
Hot Press
Financial Times
Fingerpost Monthly
Foreign Affairs
Fortnight
Independent
Ireland on Sunday
Irish News
Irish Times
Observer
Parliamentary Brief
Republican News
Starry Plough
Studies
Sunday Independent
Sunday Times

Sunday Tribune
Ulster News-Letter

(4) Books, Articles, Pamphlets and Theses

Adams, Gerry, *The Politics of Irish Freedom* (Dublin 1986)

Adams, Gerry, *Free Ireland: Towards a Lasting Peace* (Dublin 1995)

Adamson, Ian, *The Identity of Ulster* (Belfast 1982)

Anderson, Don, *14 May Days: The Inside Story of the Loyalist Strike of 1974* (Dublin 1994)

Arthur, Paul, *The People's Democracy 1968-73* (Belfast 1974)

Arthur, Paul, *Government and Politics of Northern Ireland* (Essex 1980)

Arthur, Paul and Keith Jeffrey, *Northern Ireland since 1968* (Oxford 1988)

Aughey, Arthur, *Under Siege: Ulster Unionism and the Anglo-Irish Agreement* (Belfast 1989)

Aughey, Arthur, 'Unionism and Self-Determination' in Patrick J. Roche and Brian Barton (eds), *The Northern Ireland Question: myth and reality* (Aldershot, 1991)

Bardon, Jonathan, *A History of Ulster* (Belfast 1992)

Barritt, D.P. and Charles F. Carter, *The Northern Ireland Problem: A Study in Group Relations* (Oxford 1962)

Barton, Brian, *Brookeborough: The Making of a Prime Minister* (Belfast 1988)

Barton, Brian, *Northern Ireland in the Second World War* (Belfast 1995)

Bell, Desmond, *Acts of Union: Youth Culture and Sectarianism in Northern Ireland* (London 1990)

Bell, J. Bowyer, *The Secret Army: The IRA 1916-1979* (Dublin 1979)

Bell, J. Bowyer, *The Irish Troubles: A Generation of Violence 1967-1992* (Dublin 1993)

Beresford, David, *Ten Men Dead: The Story of the 1981 Irish Hunger Strike* (London 1987)

Bew, Paul, *Conflict and Conciliation in Ireland 1890-1910: Parnellites and Radical Agrarians* (Oxford 1987)

Bew, Paul, Peter Gibbon and Henry Patterson, *Northern Ireland: Political Forces and Social Classes 1921-1994* (London 1995)

Bew, Paul, Kenneth Darwin and Gordon Gillespie, *Passion and Prejudice: Nationalist-Unionist Conflict in Ulster in the 1930s and the Foundation of the Irish Association* (Belfast 1993)

Bew, Paul and Gordon Gillespie, *Northern Ireland: A Chronology of the Troubles 1968-1993* (Dublin 1993)

Bew, Paul and Gordon Gillespie, *The Northern Ireland Peace Process 1993-1996 A Chronology* (London 1996)

Bew, Paul, Henry Patterson and Paul Teague, *Northern Ireland: Between War and Peace. The Political Future of Northern Ireland* (London 1997)

Birrell, Derek and Alan Murie, *Policy and Government in Northern Ireland: Lessons of Devolution* (Dublin 1980)

Bishop, Patrick and Eamon Mallie, *The Provisional IRA* (London 1987)

Bloomfield, Ken, *Stormont in Crisis: A Memoir* (Belfast 1994)

Bowman, John, *De Valera and the Ulster Question 1917-1973* (Oxford 1982)

Boyce, D.G., 'British Conservative Opinion, The Ulster Question and the Partition of Ireland, 1912-1921' in *Irish Historical Studies* No.65 Vol.XVII 1970

Boyce, D.G., 'British Opinion, Ireland and the War' in *Historical Journal* No.3 Vol. 17 1974

Boyce, D.G. and John Stubbs, 'F.S. Oliver, Lord Shelbourne and Federalism' in *Journal of Imperial and Commonwealth History* Vol. 5 1976

Boyce, D.G., *Nationalism in Ireland* (London 1982)

Boyce, D.G., *The Irish Question and British Politics 1868-1986* (London 1988)

Boyce, D.G. (ed.), *The Revolution in Ireland 1879-1923* (London 1988)

Boyce, D.G., 'Edward Carson and Irish Unionism' in Ciaran Brady (ed.) *Worsted in the Game: Losers in Irish History* (Dublin 1989)

Boyce, D.G., *Nineteenth-Century Ireland: The Search for Stability* (Dublin 1991)

Boyce, D.G., R. Eccleshall and V. Geoghegan (eds), *Political Thought in Ireland Since the Seventeenth Century* (London 1993)

Boyd, Andrew, *Brian Faulkner and the Crisis of Ulster Unionism* (Kerry 1972)

Boyle, Kevin and Tom Hadden, *Ireland: A Positive Proposal* (Harmondsworth 1985)

Boyle, Kevin and Tom Hadden, *Northern Ireland: the Choice* (London 1994)

Brewer, John D. with Kathleen Magee, *Inside the RUC: Routine Policing in a Divided Society* (Oxford 1991)

Brooke, Peter, *Ulster Presbyterianism: The Historical Perspective 1610-1970* (Dublin 1987)

Bruce, Steve, *God Save Ulster! The Religion and Politics of Paisleyism* (Oxford 1986)

Bruce, Steve, *The Red Hand: Protestant Paramilitaries in Northern Ireland* (Oxford 1992)

Bruce, Steve, 'Loyalists in Northern Ireland: Further Thoughts on "Pro-State Terror"', in *Terrorism and Political Violence*, Vol. 5, No. 4, Winter 1993 pp 262-3

Bruce, Steve, *The Edge of the Union: The Ulster Loyalist Political Vision* (Oxford 1994)

Bruce, Steve and Fiona Alderdice, 'Religious Belief and Behaviour' in *Social Attitudes in Northern Ireland: The Third Report 1992-1993* edited by Peter Stringer and Gillian Robinson (Belfast 1993)

Bryson, Lucy and Clem McCartney, *Clashing Symbols? a report on the use of flags, anthems and other national symbols in Northern Ireland* (Belfast 1994)

Buckland, Patrick, *Irish Unionism 1: The Anglo-Irish and the New Ireland 1885-1922* (Dublin 1972)

Buckland, Patrick, *Irish Unionism 2: Ulster Unionism and the Origins of Northern Ireland 1886-1922* (Dublin 1973)

Buckland, Patrick, *Irish Unionism 1885-1923: A Documentary History* (Belfast 1973)

Buckland, Patrick, *The Factory of Grievances: Devolved Government in Northern Ireland 1921-39* (Dublin 1979)

Buckland, Patrick, *James Craig, Lord Craigavon* (Dublin 1980)

Buckland, Patrick, *A History of Northern Ireland* (Dublin 1981)

Budge, Ian and Cornelius O'Leary, *Belfast: Approach to Crisis: A Study of Belfast Politics 1613-1970* (London 1973)

Burton, Frank, *The Politics of Legitimacy: Struggles in a Belfast Community* (London 1978)

Campbell, Brian, Laurence McKeown and Felim O'Hagan (eds), *Nor Meekly Serve My Time: The H-Block Struggle 1976-1981* (Belfast 1994)

Campbell, Colm, *Emergency Law in Ireland 1918-1925* (Oxford 1994)

Campbell, T.J., *Fifty Years of Ulster: 1890-1940* (Belfast 1941)

Cash, John D., *Identity, Ideology and Conflict: the Structuration of Politics in Northern Ireland* (Cambridge 1996)

Cathcart, Rex, *The Most Contrary Region: The BBC in Northern Ireland 1924-1984* (Belfast 1984)

Coldrey, B.M., *Faith and Fatherland: The Christian Brothers and the Development of Irish Nationalism 1838-1921* (Dublin 1988)

Connolly, Michael, *Politics and Policy Making in Northern Ireland* (London 1990)

Connolly, Michael and Andrew Erridge, 'Central Government in Northern Ireland', in *Public Policy in Northern Ireland: Adoption or Adaption?*, edited by M.E.H. Connolly and S. Loughlin (Belfast and Coleraine 1990)

Coogan, Tim Pat, *The IRA* (London 1970)

Coogan, Tim Pat, *Michael Collins: A Biography* (London 1990)

Coogan, Tim Pat, *De Valera: Long Fellow, Long Shadow* (London 1993)

Coogan, Tim Pat, *The Troubles: Ireland's Ordeal 1966-1995 and the Search for Peace* (London 1995)

Cormack, R.J. and R.D. Osborne (eds), *Religion, Education and Employment: Aspects of Equal Opportunity in Northern Ireland* (Belfast 1983)

Cormack, R.J. and R.D. Osborne (eds), *Discrimination and Public Policy in Northern Ireland* (Oxford 1991)

Cormack, R.J. and R.D. Osborne, 'The evolution of a Catholic middle class' pp 67-76, in *New Perspectives on the Northern Ireland Conflict* (Aldershot 1994)

Cormack, R.J. and Robert Osborne, 'Education in Northern Ireland: The Struggle for Equality' in *Irish Society: Sociological Perspectives* edited by Patrick Clancy, Sheelagh Drudy, Kathleen Lynch and Liam O'Dowd (Dublin 1995)

Coulter, Colin, 'The Character of Unionism', *Irish Political Studies*, Vol. 9, 1994 pp 1-24

Crawford, Robert G., *Loyal to King Billy: A Portrait of the Ulster Protestants* (Dublin 1987)

Crozier, Maurna (ed.), *Cultural Traditions in Northern Ireland: Varieties of Irishness* (Belfast 1989)

Crozier, Maurna (ed.) *Cultural Traditions in Northern Ireland: Varieties of Britishness* (Belfast 1990)

Crozier, Maurna (ed.), *Cultural Traditions in Northern Ireland: All Europeans Now?* (Belfast 1991)

Cunningham, Michael J., *British Government Policy in Northern Ireland 1969-89: Its Nature and Execution* (Manchester 1991)

Curran, Frank, *Derry: Countdown to Disaster* (Dublin 1986)

Cusack, Jim and Max Taylor, 'The Resurgence of a Terrorist Organization – Part 1 the UDA, A Case Study', in *Terrorism and Political Violence* Vol. 5, Autumn 1993, No. 3

Daly, Cathal, *The Price of Peace* (Belfast 1991)

Darby, John, *Northern Ireland: the Background to the Conflict* (Belfast 1983)

Darby, John, *Intimidation and the Control of Conflict* (Dublin 1986)

Darby, John, 'Legitimate Targets: a control on violence?', in *New Perspectives on the Northern Ireland Conflict*, edited by Adrian Guelke (Aldershot 1994)

Davis, Richard, *Arthur Griffith and Non-Violent Sinn Féin* (Tralee 1974)

de Baróid, Ciarán, *Ballymurphy and the Irish War* (Dublin 1989)

Devlin, Bernadette, *The Price of My Soul* (London 1969)

Devlin, Paddy, *The Fall of the N.I. Executive* (Belfast 1975)

Devlin, Paddy, *Straight Left: An Autobiography* (Belfast 1993)

Duggan, John P., *A History of the Irish Army* (Dublin 1991)

Dunlop, John, *A Precarious Belonging: Presbyterians and the Conflict in Ireland* (Belfast 1995)

Dunn, Seamus and Valerie Morgan, *Protestant Alienation in Northern Ireland: A Preliminary Survey* (Coleraine 1994)

Dunn, Seamus and Thomas Hennessey, 'Ireland' in *Europe and Ethnicity: World War One and Contemporary Ethnic Conflict*, edited by T.G. Fraser and Seamus Dunn (London 1996)

Dwyer, T. Ryle, *Éamon de Valera* (Dublin 1980)

Eames, Robin, *Chains to be Broken: A Personal Reflection on Northern Ireland and its People* (London 1992)

Edwards, Ruth Dudley, *Patrick Pearse: The Triumph of Failure* (Dublin 1977)

English, Richard and Graham Walker, *Unionism in Modern Ireland: New Perspectives on Politics and Culture* (Dublin 1996)

Ervine, St John, *Craigavon, Ulsterman* (London 1949)

Eversley, David, *Religion and Employment in Northern Ireland* (London 1989)

Farrell, Brian, *The Founding of Dáil Éireann: Parliament and Nation-Building* (Dublin 1971)

Farrell, Michael, *Northern Ireland: The Orange State* (London 1976)

Farrell, Michael, *Arming the Protestants: The Formation of the Ulster Special Constabulary and the Royal Ulster Constabulary 1920-27* (London 1983)

Faulkner, Brian, *Memoirs of a Statesman* (London 1978)

Fisk, Robert, *In Time of War: Ireland, Ulster and the Price of Neutrality* (London 1985)

FitzGerald, Garret, *All in a Life* (Dublin 1991)

Flackes, W.D. and Sydney Elliott, *Northern Ireland: A Political Directory 1968-88* (Belfast 1989)

Follis, Brian, *A State Under Siege: The Establishment of Northern Ireland 1920-1925* (Oxford 1995)

Forester, Margery, *Michael Collins: The Lost Leader* (London 1971)

Forum for Peace and Reconciliation, *Paths to a Political Settlement in Ireland: Policy Papers Submitted to the Forum for Peace and Reconciliation* (Belfast 1995)

Foster, R.F., *Modern Ireland 1600-1972* (London 1988)

Fulton, John, *The Tragedy of Belief: Politics and Religion in Northern Ireland* (Oxford 1991)

Gailey, Andrew (ed.), *Crying in the Wilderness; Jack Sayers: A Liberal Editor in Ulster 1939-69* (Belfast 1995)

Gallagher, Anthony M., 'The Approach of Government: Community Relations and Equity' in *Facets of the Conflict in Northern Ireland*, edited by Seamus Dunn (London 1995)

Gallagher, Eric and Stanley Worrall, *Christians in Ulster 1968-1980* (Oxford 1982)

Gallagher, Frank, *The Indivisible Island* (London 1957)

Galliher, John F. and Jerry L. de Gregory, *Violence in Northern Ireland: Understanding Protestant Perspectives* (Dublin 1985)

Garvin, Tom, *The Evolution of Irish Nationalist Politics* (Dublin 1981)

Garvin, Tom, *Nationalist Revolutionaries in Ireland 1858-1928* (Oxford 1987)

Gearty, Conor, *Terror* (London 1991)

Gibbon, Peter, *The Origins of Ulster Unionism: The Formation of Popular Protestant Politics and Ideology in Nineteenth-Century Ireland* (Manchester 1975)

Gordon, David, *The O'Neill Years: Unionist Politics 1963-1969* (Belfast 1989)

Guelke, Adrian, *Northern Ireland: The International Perspective* (Dublin 1988)

Guelke, Adrian, 'Paramilitaries, Republicans and Loyalists' in *Facets of the Conflict in Northern Ireland*, edited by Seamus Dunn (London 1995)

Hadfield, Bridgid, *The Constitution of Northern Ireland* (Belfast 1989)

Hadfield, Bridgid, 'Legislating for Northern Ireland at Westminster' in *Public Policy in Northern Ireland: Adoption or Adaption?*, edited by M.E.H. Connolly and S. Loughlin (Belfast and Coleraine 1990)

Hadfield, Bridgid, *Northern Ireland: Politics and the Constitution* (Milton Keynes 1992)

Hadfield, Bridgid, 'The Belfast Agreement, Sovereignty and the State of the Union', *Public Law*, Winter 1998

Hamill, Desmond, *Pig in the Middle: The Army in Northern Ireland 1969-1985* (London 1985)

Hamilton, Andrew and Linda Moore, 'Policing a Divided Society', in *Facets of the Conflict in Northern Ireland*, edited by Seamus Dunn (London 1995)

Hand, Geoffrey J., *Report of the Irish Boundary Commission 1925* (Dublin 1969)

Harbinson, John F., *The Ulster Unionist Party 1882-1973: Its Development and Organisation* (Belfast 1973)

Harkness, David, *Northern Ireland since 1920* (Dublin 1983)

Harris, Mary, *The Catholic Church and the Foundation of the Northern Irish State* (Cork 1993)

Harris, Rosemary, *Prejudice and Tolerance in Ulster: A Study of Neighbours and Strangers in a Border Community* (Manchester 1972)

Harrison, Richard T., 'Industrial Development in Northern Ireland – The Industrial Development Board' in *Public Policy in Northern Ireland: Adoption or Adaption?*, edited by M.E.H. Connolly and S. Loughlin (Belfast and Coleraine 1990)

Heath, Edward, *The Course of My Life. The Autobiography of Edward Heath* (London 1998)

Hempton, David and Myrtle Hill, *Evangelical Protestantism in Ulster Society 1740-1890* (London 1992)

Hennessey, Thomas, 'Ulster Unionist Territorial and National Identities 1886-1893: province, island, kingdom and empire', *Irish Political Studies*, Vol. 8, 1993

Hennessey, Thomas, *A History of Northern Ireland 1920-1996* (Dublin 1997)

Hennessey, Thomas, *Dividing Ireland: World War One and Partition* (London 1998)

Heskin, Ken, *Northern Ireland: A Psychological Analysis* (Dublin 1980)

Hickey, John, *Religion and the Northern Ireland Problem* (Dublin 1984)

Hogan, Gerald and Clive Walker, *Political Violence and the Law in Ireland* (Manchester 1989)

Holland, Jack and Henry McDonald, *INLA: Deadly Divisions* (Dublin 1994)

Holt, E., *Protest in Arms: The Irish Troubles 1916-1923* (London 1963)

Howell, David, *A Lost Left: Three Studies in Socialism and Nationalism* (Manchester 1986)

Hume, John, *Personal Views: Politics, Peace and Reconciliation in Ireland* (Dublin 1996)

Hutchinson, John, *The Dynamics of Cultural Nationalism: the Gaelic Revival and the Creation of the Irish Nation State* (London 1987)

Hyde, H. Montgomery, *Carson; the Life of Lord Carson of Duncairn* (London 1953)

Jackson, Alvin, *The Ulster Party: Irish Unionists in the House of Commons, 1884-1911* (Oxford 1989)

Jackson, Alvin, 'Unionist Myths 1912-1985' in *Past and Present*, No. 136

(August 1992), pp 164–85

Jackson, Alvin, *Sir Edward Carson* (Dundalk 1993)

Jackson, Alvin, 'Irish Unionism, 1905–21' in Peter Collins (ed.), *Nationalism and Unionism: Conflict in Ireland 1885–1921* (Belfast 1994)

Jalland, Patricia, *The Liberals and Ireland: The Ulster Question in British Politics to 1914* (Brighton 1980)

Kee, Robert, *The Green Flag* (London 1972)

Keena, Colm, *A Biography of Gerry Adams* (Dublin 1990)

Kelly, Henry, *How Stormont Fell* (Dublin 1972)

Kendle, John, *Ireland and the Federal Solution: the Debate over the United Kingdom Constitution 1870–1921* (Kingston 1989)

Kennedy, Dennis, *The Widening Gulf: Northern Attitudes to the Independent Irish State 1919–1949* (Belfast 1988)

Kennedy-Pipe, Caroline, *The Origins of the Present Troubles in Northern Ireland* (Essex 1997)

Keogh, Dermot, *Twentieth-Century Ireland: Nation and State* (Dublin 1994)

Knox, Colin, 'Local Government in Northern Ireland – Adoption or Adaption?' pp 35–8 in *Public Policy in Northern Ireland: Adoption or Adaption?*, edited by M.E.H. Connolly and S. Loughlin (Belfast and Coleraine 1990)

Laffan, Michael, *The Partition of Ireland 1911–1925* (Dundalk 1983)

Lawlor, Sheila, *Britain and Ireland 1914–23* (Dublin 1983)

Lawrence, R.J., *The Government of Northern Ireland* (Oxford 1965)

Lee, J.J., *Ireland 1912–1985: Politics and Society* (Cambridge 1989)

Longford, Lord and Anne McHardy, *Ulster* (London 1981)

Longley, Edna, 'The Rising, the Somme and Irish Memory' in Máirín Ní Dhonnchadha and Theo Dorgan (eds), *Revising the Rising* (Derry 1991)

Loughlin, James, *Gladstone, Home Rule and the Ulster Question 1882–93* (Dublin 1986)

Loughlin, James, *Ulster Unionism and British National Identity since 1885* (London 1995)

Lyons, F.S.L., *Ireland since the Famine* (London 1973)

McAllister, Ian, *The Northern Ireland Social Democratic and Labour Party: Political Opposition in a Divided Society* (London 1977)

McAuley, James W., *The Politics of Identity: A Loyalist Community in Belfast* (Aldershot 1994)

McCabe, Ian, *A Diplomatic History of Ireland 1948–49: The Republic, the Commonwealth and NATO* (Dublin 1991)

McCann, Eamon, *War in an Irish Town* (London 1980)

McDowell, R.B., *The Irish Convention 1917–18* (London 1970)

McElroy, Gerald, *The Catholic Church and the Northern Ireland Crisis 1969–86* (Dublin 1991)

McGarry, John and Brendan O'Leary (eds), *The Future of Northern Ireland* (Oxford 1990)

McGarry, John and Brendan O'Leary, *Explaining Northern Ireland: Broken Images* (Oxford 1995)

McGuire, Maria, *To Take Arms: A Year in the Provisional IRA* (London 1973)

McIntyre, Anthony, 'Modern Irish Republicanism: The Product of British State Strategies', in *Irish Political Studies*, Vol. 10, 1995

McKeown, Ciaran, *The Passion of Peace* (Belfast 1984)

McKeown, Michael, *The Greening of a Nationalist* (Lurgan 1986)

McMahon, Deirdre, *Republicans and Imperialists: Anglo-Irish Relations in the 1930s* (Yale 1984)

McNeill, Ronald, *Ulster's Stand for Union* (London 1922)

Mac Stiofáin, Seán, *Revolutionary in Ireland* (Farnborough 1974)

MacVeigh, Jeremiah, *Home Rule in a Nutshell* (London 1911)

Major, John, *The Autobiography* (London 1999)

Mallie, Eamon and David McKittrick, *The Fight for Peace: The Secret Story Behind the Irish Peace Process* (London 1996)

Mansergh, Nicholas, *The Unresolved Question: the Anglo-Irish Settlement and its Undoing 1912-72* (Yale 1991)

Marjoribanks, Edward and Ian Colvin, *The Life of Lord Carson*, 3 Volumes (London 1932-4)

Miller, David, *Queen's Rebels: Ulster Loyalism in Historical Perspective* (Dublin 1978)

Mitchell, George J., *Making Peace* (London 1999)

Moloney, Ed and Andy Pollock, *Paisley* (Dublin 1986)

Moxon-Browne, Edward, *Nation, Class and Creed in Northern Ireland* (Aldershot 1983)

Murphy, Brian P., *Patrick Pearse and the Lost Republican Ideal* (Dublin 1991)

Murphy, Richard, 'Faction in the Conservative Party and the Home Rule Crisis 1912-14' in *History* No. 232, Vol. 71 1986

Murray, Dominic, *Worlds Apart: Segregated Schools in Northern Ireland* (Belfast 1985)

Murray, Raymond, *The SAS in Ireland* (Dublin 1990)

Nelson, Sarah, *Ulster Uncertain Defenders: Loyalists and the Northern Ireland Conflict* (Belfast 1984)

O'Brien, Brendan, *The Long War: The IRA and Sinn Féin 1985 to Today* (Dublin 1993)

O'Brien, William, *The Irish Revolution and How it Came About* (Dublin 1923)

O'Connor, Fionnuala, *In Search of a State: Catholics in Northern Ireland* (Belfast 1993)

O'Dowd, Liam, Bill Rolston and Mike Tomlinson, *Northern Ireland: Between Civil Rights and Civil War* (London 1980)

O'Dowd, Liam, 'Development or Dependency? State, Economy and Society in Northern Ireland' in *Irish Society: Sociological Perspectives* edited by Patrick Clancy, Sheelagh Drudy, Kathleen Lynch and Liam O'Dowd (Dublin 1995)

O'Halloran, Clare, *Partition and the Limits of Irish Nationalism* (Dublin 1987)

O'Leary, Brendan and John McGarry, *The Politics of Antagonism: Understanding Northern Ireland* (London 1993)

O'Malley, Pádraig, *The Uncivil Wars: Ireland Today* (Belfast 1983)

O'Malley, Pádraig, *Biting at the Grave: The Irish Hunger Strikes and the Politics of Despair* (Belfast 1990)

O'Malley, Pádraig, *Northern Ireland: Questions of Nuance* (Belfast 1990)

O'Neill, Terence, *Ulster at the Crossroads* (London 1969)

O'Neill, Terence, *The Autobiography of Terence O'Neill: Prime Minister of Northern Ireland 1963-1969* (London 1972)

Orr, Philip, *The Road to the Somme: Men of the Ulster Division Tell Their Story* (Belfast 1987)

Patterson, Henry, *Class Conflict and Sectarianism: The Protestant Working Class and the Belfast Labour Movement 1868-1920* (Belfast 1980)

Patterson, Henry, *The Politics of Illusion: Republicanism and Socialism in Modern Ireland* (London 1989)

Phoenix, Eamon, 'Northern Nationalists, Ulster Unionists and the Development of Partition 1900-1921' in *Nationalism and Unionism: Conflict in Ireland 1885-1921* edited by Peter Collins (Belfast 1994a)

Phoenix, Eamon, *Northern Nationalism: Nationalist Politics, Partition and the Catholic Minority in Northern Ireland 1890-1940* (Belfast 1994b)

Pollack, Andy (ed.), *A Citizens' Inquiry: The Opsahl Report on Northern Ireland* (Dublin 1993)

Purdy, Ann, *Molyneaux: The Long View* (Belfast 1989)

Purdy, Bob, *Politics in the Streets: The Origins of the Civil Rights Movement in Northern Ireland* (Belfast 1990)

Rea, Desmond (ed.), *Political Co-operation in Divided Societies: A Series of Papers Relevant to the Conflict in Northern Ireland* (Dublin 1982)

Rolston, Bill (ed.), *The Media and Northern Ireland: Covering the Troubles* (London 1991)

Rose, Richard, *Governing Without Consensus: An Irish Perspective* (London 1971)

Rowan, Brian, *Behind the Lines: The Story of the IRA and Loyalist Ceasefires* (Belfast 1995)

Rowthorn, Bob and Naomi Wayne, *Northern Ireland: The Political Economy of Conflict* (Cambridge 1988)

Ruane, Joseph and Jennifer Todd, *The Dynamics of Conflict in Northern Ireland: Power, Conflict and Emancipation* (Cambridge 1996)

Ryder, Chris, *The RUC: A Force Under Fire* (London 1989)

Ryder, Chris, *The Ulster Defence Regiment: An Instrument of Peace?* (London 1991)

Shea, Patrick, *Voices and the Sound of Drums: An Irish Autobiography* (Belfast 1981)

Sinn Féin, *Colonial Home Rule: What it means* (Dublin 1917)

Smith, Alan, 'Education and the Conflict in Northern Ireland' in *Facets of the Conflict in Northern Ireland*, edited by Seamus Dunn (London 1995)

Smith, Alan and Alan Robinson, *Education for Mutual Understanding: The Initial Statutory Years* (Coleraine 1996)

Smith, David and Gerald Chambers, *Inequality in Northern Ireland* (Oxford 1991)

Smith, M.L.R., *Fighting for Ireland: The Military Strategy of the Irish Republican Movement* (London 1995)

Smyth, Clifford, *Ian Paisley: Voice of Protestant Ulster* (Edinburgh 1987)

Stewart, A.T.Q., *The Ulster Crisis: Resistance to Home Rule 1912-14* (London 1967)

Stewart, A.T.Q., *The Narrow Ground: the Roots of Conflict in Ulster* (London 1977)

Stewart, A.T.Q., *Edward Carson* (Dublin 1981)

Stringer, Peter and Gillian Robinson (eds), *Social Attitudes in Northern Ireland* (Belfast 1991)

Stringer, Peter and Gillian Robinson (eds), *Social Attitudes in Northern Ireland: The Second Report* (Belfast 1992)

Stringer, Peter and Gillian Robinson (eds), *Social Attitudes in Northern Ireland: The Third Report* (Belfast 1993)

Stubbs, John, 'Unionists and Ireland, 1914-1918' in *Historical Journal* No. 33, Vol. 4 1990

Sugden, John, 'Sport, Community Relations and Community Conflict in Northern Ireland' in *Facets of the Conflict in Northern Ireland*, edited by Seamus Dunn (London 1995)

Sunday Times Insight Team, *Ulster* (London 1972)

Teague, Paul (ed.), *Beyond the Rhetoric: Politics, the Economy and Social Policy in Northern Ireland* (London 1987)

Thatcher, Margaret, *The Downing Street Years* (London 1993)

Todd, Jennifer, 'Two traditions in unionist political culture' in *Irish Political Studies*, Vol. 5, 1990

Tools, Kevin, *Rebel Hearts: Journeys within the IRA's Soul* (London 1995)

Townshend, Charles (ed.), *Consensus in Ireland* (Oxford 1983)

Townshend, Charles, *Political Violence in Ireland: Government and Resistance since 1848* (Oxford 1983)

Travers, Pauric, *Settlements and Divisions: Ireland 1870-1922* (Dublin 1988)

Trew, Karen, 'National Identity' in *Social Attitudes in Northern Ireland: The Fifth Report 1995-1996* edited by Richard Breen, Paul Devine and Lizanne Dowds (Belfast 1996)

Urban, Mark, *Big Boys' Rules: The Secret Struggle Against the IRA* (London 1992)

Walker, B.M., *Ulster Politics: The Formative Years 1868-86* (Belfast 1989)

Walker, Graham, *The Politics of Frustration: Harry Midgley and the Failure of Labour in Northern Ireland* (Manchester 1985)

Walsh, Pat, *From Civil Rights to National War: Northern Ireland Catholic Politics 1964-74* (Belfast 1989)

Walsh, Pat, *Irish Republicanism and Socialism: the Politics of the Movement 1905 to 1994* (Belfast 1994)

Ward, Margaret, *Unmanageable Revolutionaries: Women and Irish Nationalism* (London 1983)

White, Barry, *John Hume: Statesman of the Troubles* (Belfast 1984)

Whyte, J.H., *Church and State in Modern Ireland 1923-1979* (Dublin 1979)

Whyte, J.H., 'How much discrimination was there under the unionist regime 1921-1968?' in *Contemporary Irish Studies* edited by Tom Gallagher and James O'Connell (Manchester 1983)

Whyte, John, *Interpreting Northern Ireland* (Oxford 1990)

Wichert, Sabine, *Northern Ireland Since 1945* (Essex 1991)

Wilson, Derick and Jerry Tyrrell, 'Institutions for Conciliation and Mediation' in *Facets of the Conflict in Northern Ireland*, edited by Seamus Dunn (London 1995)

Wilson, Tom, *Ulster: Conflict and Consent* (Oxford 1989)

Wright, Frank, *Northern Ireland: A Comparative Analysis* (Dublin 1987)

Index